SOCIAL EMOTIONAL STORIES

Lessons and Learning from Plants and Animals

BARBARA A. LEWIS

free spirit
PUBLISHING®

Library of Congress Cataloging-in-Publication Data
Names: Lewis, Barbara A., 1943- author.
Title: Social emotional stories : lessons and learning from plants and animals / by Barbara A. Lewis.
Other titles: Building character with true stories from nature
Description: [updated edition]. | Minneapolis, MN : Free Spirit Publishing Inc., [2020] | Includes bibliographical references and index.
Identifiers: LCCN 2019060160 | ISBN 9781631985140 (paperback) | ISBN 9781631985157 (pdf) | ISBN 9781631985164 (epub)
Subjects: LCSH: Moral education. | Character—Study and teaching—Activity programs. | Nature study—Activity programs. | Animal ecology—Study and teaching.
Classification: LCC LC268 .L465 2020 | DDC 370.11/4—dc23
LC record available at https://lccn.loc.gov/2019060160

Free Spirit Publishing does not have control over or assume responsibility for author or third-party websites and their content. At the time of this book's publication, all facts and figures cited within are the most current available. All telephone numbers, addresses, and website URLs are accurate and active; all publications, organizations, websites, and other resources exist as described in this book; and all have been verified as of April 2020. If you find an error or believe that a resource listed here is not as described, please contact Free Spirit Publishing. Parents, teachers, and other adults: We strongly urge you to monitor children's use of the internet.

Photos from Dreamstime and Wikimedia

Edited by Alison Behnke
Cover and interior design by Shannon Pourciau

10 9 8 7 6 5 4 3 2 1
Printed in the United States of America

Free Spirit Publishing Inc.
Minneapolis, MN
(612) 338-2068
help4kids@freespirit.com
freespirit.com

FSC
www.fsc.org
MIX
Paper from
responsible sources
FSC® C005010

DEDICATION

To my grandchildren, who still see the magic of nature:
Adam, Anderson, Andrew, Chloe, Clara, Houston, Jordan, Lizzie, Maddy, and Ruby

ACKNOWLEDGMENTS

A special thanks to my publisher, Judy Galbraith, for her continued confidence in my work and her belief that good books can inspire the lives of kids. And a special thank you to Alison Behnke, who provided great guidance and outstanding editing. Thanks to all the Free Spirit Publishing team for their efforts in producing this book. I must recognize the Character Education Partnership, which continues to provide a proven path for the development of positive character traits—along with the many national organizations dedicated to developing character among young people. And thanks to Dr. Marvin Berkowitz for his wise advice and great example of what good character education should be.

Always, I thank my dear husband and best friend, Lawrence, for his love and support in this endeavor.

CONTENTS

LIST OF REPRODUCIBLE PAGES

INTRODUCTION

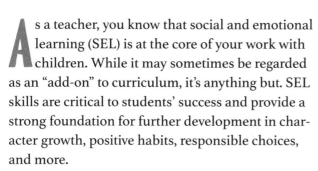

> "After nourishment, shelter, and companionship, stories are the thing we need most in the world."
>
> —**Philip Pullman**

As a teacher, you know that social and emotional learning (SEL) is at the core of your work with children. While it may sometimes be regarded as an "add-on" to curriculum, it's anything but. SEL skills are critical to students' success and provide a strong foundation for further development in character growth, positive habits, responsible choices, and more.

One of the greatest ways to set the stage for building these essential social and emotional skills in grades two through five (and beyond) is through stories. Storytelling is fundamental to our experience as humans. And powerful, well-told stories prepare our minds and hearts for growth, making storytelling a natural fit for pursuing SEL goals. Becoming absorbed in a story actively engages kids' critical thinking skills as well as their empathy. In this book, you'll learn and explore ways to use stories to build and strengthen your students' SEL skills.

WHAT HAPPENS TO A BRAIN ON STORIES?

From drawings on cave walls to Hans Christian Andersen's fairy tales to traditional storytellers around the world, stories have been a major way to pass on knowledge, ideas, and values throughout human history. Stories can motivate us to change our attitudes, build relationships, and feel empathy for others.

Storytelling can engage listeners, spark change, provoke emotions, and teach skills. This makes stories a perfect way to help children develop socially and emotionally as they live imaginatively through the characters' experiences. When the brain is hooked on a story, there's an explosion of activity, creating connections between neurons. This helps listeners and readers understand and participate in the story. As the tension builds in the narrative, the story follows the dramatic arc to its pinnacle. It transports its audience into the world of the character.

The boosted brain activity stimulated by a story increases the listener's or reader's ability to remember by seven times (Narrative IQ 2014). Especially when combined with thought-provoking questions, storytelling can increase children's critical thinking skills, help kids develop social and emotional skills, and encourage them to develop positive character traits (Agosto 2013). All of these benefits make storytelling a great tool for teachers or anyone else working with young people.

What does a brain on stories *look* like? Researchers using MRI technology (magnetic resonance imaging) have traced blood flow to the parts of the brain that become involved with stories and have found that the brain lights up on a well-told story. The areas receiving blood flow are actively engaged. A story can sometimes lead to a nearly global engagement of the brain, as the imagination explodes with ideas (Yuan, Major-Girardin, and Brown 2018). This response shows that listeners or readers are feeling emotions which in turn can motivate them to better understand themselves and others, manage challenging emotions, and grow in positive behavior.

IMAGI-NATION

I like to think of the imagination as a special place where each person is in charge of their own country or kingdom. Anything can happen there. It's a bustle of activity where creative ideas are born. One child might dream up an idea for how to make a hover board, while another child envisions how to make a friendship. We all have a kind of "mental workspace" in the brain that coordinates input in creative and personal ways (Schlegel et al. 2013). That's the imagination at work. But it doesn't happen in a vacuum. It depends upon past experiences and connections that are already in the brain. And it depends upon reality. As the imagination molds these elements together in new ways, creative ideas are born. Stories help us spark this process in students.

Further, if someone tells a compelling story, the listener's brain can synchronize or match with the storyteller. In one study, a woman told a story to volunteers. The same areas of the listeners' brains were stimulated as in the storyteller's brain. When the storyteller felt emotion, an emotional response also took place in the brains of the listeners (Stephens, Silbert, and Hasson 2010).

Storytelling provides an effective tool for teaching social and emotional skills because stories can activate the same areas of the brain as experience does. In other words, imagining a sound or a shape changes how we see the world around us in the same way as actually hearing that sound or seeing that shape. So, *think* of a pickle, or a roaring stream, or your hair when you wake up in the morning. Your brain will react in similar ways as it would if you *held* a pickle, walked beside the roaring stream, or looked in shock at your hair in the mirror. "The brain, it seems, does not make much of a distinction between reading about an experience and encountering it in real life. The same neurological regions are stimulated," explains Keith Oatley, a researcher in cognitive psychology (Paul 2012).

Storytelling can light the brain globally and make learning come alive. This does not mean that hearing a story is the same exact experience as real life. Still, it shows that you don't have to bring an elephant into your school—or even be sitting outside in nature—to have your nature story be successful! Well-told stories about animals and plants can teach social and emotional growth skills right from where you are sitting inside your classroom.

Other research taps into how stories are related to empathy—one of the cornerstones of social and emotional learning. Paul Zak, a professor of neuro-economics, conducted research on chemical changes in the brain that took place when people watched and listened to an emotional story (Future of StoryTelling 2012). Before and after the story, blood samples were collected from participants. The samples showed that two chemicals were released in their brains while watching the story. Those two chemicals were cortisol and oxytocin.

Cortisol is a neurochemical produced in the brain. It is released when people feel stressed and causes people to focus their attention. The participants who felt distressed by the story had elevated levels of cortisol.

Oxytocin is another neurochemical. The brain releases it when people feel empathy. In Zak's study, the participants who felt the most empathy for the characters in the story had more oxytocin in their bodies after the story than before. Participants also had higher heart rates and respiration. This showed the strong influence of a story on stimulating caring for others.

After the experiment, the participants were given a chance to share or donate money with a stranger or with a charity. The researchers found they could predict with 80 percent accuracy which

Powerful, well-told stories prepare our minds and hearts for growth.

participants would donate money. How? By the amount of oxytocin in their blood samples. Elevated oxytocin meant greater generosity (Zak 2013). As Zak reported, we can "change behavior by changing our brain chemistry" (Rodriguez 2017). A story can do this by inspiring the listeners to feel empathy for its characters. And that can transfer to real life.

In another study, researchers studied the influence of public service announcements or ads, which often use mini-stories to communicate their messages. Their findings showed that after viewing effective ads, participants had higher levels of oxytocin in their blood. A second result? People with the most oxytocin donated more to charities (Lin et al. 2013).

In still another pair of studies, led by psychologist Dan Johnson, researchers had some people read part of a novel about a Muslim woman. Other participants did not read the story. Afterward, the people who read the story showed a lower amount of bias and less stereotyping in response to photos of people from various cultural backgrounds. Reporting on the findings, the researchers said, "There is growing evidence that just reading a story engages many of the same neural networks involved in empathy" (Jacobs 2014; Johnson, Huffman, and Jasper 2014).

A story that creates empathy and releases oxytocin has another benefit too. It not only helps people be more compassionate, charitable, and trustworthy; it can also help people notice and understand social cues better (Firth 2015). This is another goal of SEL: to help children recognize and understand how to interact socially with others.

As a teacher, I am inspired and motivated by this research showing so vividly that a good story can set the stage for behavior change. You can help your students grow emotionally, build social skills, and strengthen positive character traits through good storytelling.

WHAT IS SOCIAL AND EMOTIONAL LEARNING?

We know that stories can help direct and strengthen SEL, as well as character education and academic learning. But what exactly *is* SEL? A good definition comes from CASEL (Collaborative for Academic, Social, and Emotional Learning): "Social and emotional learning (SEL) is the process through which children and adults understand and manage emotions, set and achieve positive goals, feel and show empathy for others, establish and maintain positive relationships, and make responsible decisions" (CASEL 2019, "What is SEL?").

Psychologist Daniel Goleman sums up the far-reaching importance of these skills, saying, "If your emotional abilities aren't in hand, if you don't have self-awareness, if you are not able to manage your distressing emotions, if you can't have empathy and have effective relationships, then no matter how smart you are, you are not going to get very far" (Treher, Piltz, and Jacobs 2011). In fact, research shows that most employers value emotional intelligence over other traits, including IQ (Ovans 2015; Barker 2017). The good news? Children and adults can learn, strengthen, and refine these skills.

The history of teaching social and emotional skills goes back at least as far as Plato's *Republic*. Plato's philosophy and vision for education included "good character." Along the historical path, many other educators and researchers have promoted teaching positive character and behavior, and modern education still involves teaching more than academic skills.

In the United States, federal policy has begun to include social and emotional and behavioral factors into educational accountability metrics, including through the 2015 Every Student Succeeds

Act (ESSA), and as part of school climate initiatives, anti-bullying work, and positive behavior programs.

CASEL is a leader in the SEL movement, having launched an initiative to support states as they develop policies, standards, and guidelines for SEL in schools. The organization identifies the following domains or competencies of growth within SEL (CASEL 2019, "Core SEL Competencies" and "Overview of SEL"). (I have elaborated on their descriptions.) The lessons and stories in this book will help you use stories to build each of these domains:

- **Self-awareness:** Understand personal feelings and the vocabulary of emotions; recognize emotions as they happen; understand and accept emotions, beliefs, and behavior patterns; develop self-confidence; understand personal strengths and weaknesses; create inner peace

- **Self-management:** Develop skills for relaxing and coping; develop self-motivation; increase self-regulation and self-control of personal behavior, including organization and goal-setting; understand and grow in trustworthiness and adaptability; maintain healthy habits

- **Social awareness:** Understand non-verbal communication and social cues from others; develop positive views of others; develop empathy; understand the emotional needs of others; serve others

THE SCOPE OF SEL

Exploring CASEL's domains and competencies illuminates how fundamental these skills are, as well as how much they align with other areas of education, and prompts many of us to reflect on how we teach these concepts. For example, we can teach students about the idea of respect through a self-contained lesson on respecting others. But respect develops more deeply in children when they also learn to accept and respect themselves. Further, when children truly grasp respect, they also better understand other people and their feelings, and in turn they can begin to see how showing respect and kindness to others develops and strengthens friendships.

And SEL is anything but a stand-alone initiative. Some people view it as overlapping with character education, for instance. CASEL describes character education as aligning with SEL. Still others consider character education an extension of SEL. It can get confusing! In my view, character education promotes behaviors and traits such as moral sensitivity, ethical reasoning, and basic positive character, while SEL addresses the *core* of behavior. It is the social emotional backbone that supports and strengthens the individual character traits and actions that can extend from it.

It's also worth noting that the umbrella of SEL encompasses many other skills and benefits. A range of valuable programs, curricular goals, and educational initiatives are involved in developing social and emotional learning, including:

- character education
- non-cognitive skills and development
- twenty-first-century skills
- service learning
- bullying prevention
- conflict resolution
- social skills training
- growth mindset
- resilience and grit

This book will give you new ways of incorporating SEL every day.

- 👁 **Relationship skills:** Learn communication skills, listening, and understanding; develop inspiring leadership skills; learn conflict management skills; build bonds with others; learn teamwork and collaboration skills; help others develop skills
- 👁 **Responsible decision-making:** Solve problems; make positive choices; analyze and evaluate choices; reflect on past decisions; behave ethically and responsibly

At the beginning of each lesson you'll find a list of key words and phrases showing ways to connect individual traits, emotions, or behaviors to each of these five CASEL competencies or domains. You will notice that most or even all of the words and phrases listed could be placed in other domains as well, and you will also surely think of additional traits, emotions, and behaviors that would fit into these domains and have connections to the lesson and story. These lists of key words are simply a starting point, intended to suggest ways of inspiring positive SEL growth through the stories.

You probably already have ideas and approaches for integrating core SEL skills into curricular areas. I hope this book will expand on the strategies you have and give you new ways of incorporating SEL every day through inspiring stories. As professors Joseph E. Zins and Maurice J. Elias have put it, SEL is "the capacity to recognize and manage emotions, solve problems effectively, and establish positive relationships with others, competencies that clearly are essential for all students" (Zins and Elias 2006). Young people need these skills to navigate successfully through the choices and challenges of life.

HOW MANY EMOTIONS DO WE HAVE?

In the 1600s, Rene Descartes said that humans have only six primary emotions. If you watched the movie *Inside Out*, you might think that there are only five: joy, sadness, fear, anger, and disgust. However, recent thought identifies far more emotions, with one study identifying twenty-seven distinct emotions and other sources theorizing that the number of secondary emotions could be in the hundreds or even thousands (Anwar 2017).

In fact, many emotions are similar shades of another emotion—happiness and joy, sadness and grief, anticipation and surprise. They are slightly different. This book will show that stories can unleash many emotions that can motivate social and emotional growth in children so that they can respond with positive behavior.

WHY USE STORIES ABOUT PLANTS AND ANIMALS?

Clearly, stories are a powerful tool for developing social and emotional skills. And clearly, social and emotional skills are crucial to healthy, happy, and successful lives, for both children and adults. But why focus on stories about plants and animals, specifically, in teaching these skills?

Stories from nature can be particularly powerful and non-threatening to young listeners and readers. One reason for this is that most kids enjoy nature and are drawn to stories about animals and plants. Additionally, contact with nature can promote children's mental, emotional, and social health. Research has shown that hands-on contact with nature can help improve children's self-esteem, their engagement with school, and their sense of empowerment (Maller 2009). While the stories and lessons in this book cannot serve as a substitute for this direct

Stories are a powerful tool for developing social and emotional skills. And social and emotional skills are crucial to healthy, happy, and successful lives.

contact, they *can* draw on that fundamental connection that humans feel with the natural world.

Just as important, using stories about plants and animals—rather than about humans—provides a unique benefit. When a story is powerful or painful, nature is a safe distance from children. They do not feel in competition with a dog or a tree, as they can feel when presented with comparisons to people. Nature can illuminate and explore important lessons and ideas without pointing a finger at children or leading to feelings of inferiority, shame, or guilt.

For example, suppose you were to consider the dependability of two students. Sasha always remembers to do her homework. Nick can't seem to remember to take his assignments home. If you compare the two children with the intention of encouraging Nick to become dependable, Nick is more likely to feel embarrassed and hurt than encouraged or motivated. He may also feel resentment toward Sasha. He might feel attacked or view the comparison as unfair. Nick's thought process can get sidetracked by his resentment, hurt feelings, and anger. Meanwhile, your comparison gets ignored. The opportunity for helping Nick to develop dependability and responsibility—which, in turn, are social emotional skills of self-management—may be lost.

Nature, however, offers that reassuring sense of separation from human behavior. If a teacher or parent had read Nick the story "Dedicated Dogs" in lesson 10, he might have grasped the value of dependability demonstrated by dogs without feeling threatened by it. Nick may also have found the story to be emotionally moving or resonant. And through the related discussion and activities, Nick could gain a deeper understanding of responsibility and its importance. In the process, his brain could begin building a new neural pathway toward self-management and being more dependable.

Stories from nature allow us to teach social skills, including by highlighting characters who break the rules and whose actions—and their consequences—communicate important messages and lessons. We can see this in folk tales such as *Anansi the Spider*, stories like *Little Red Riding Hood,* and series such as The Berenstain Bears. Another example of a familiar and inspiring animal story is Hans Christian Andersen's famous fairy tale *The Ugly Duckling.* It resonates with anyone who has ever been left out, teased, or lonely—which is just about all of us. Hearing this story, children can feel empathy for the misjudged ugly duckling. It can create feelings of respect and appreciation for those who are different. And when the duck discovers he is a beautiful swan, it gives hope to everyone that when we discover our own identity, we can also become beautiful.

Reinforcement and Repetition of Stories Can Foster Positive Change

When any story, behavior, thought pattern, or message is repeated frequently enough, the brain's neurons create a pathway—and a habit. Over time, the habit seems easier and more natural. It's easy to understand this process through an analogy: Have you ever watched children make a sled run in the snow? If the hill isn't very steep, they first have to make the snow slick enough so that the sleds will slide down easily. Otherwise, they will get stuck in the snow. Children pull their sleds down the same path over and over again. Eventually, the repeated process creates a slippery surface for sledding.

When you use the lessons and stories in this book, you help remind students of how their behavior affects others—and vice versa. Children gain perspective of and empathy for the feelings of others. They begin to improve their own self-regulation, creating new pathways in their brains.

And as they repeatedly hear and discuss these stories, their thoughts and emotions can travel those pathways more quickly, like that slippery sled path. They begin to create positive emotional and social habits. Those habits can be further developed through stories in several ways:

- **Attention:** Stories have the potential to grab students' attention immediately, engaging their brains on many levels.

- **Participation:** When students participate vicariously in what is happening in a story, the brain is more deeply engaged in a way that rivals the level of engagement that would take place in a real-life experience.

- **Emotion:** Stories can release emotion in children as they feel empathy, curiosity, sadness, and other emotions for the characters. For example, lesson 4, about the bristlecone pine tree, can help students feel empathy for the tree's struggle to survive. It can speak to a kid who is struggling with math, with reading, or with finding a friend. Children can see that the tree's struggle has made it strong. They can be encouraged to understand that doing difficult things requires courage and inner strength.

- **Change:** Emotions can motivate change and growth in behavior and beyond far better than rules and lectures. For example, children could be reminded of lesson 6 and the story "Creeping Coconut Crabs" to help them keep trying when things are hard, and they can grow in resilience and perseverance. Repetition helps build new habits. Slowly but surely the pathways form in the brain, and change can come.

In your work with children, you have the chance to make a big difference. You can help shape the kinds of people your young students become. *Social Emotional Stories* gives you simple, effective ways to help kids to grow both socially and emotionally through storytelling. They can learn how to be more aware of their own personal feelings and those of others. They can learn to recognize problems and make better decisions and even show positive leadership.

WHAT IS A STORY?

For this book's purposes, the definition of a story is a narrative that is true or fiction, legend or biographic, written or in visual or audio format. It can be prose or verse, short or long. It will usually have a dramatic arc, including a hook to catch attention, a setting, plot, conflict, and a resolution of that conflict. It will aim to inspire empathy, curiosity, or other emotions that can that motivate behavior and positive growth.

HOW TO USE THIS BOOK

Each of the twenty-four lessons in this book is centered on a story that explores the characteristics and qualities of a fascinating animal or plant. You don't have to use these lessons or stories in any order. You can choose one that relates to something else your class is studying, one that includes a social or emotional idea, skill, or trait you want to address, or simply one that sounds especially interesting. As discussed earlier, each lesson opens with a list of key words and concepts tied to the story's ideas, broken down into the five SEL domains. You can also explore the Key Word Reference Charts that begin on page 16, which offer a quick overview of which lessons explore specific themes.

When you've chosen a lesson, read the story to familiarize yourself with it before using it in class. If you think that some of the vocabulary may be challenging for your students, see the glossary for kid-friendly definitions. You can tell the story animatedly as they listen. Telling the story usually has a greater emotional impact on the students. But you can also choose to pass it out and read it aloud. After you have presented the story, students can also read it themselves or as a group. If you like, display the picture of the lesson's subject on an interactive whiteboard or other surface. (All pictures are in the digital content. See page 168 for download instructions.)

Students may surprise you with the intuitive comments and connections they make on their own.

Accompanying each story is a list of discussion questions that will help your students make connections between the animals and plants explored in the lesson and SEL topics—human character traits, emotions, and relationships. Keep in mind that these questions are simply jumping-off points. Feel free to create your own! Similarly, the sample answers following each question are just to get you started. Your students may surprise you with the intuitive comments and connections they make on their own.

Each story is also paired with several activities specifically related to the lesson's SEL focus areas and to its animal or plant. These activities will help you engage your students in deeper exploration. Most require only minimal preparation and basic materials, and many include prepared handouts, which you will also find in the digital content. These activities can be adapted to work with kids of different ages, interests, abilities, and needs. You know your group best. Do what works for you.

Similarly, you can find creative and natural ways to work these lessons into your day. One option is to use one lesson per week in ten- to fifteen-minute blocks each day. For instance, you could read the story on a Monday, do discussion activities Tuesday through Thursday, and conduct review and reflection on Friday. You are the expert on what will be most effective in your classroom.

If you want to take a lesson even further, turn to Jump-Start Lessons for Social and Emotional Learning on page 13. There you'll find descriptions of hands-on activities that can be used in connection with any of the book's stories. And in the section Integrating This Book's Lessons and Stories Across Subject Areas on page 9, you'll find a sample story followed by interdisciplinary examples of how to integrate story across subject areas. Additionally, if you are comfortable embracing dramatic storytelling, you'll find tips in the following section for delivering stories. I invite you to look at this book as a toolbox of stories and lessons that will help you integrate SEL in an inspiring and exciting way.

Hints for Stronger Storytelling

Storytelling provides a springboard that can lead to discussions, activities, problem-solving, and behavior change in developing social and emotional growth. You are probably well acquainted with storytelling, and you might already be a pro. But if you choose to deliver stories aloud to your students, the following tips may be helpful. And remember: Good storytelling takes practice, so be patient with yourself. When you grow comfortable with telling stories, it will become natural, and you will enjoy the power of storytelling.

- Become familiar with your story ahead of time. You could write a few words on a slip of paper to remind you of important parts of the story. Then you can peek down at the paper if you need a cue. As you learn the story, it will become easier to repeat it without any notes.

- Stories do not need to be memorized, and you don't have to use the exact same words every time you tell a story. In fact, it is better if you don't. You might trip over your tongue trying to remember exact words, or it may sound robotic. Instead, focus on delivering the content and the message rather than a script.

- Practice telling the story to a kind person—or a mirror. The mirror won't talk back, but it will mimic what you do and help you refine your skills.

- Create a story from your personal life. Your story will be stronger if it has emotional impact. It can create understanding for children to learn to manage their emotions better and to set goals to achieve benchmarks.

WHAT THIS BOOK WILL NOT DO

This book offers you hands-on, practical ways to combine storytelling and SEL. But it does not attempt to cover all challenging situations with a story. And it does not indicate that stories are the only way to teach SEL. Additionally, if you have students who struggle with significant challenges to their mental or emotional health, those issues are beyond the scope of this book. Nevertheless, stories have the potential to reach any and all children in powerful ways, gaining their attention and encouraging such feelings as empathy, curiosity, loyalty, or cooperation.

- 👁 Be animated in your facial expressions and physical gestures. Open your eyes wide for dramatic surprise. Move about and use the space you have. Use visuals, if you want to, but you can tell your story without them.

- 👁 Change your voice level and pitch. See the power of suddenly speaking softly. Build tension as you slowly speak louder. Occasionally use a sudden loud burst to add drama. Interject silences and pauses.

- 👁 Use different character voices if you can.

- 👁 Employ metaphors to spark critical and creative thinking.

- 👁 Use language that fires up the senses: the sight of crystalline raindrops dripping off leaves; the smell of fresh cedar; the creamy taste of chocolate milk; the faint sound of footsteps; the feeling of touching a prickly cactus. Engaging the senses helps engage the brain and set the stage for empathy and growth. And remember, empathy is key. As psychologist Perry Firth has written, "War has built empires, but it is empathy and love that have sustained the human species."

INTEGRATING THIS BOOK'S LESSONS AND STORIES ACROSS SUBJECT AREAS

Stories can serve as "connective tissue" that helps tie together curricular areas and SEL. A good story, told well, might be used to introduce a unit of history, generate an art project, motivate emotions of courage or empathy, spark problem-solving, teach the use of metaphors, build self-confidence, or encourage patience. You get the idea!

To show you what I mean in more detail, what follows is an example of a legend in which a spider becomes a hero. After, you'll find ways you might integrate this story and its ideas across multiple academic subjects and also incorporate SEL concepts. As you read this book's stories with your students, keep these ideas in mind. They can be used across all the subjects and SEL domains you teach.

Robert the Bruce and the Spider

A great military leader by the name of Robert the Bruce lay hidden on a bed of straw in a cold, damp hut where he hoped his enemies would not find him. The year was 1306, and Bruce rightfully should have been the king of Scotland. But there was no Scotland, and he was no king. Instead, he was on the verge of defeat after a long fight against England's armies.

Bruce had gathered an army of his own to fight for Scottish independence from England. Their greatest wish was to become their own nation. But England's soldiers had defeated Bruce and his tattered army six times. Bruce's castle had been sacked, his brother executed, and his wife imprisoned. Bruce and his followers were nearly ready to throw down their weapons and give up their freedom.

As the discouraged Bruce lay in that cave, with wind howling outside, he saw a spider swinging from a web. Bruce watched the spider try to attach its web to the wall on the other side of the bed. Six times the spider failed in its wobbly attempts.

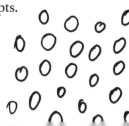

Bruce thought, "My soldiers and I have been defeated six times too. Now if this spider fails on its seventh try, I too shall give up the fight for Scotland."

Bruce watched closely. The spider swung toward the wall again with all its tiny strength. And to Bruce's surprise, on the seventh try, the spider reached the wall and finally connected its web. Bruce wanted to cheer. His attitude of defeat began to lift. He jumped up from the bed of straw and resolved to try again.

The spider's action rallied Bruce from his discouragement. Bruce rallied his troops. It wasn't easy, but ultimately, they won Scottish independence, and Bruce became king of Scotland. This story of one small spider—part truth, part legend—remains an inspiration to all who seek the courage to not give up.

Interdisciplinary Connections with the Story

In this section you'll find examples of how you can use a story from nature—in this case, "Robert the Bruce and the Spider"—to create an interdisciplinary unit for your class or grade level, or even a whole school. These activity and discussion ideas are broken down by subject area, and within each subject area you'll also find specific ideas for connecting SEL themes to discussion of the story. Two domains are explored in each area below, but as you use the stories and lessons in the book, you might discover that you can connect all domains to each story.

Language Arts

- Invite your group to create metaphors or similes about spiders.

- Discuss how facing challenges can sometimes help us find courage and resolve, as in the story of Robert the Bruce and the spider. Ask children to write or tell stories about times when they showed courage in their own lives. Did they ever do something that was frightening or hard? Did they get stronger by doing it? Did they feel discouraged like Robert the Bruce?

- Make SEL connections:

  - **Social awareness:** Children can feel empathy for Bruce, his tattered soldiers—maybe even the spider. They could write stories or poems from the perspective of one of these characters.

  - **Relationship skills:** Discuss the inspiring leadership of Robert the Bruce and his courage to not give up. You might also discuss the importance of teamwork in solving problems. Ask children to discuss other stories that share these themes.

Math

- Select students to conduct a survey of your class, grade level, school, or other group. The survey might seek to learn how many people are afraid of spiders, and how afraid (for example, 1. Very afraid; 2. Somewhat afraid; 3. Not afraid at all). Guide students in collecting the results and making a graph with percentages, perhaps also gathering data on other characteristics, such as age or gender. Discuss the findings.

- Make SEL connections:

  - **Self-awareness:** What did the survey help children learn about the fear of spiders? Is it common? Does it seem to be related to age or other factors?

  - **Relationship skills:** Ask the children to work in small groups to discuss the survey results. If applicable to your group, allow children who have learned how to calculate percentages to explain the idea to their group members. If you like, you could reconvene the large group to discuss the importance of clear communication and attentive listening.

Science and Technology

- Help students investigate how spiders spin their webs. You can look for information in print and online, and you may want to show students videos of the web-building process.

- As a group, explore and discuss inventions that have been inspired by spiders and their webs.

Examples include liquid wire, spiderweb glass, sound-proof metamaterial, and synthetic spider silk for use in textiles including bulletproof vests, and more.

👁 Make SEL connections:

- **Self-awareness:** Talk as a group about how science and technology depend on imagination. The imagination can help us discover new solutions, cures, inventions, and even games. From Robert the Bruce to innovative scientists, everyone has an imagination that helps them solve problems. We can develop our imaginations in many ways, such as drawing, writing, singing, playing, listening, and letting our thoughts wander through ideas.

- **Relationship skills:** To defeat England's armies, Robert the Bruce and his soldiers had to demonstrate a lot of teamwork. With your group, explore the idea that scientists also have to work together to invent things. Ask questions to spark discussion: "How do you think it helps scientists to work in teams, listen to each other, and learn to communicate clearly?" "How do scientists consider everyone's ideas and perspectives and then choose the best ones to explore?"

Social Studies

👁 A tiny spider inspired an army. What other small things or small actions have made a difference in history, in your community, or in society?

👁 Ask kids whether they think anyone can contribute if they summon up the courage. What are examples of this in history?

👁 Make SEL connections:

- **Self-management:** Discuss with the children what to do with their emotions. Most might decide they just try to keep a respectful distance from spiders.

- **Responsible decision-making:** Robert the Bruce made the courageous decision to keep fighting for his nation. Guide children though some steps for making courageous and

positive choices, such as brainstorming possible ideas; researching those ideas; choosing one; making a plan and carrying it out; reflecting and evaluating how it went in order to learn new approaches for the next decision.

Physical Education

👁 What can the tiny spider's determination teach us about physical ability? What helps a young person perform well in sports? Is it size? What might be the most important qualities to develop to make contributions in sports?

👁 Invite students to discuss or write about this statement and what it means to them in the context of physical education: "Perseverance pays off."

👁 How do you find courage to not give up in a losing game?

👁 Make SEL connections:

- **Self-management:** Robert the Bruce and the spider both had to bounce back from defeat. Talk with students about how this kind of resilience is important in sports and beyond. How do they get back up after being knocked down? How do they cope with defeat and disappointment? How do they control their emotions when losing a game or contest?

- **Social Awareness:** Robert the Bruce had to develop skills in communicating with his soldiers and understanding how they felt in order to keep their support. In what ways do you communicate on a team while playing a sport? How can you read what your teammates are thinking and feeling?

Art

👁 Invite children to find photographs of various spiders and insects (printed from online sources, cut out of magazines, or copied from books) and make a collage out of the photos.

👁 Have kids create spider-shaped crafts using materials such as pom poms, paper, craft straws, googly eyes, and more. They could even attach their creations to paper webs.

"You may tell a tale that takes up residence in someone's soul, becomes their blood and self and purpose. That tale will move them and drive them and who knows what they might do because of it, because of your words. That is your role, your gift."

—**Erin Morgenstern**

👁 Make SEL connections:

- **Self-management:** Ask children to show their spider creations or other artwork to the group. They might talk about what their art shows or explain what it means to them. Having the courage to share your gifts without embarrassment or shyness can help develop self-confidence and self-management.

- **Relationship skills:** Work as teams to create an art mural or collage together depicting the story of Robert the Bruce and the spider. Remember that everyone contributes to a beautiful mural. It is important for children to listen to each other's ideas so they can work together on creating the mural or collage.

Music

👁 There are many children's songs about spiders, from "The Itsy Bitsy Spider" to "A Spider on the Floor" by Raffi to "Spunk the Spider"—another spider that didn't give up (you can find music and lyrics here: songsforteaching.com/animalsongs/spunkthespider.php). Teach students one of these songs, or have them write their own.

👁 Make SEL connections:

- **Self-awareness:** Talk about how children felt individually when they heard songs about spiders. Were they frightened? Did they laugh and think it was funny? Help them explore how recognizing and accepting our emotions is part of self-awareness, and discuss the idea that music can help us feel emotions.

- **Responsible decision-making:** Robert the Bruce made a decision to learn from the spider's perseverance, despite the many differences between him and the spider. Even when we feel that we are different from the people around us, we can decide to sing together. We can create more beautiful music as a chorus. We can decide to listen to each other's voices so that we blend together in harmony. We can choose to enrich our lives and the lives of others—through our songs and through our actions.

A FINAL WORD

I would love to hear how *Social Emotional Stories* works for you and your students. Please feel free to share your experiences by emailing me at help4kids@freespirit.com, or by writing to me in care of the following address:

Free Spirit Publishing
6325 Sandburg Road, Suite 100
Minneapolis, MN 55427-3674

Best wishes to you,
Barbara A. Lewis

JUMP-START LESSONS FOR SOCIAL AND EMOTIONAL LEARNING

You can use these activities with any of the lessons or stories in this book. These activities will help children become more aware of their feelings and emotions, which in turn can help them manage those feelings better. They also can help children understand, communicate with, and empathize with others; strengthen positive habits; make productive decisions; and engage in discussion and reflection. Getting kids active and engaged through these activities can boost blood flow to the brain, bolster your classroom community, and build SEL skills all at the same time.

Nature is a powerful teaching tool—and it is always near! Most children love to touch, hear, smell, and see the outside world. They relate to weather, animals, plants, and even dirt. Take kids outside and ask them to look at the clouds above. What animals and plants do they see in the clouds? Seeing something within something else is a beginning step in understanding different perspectives. Ask kids to draw the outlines of clouds and, within these outlines, to draw what they see in the clouds. If you can't go outside, you can do this activity by displaying photographs of clouds on a projector or interactive whiteboard.

Focus on feelings. Pair up students and ask them to sit facing their partners, without talking. When everyone is still and quiet, invite kids to try to figure out how their partners are feeling, just by looking closely at their faces, posture, and so forth. Practice in becoming a thoughtful observer is an important step in learning to read social cues and in developing empathy.

Fill a jar with slips of paper, on each of which is written an emotion. Pair up students and have one member of each pair draw a slip without showing what it says to the partner. These students will then act as though they are feeling that emotion, while the partners try to guess it. This helps students learn to watch for subtle signs of different emotions and to empathize with others.

Teach children that communication goes beyond our words. Discuss how voice, body language, and facial expressions can change the meaning of what we're saying. We might communicate one thing with our tone of voice while our actions communicate the opposite meaning. Students will see the difference when role-playing the examples below. You can add many more phrases and have them role-play those as well. If needed, you can demonstrate first and then have children try.

👁 **Words:** "I really like you."
    Nonverbal communication: First, say this with a loud, sarcastic voice and a sneering expression. Wiggle your hands back and forth in a mocking way. Next, say the same sentence with a kind voice, a smile, and a thumbs-up gesture.

👁 **Words:** "I'm so happy!
    Nonverbal communication: First, say this with a loud, mad voice, a frowning or sad face, and drooped or hunched shoulders. Next, say the same sentence with a cheerful voice and a huge smile while clapping your hands.

What do students notice about each example?

Choose one story from the book and examine the positive SEL skills of the lesson's subject. Talk with your group about how everyone can practice developing or strengthening one of those skills for one week. For example, dogs appear to show forgiveness and caring for humans. Can kids practice forgiveness, caring, and empathy each day? Brainstorm specific ideas for doing so. Talk about this goal daily to remind children what they're working toward. At the end of the week, discuss their experiences. Did kids find that practicing the trait or behavior got easier as the week went on? Did the experiences help the children understand other people's feelings better? Invite kids to journal about their experiences and what they learn.

Invite students to make lists of their favorite creatures, plants, or objects in nature. Then have each child pick five of them and talk about comparisons and connections to human behaviors. *Example:* A mouse is small and can seem timid. It hides in small, dark places. Mice hide to protect themselves. Do people sometimes stay isolated or closed off because they are afraid to reveal themselves? Can it be scary to leave somewhere familiar and venture into the unknown, like when you move or change schools? These discussions can yield powerful realizations but can also be complex, and children may need extra help to understand the comparisons drawn.

Pass out handouts of a story to kids and ask them to highlight passages or facts that especially grab their attention. Use these as starting points for drawing connections to SEL skills in people, such as dependability as illuminated by the "Heroic Horses" story in lesson 14.

Divide your group into pairs and have each pair write and perform a skit. Assign two plants or animals to each pair and ask kids to act out a scene between these two characters. For example, suppose one pair is assigned "dog" and "cat." What kind of scene could these animals share? Would they agree or disagree? How are they the same or different? How might they resolve differences and conflicts? Give kids time to work on their ideas and prepare their skits, and help as necessary. As time allows, have students perform their skits for the group.

Play the following game with your students. It works especially well after you have read all or most of the stories in this book, but you can apply it to a smaller group of lessons as well.

Obtain a soft, squishy ball. One student begins as the leader and stands in front of the group, holding the ball. The leader says the name of something from nature, such as "tree," "cow," or "thunderstorm." Each group member quickly thinks of a quality (positive or negative) shown by the named object from nature. When students have their ideas in mind, they raise their hands. Then the leader calls on the first person who raises a hand and throws the ball to that person. That person answers by saying the positive or negative quality, and then says the name of another object in nature and throws the ball to a third person who raises a hand.

Example: Jessie says, "dolphin," and throws the ball to Lukas, who has his hand up. Lukas answers, "friendship." Then he says, "metalmark moth," and throws the ball to Senji, who is waving his arm. Senji catches the ball and responds, "copying." Play continues until everyone has had at least one turn.

Variation: Divide your group into two teams. Have each team stand in a line, facing the opposite team. Throw the ball from person to person on opposite sides down the line, asking questions and giving answers. Establish a time limit for responses—possibly ten to fifteen seconds to ask or answer.

Ask each kid to draw any plant or creature that they like. Each day or so, invite a few students to show their drawings to the class. As a group, talk about what positive qualities the subject of each

drawing might show. As the class brainstorms, write their answers and ideas on the board. Then choose one trait that is especially interesting and invite the group to write poems or short stories about this good quality and the animal or plant that shows it. They could work individually or in small groups. Once they've finished, pair the artwork with the written work and create a display. As more kids present their artwork, the character display will continue to grow.

Choose one of the animals or plants in the book and have kids write an acrostic poem using the first letters of the animal or plant's name, focusing on positive behaviors. Kids could do this individually and then share their compositions, or the group might brainstorm the poem together. For example:

Dedicated
Outgoing
Good friend

Play a game based on circle tag. Have students stand in a circle, with one person (Player 1) outside the circle. She stops behind a person (Player 2) and says something complimentary or appreciative about Player 2. Player 2 leaves their spot and runs around the outside of the circle, while Player 1 tries to beat Player 2 back to their place in the circle. Player 2 then repeats the pattern. As the game progresses, no person can be chosen twice. The choices become fewer and more challenging to the memory. This helps kids to think kind thoughts about the others and to concentrate, so as to remember which people have not been selected yet. If they make a mistake, they have to sit in the middle of the circle. At the end of the game, the person, who is "it" says, "I let Tony out of the circle, because he shared his pencil with me" and so on, until all children have left the inside of the circle.

Variation: Have children stand or sit in two equal lines facing each other and take turns saying something kind or appreciative to the people across from them.

KEY WORD REFERENCE CHARTS

Looking for a specific idea to investigate and discuss with your group? Use these charts to find out which major SEL ideas, skills, and character traits are discussed in each lesson. The key words and phrases that follow are broken into the five SEL domains defined by CASEL, but you'll see that some appear in multiple domains. Indeed, all of these ideas overlap, align, and intertwine. A trait, feeling, behavior, or idea might fall more neatly into the domains of self-awareness and self-management when focused inward, while seeming more tied to social awareness or relationship skills when outwardly focused—and the responsible decision-making domain can easily encompass inwardly or outwardly focused actions. For example, *goal-setting* could fall into both self-management and responsible decision-making. *Integrity* might typically fall under self-management but could reasonably be applied to any domain.

SELF-AWARENESS

KEY WORD	LESSON #
Balance	17, 18
Courage and Boldness	3, 4, 10, 17, 21
Curiosity	5, 21, 23
Fear	1, 3, 23, 24
Frustration	2, 9, 14
Gratitude	1, 19, 24
Happiness and Joy	9, 11, 13, 19
Imagination	2, 7, 23
Inner Strength	2, 4, 7, 13, 14, 15, 16, 17, 19, 20, 22
Love	1, 10, 12, 14, 19
Mindfulness	4, 6, 9
Peacefulness	6, 12
Self-Confidence	2, 8, 11, 13, 22
Understanding Personal Strengths and Weaknesses	4, 7, 8

SELF-MANAGEMENT

KEY WORD	LESSON #
Adaptability	4, 8, 9, 14, 17, 20, 23
Anger and Impulse Management	1, 12, 23
Assertiveness	7, 9, 15
Coping Skills and Stress Management	2, 3, 4, 6, 14
Courage and Boldness	6, 14, 15, 19
Goal-Setting	9, 10, 11, 18, 21
Hard Work	2, 4, 9, 10, 14, 21
Healthy Habits	2, 3, 5, 8, 9, 10, 16, 20
Honesty	6, 8, 13, 15, 16, 24
Integrity	8, 13, 15, 16, 20
Organization and Self-Motivation	9, 18, 21
Patience	2, 4, 14
Peacefulness	4, 12
Perseverance	2, 4, 6, 14
Planning and Preparation	3, 21, 24
Responsibility	2, 10, 14, 18, 22, 23
Sadness	5, 10, 12
Safety	3, 5, 6
Self-Regulation	3, 5, 20, 23
Trust and Trustworthiness	1, 2, 8, 10, 12, 21, 24

SOCIAL AWARENESS

KEY WORD	LESSON #
Acceptance of Others	3, 4, 6, 7, 8, 9, 12, 18, 19, 22
Caring and Kindness	1, 10, 11, 12, 20, 23, 24
Communication	5, 7, 10, 24
Discernment	3, 8, 16
Empathy	1, 5, 10, 11, 12, 14, 17, 19, 21
Fairness and Equality	15, 16, 22
Helpfulness	1, 10, 11, 12, 14
Perspective-Taking	1, 2, 3, 4, 5, 6, 7, 9, 16, 19, 21, 22, 23

KEY WORD	LESSON #
Reading Social Cues	1, 5, 8, 10, 11, 15, 22, 23
Respect	7, 8, 11, 12, 16, 19, 22
Service to Others	13, 14, 21, 24
Understanding Others	5, 11, 13, 17

RELATIONSHIP SKILLS

KEY WORD	LESSON #
Bullying Prevention	7, 15, 17, 20, 22
Citizenship	9, 22, 24
Communication	1, 11, 17, 18, 21
Conflict Management and Resolution	1, 7, 12, 23
Cooperation, Collaboration, and Teamwork	2, 7, 11, 14, 15, 18, 20, 22, 24
Forgiveness	1, 10, 24
Friendship	10, 11, 12, 17, 23, 24
Helpfulness	2, 10, 11, 14, 16, 19, 21
Humor	6, 9, 17
Leadership	2, 10, 18, 19, 22, 23
Listening	1, 3, 4, 5, 7
Loyalty	10, 14, 16, 18, 24
Playfulness	5, 11, 17, 18
Resisting Social Pressure	8, 14, 15, 23
Service to Others	5, 10, 13, 14

RESPONSIBLE DECISION-MAKING

KEY WORD	LESSON #
Analyzing and Evaluating	3, 5, 11, 13, 15, 16, 18, 24
Conservation	4, 21
Discernment	3, 8, 16
Healthy Habits	8, 13
Identifying Challenges	3, 5, 19, 24
Positive and Ethical Choices	1, 3, 4, 5, 6, 12, 13, 14, 15, 16, 19, 22, 23
Problem-Solving	1, 2, 6, 7, 9, 10, 11, 14, 16, 17, 18, 19, 20, 21, 23
Safety	8, 10, 16, 23
Understanding Consequences	3, 5, 8, 13, 15, 23
Wisdom and Learning	17, 19, 21

LESSON 1
APES

Key Words

The behaviors, traits, and emotions below are just starting points for aligning SEL, character education, and this lesson's story. Most of these ideas can easily be connected with more than one competency or domain.

Self-Awareness: Fear • Gratitude • Love

Self-Management: Anger and Impulse Management • Trust and Trustworthiness

Social Awareness: Caring and Kindness • Empathy • Helpfulness • Perspective-Taking • Reading Social Cues

Relationship Skills: Communication • Conflict Management and Resolution • Forgiveness • Listening

Responsible Decision-Making: Positive and Ethical Choices • Problem-Solving

Students will

- learn about apes, a group of mammals that includes gorillas and chimpanzees
- think about ways to help and care for those who might be in trouble
- discuss and consider what might happen when someone treats an animal or a person with kindness and love
- consider the behavior of the gorilla Binti Jua, and think about what might encourage people to trust and forgive others, even after they have been hurt

Overview

This story of the gorilla Binti Jua can unleash empathy in students as they read or listen to it. This is powerful: research shows that people are more willing to help and share with others when they feel empathy in response to a story (see the introduction for more information on this). Helping children feel empathy is an important part of social and emotional learning.

Apes are among the most intelligent animals on the planet. They share close genetic ties with humans, and they demonstrate behaviors that seem similar to character traits in people, such as understanding the needs of others and possibly even feeling empathy and love. These traits also can be similar to helpfulness, caring for others, and communication.

After learning the stories of the gorillas Koko and Binti Jua, students will enjoy discussing and considering what might happen if people treat animals, and other people, with kindness, love, and respect rather than anger and violence. Binti Jua cradled a small and vulnerable boy, protecting him from the other gorillas. Her story is a peaceful example of stopping a conflict before it happens.

Story

Awesome Apes

AWESOME APES

Koko was a famous gorilla. Her trainer, Francine, taught her hundreds of words in sign language. Scientists aren't sure just what Koko understood. She probably didn't think about language the same way people do. But Koko *did* communicate. Francine says that Koko used sign language to ask for a pet kitten. Koko played with the kitten and cuddled with it.

Many apes also seem to be good helpers. Have you ever heard this saying? *"I'll scratch your back if you'll scratch mine."* It means, "I'll help you if you'll help me." Apes seem to follow this saying. They help clean each other's fur. Sometimes they get food from each other in return.

Chimpanzees are a kind of ape. Scientists have studied how chimps help each other. Sometimes they're helpful even when they don't get any reward. In some tests, they help people, not just other chimps.

Chimps and other apes also love to play. They wrestle and chase each other around. They laugh too. Tickling and playing can give them the giggles.

So it seems like apes can be helpful and friendly. They can even be funny!

But gorillas are still wild animals, and they can be dangerous. An adult male can be 6 feet tall and weigh hundreds of pounds. Gorillas usually don't attack people. But sometimes it does happen.

No one was expecting anything frightening to happen at the Brookfield Zoo near Chicago one pretty day. People crowded around the gorilla enclosure. They smiled as they watched the large apes play, nap, and eat.

But suddenly the day turned scary. A three-year-old boy fell 15 feet, landing right in front of a group of big gorillas. The gorillas pawed the ground and began ambling over. The boy lay without moving on the concrete floor. People at the zoo screamed for help. They were afraid of what might happen to the small boy, because gorillas are sometimes fierce.

An unlikely hero loped into action. A female ape, Binti Jua, moved quickly over to the boy. She carried her own baby on her back. Then she did something that surprised the people watching. She gently lifted the boy off the ground. She cuddled him and protected the little boy from the other gorillas.

Binti's swift actions may have saved the boy's life. She gave zookeepers time to enter the space. Binti handed the boy over to the zookeepers, and they carried him back to his grateful mother.

The tender experience caught the world's attention. Binti had surprised the zookeepers, because Binti's own mother had ignored her when Binti was a baby. In fact, Binti's mother did not even feed her. The zookeepers felt sorry for the tiny gorilla baby. They took Binti and cradled her in their own arms and loved her. The zookeepers raised Binti like their own baby. They hand-fed her with a bottle.

As Binti grew up, she never acted mean or angry even though her mother had abandoned her. With humans, we might call that forgiveness. Binti had not learned how to nurture from her own mother. But maybe because human hands had rescued and cuddled Binti as a baby, she knew how to rescue and cradle a little human boy.

APE FACTS

- In one study, chimps worked to help others get food, even though the helper chimps received no reward.

- Orangutans are a type of ape. In the Malay language, *orangutan* means "person of the forest."

- Gibbons are another type of ape. Using their long, flexible arms, they can swing through the jungle at up to 35 miles per hour.

TALK IT OVER

Apes are not people, but we can make comparisons to them that can help us think about our own emotions and behavior. Use these questions to guide your students in considering possible similarities between the behaviors of apes and people, such as caring, empathy, forgiveness, love, helpfulness, trust, and communication.

Koko the gorilla communicated with people using sign language. Why do you think it's important for people to communicate with each other?

- When we talk with others about our thoughts and feelings—and listen to what they say too—we get closer to other people. We build trust and understanding. We also build communication skills such as the ability to interpret facial expressions, gestures, and other social cues.

- Talking about things that worry or scare us can help us feel better.

- When we are not open and honest, it can lead to misunderstandings and hurt feelings.

- It's important to communicate clearly so that everyone understands, especially when you have something meaningful to say or share.

Ask students how they felt when they heard the story about Binti Jua. Did they have feelings for Binti? Talk with students about the concept of empathy: feeling hurt on behalf of someone else and understanding how another might feel. Binti Jua took care of a little boy, even though he was very different from her. Can you think of ways that we can show caring toward people who seem to be different from us in some way?

- By learning more about people of other cultures, beliefs, and backgrounds, we change our perspectives. The more we learn about other people, the more we see how much we all have in common. We can also learn to better interpret the social cues and perspectives of others, even when they are different from our own.

- By sharing stories with people about our backgrounds and our life experiences. Everyone has a different story, and we feel good when others listen to us and care about our stories. And when we listen to others, we also begin to better understand their feelings and emotions.

- By writing letters to pen pals from other parts of the country or the world.

Scientists have seen chimpanzees perform caring acts for each other. What kind acts can you do for other people—friends, family, teachers, and others? (Encourage kids to brainstorm ideas for kind acts, large and small. Keep a list on the board or on mural paper, if you like.)

- If someone is new in class, we can be friendly and helpful. We can show the new student around, answer questions, and help the person feel comfortable in a new place.

- Everyone has different talents and skills. If you are good at math or reading, you could offer your help to someone who has a harder time with those subjects.

- Some kids don't have enough food or warm clothes. We can help get those things for them.

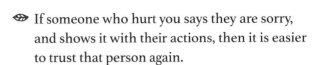
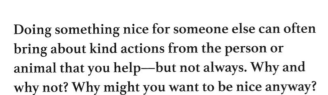

Doing something nice for someone else can often bring about kind actions from the person or animal that you help—but not always. Why and why not? Why might you want to be nice anyway?

- If someone has been nice to you, you want to be nice to them.

- We all have days when we're in a bad mood for one reason or another. At those times, it can make us feel better when people are nice to us. But other times we might be so cranky that we don't respond nicely. If you're kind to someone and they don't return your kindness right away, try again some other day.

- It can help you feel good inside to be nice to someone, even if they aren't nice back to you right away.

- Sometimes, if you keep being nice to someone who does or says mean things, that person may change their behavior. Giving kindness can bring out kindness in others. (If someone is mean to you again and again, talk to a grown-up you trust. Get help.)

Chimpanzees sometimes help each other even when they don't get any obvious reward. Do you think that people sometimes do nice things just to get a reward? Is that okay? What are some reasons other than a reward to do kind and helpful things?

- Even if someone does something nice in order to get a reward, the nice thing still gets done.

- Helping other people just makes you feel good inside. Doing the right thing is its own reward.

- Being kind and helpful to others can lead to other people being kind and helpful to us. It can also inspire people to be nice to others. Kindness spreads.

The gorilla Binti Jua learned to trust, even though she had been abandoned by her mother. How can we learn to trust when people have hurt us? Why is it sometimes important to do this? How do you tell the difference between people you can trust and those you probably should not trust?

- If someone who hurt you says they are sorry, and shows it with their actions, then it is easier to trust that person again.

- Everyone makes mistakes. We all deserve forgiveness and a second chance.

- Sometimes you need to be careful with your trust. It might be better—and safer—not to trust someone who has hurt you badly, or someone who makes you feel uncomfortable or unsafe.

Do you think people feel happier when they forgive and trust others? Why or why not?

- Carrying around anger or hurt can lead to other uncomfortable feelings. Over time, it can even make you sick. Forgiving someone can free you and help those difficult feelings go away, even though it may take a while.

- When you trust someone, you're usually happy to be with that person. You feel safe. Trusting someone can also help you relax and be yourself. (But remember: If someone has hurt you, you can choose to forgive that person. However, you do *not* need to trust someone who hurts. And you do not have to let them hurt you again. Instead, seek help from an adult you do trust.)

ACTIVITIES

Activity 1: Speaking with Signs

Materials

Sign Language Alphabet handout (in digital content)

Directions

Help kids learn to sign the alphabet in American Sign Language. Pass out copies of the Sign Language Alphabet handout. As a group, choose a few short words to learn to spell. As students practice, talk about different ways of communicating. What would it be like if they *couldn't* communicate with others? How would that make them feel? Why is it important to be able to share our thoughts and emotions?

Activity 2: The Kindness Chorus

Materials

Optional: Colored pencils and/or pens

Directions

Divide the class into small groups of two to four. Have each group work together to write a song or rap about being kind to everyone, forgiving others, or helping others without rewards. Have kids write down their compositions, and hang their papers outside your room where other students can see and enjoy them.

Optional: Invite students to perform their songs or raps for another class or at a school assembly or other event.

Activity 3: Opposites Attract

Materials

2 bar magnets (or, if possible, several pairs of bar magnets)

Directions

In front of the class, hold up the two bar magnets with the two north poles close together. Show how the magnets push each other away. Next, do the same with the south poles. They will also repel each other. Invite kids to take turns holding the magnets so that they can feel how strongly the same magnetic poles repel each other.

Next, point the north pole of one bar magnet toward the south pole of the other magnet. They will pull together. Again, offer kids the chance to do this for themselves.

Variation: If you have enough magnets, divide the class into smaller groups and allow kids to experiment and play with the magnets as you lead the discussion.

Following this simple demonstration, lead your group in making comparisons to friendships and other relationships. Like magnets, are people who are very different ever drawn to each other? Can they form strong friendships? Why do kids think that this is or isn't the case? What if two people are very similar? Can it sometimes be challenging for them to work together or to be friends? Why or why not?

Activity 4: Calming Yourself Through Your Senses

Materials

None

Directions

Help your students learn a simple calming activity to use when they feel stressed or fearful. You can do this as a group, or you can teach the skill to the children to use individually when they need to. Invite children to focus their attention on their five senses, one at a time.

- First, identify and focus on five things they can hear.
- Next, focus on four things they can feel.
- Focus on three things they can see.
- Focus on two things they can smell.
- Finally, focus on one thing they can taste.

Ask students how they felt while doing this exercise and afterward. Talk about how focusing on their senses can redirect their thoughts away from something that is stressful or scary.

LESSON 2
BAMBOO

Key Words

The behaviors, traits, and emotions below are just starting points for aligning SEL, character education, and this lesson's story. Most of these ideas can easily be connected with more than one competency or domain.

Self-Awareness: Frustration • Imagination • Inner Strength • Self-Confidence

Self-Management: Coping Skills and Stress Management • Hard Work • Healthy Habits • Patience • Perseverance • Responsibility • Trust and Trustworthiness

Social Awareness: Perspective-Taking

Relationship Skills: Cooperation, Collaboration, and Teamwork • Helpfulness • Leadership

Responsible Decision-Making: Problem-Solving

Students will

- 👁 learn about bamboo's natural qualities, including its strength and its rapid growth

- 👁 draw comparisons between bamboo's many uses and the ways people can think creatively to solve problems

- 👁 consider positive traits and behaviors such as inner strength and responsibility and talk about them with their peers

- 👁 discuss how small, negative behaviors can get quickly out of control

Overview

Kids will be fascinated by how fast bamboo grows, by its surprising strength, and by the many ways it can be used. Through discussion and activities, you can help your students see how these natural qualities can be compared to human behaviors including responsibility, strength, and problem-solving. Help your students explore real-life situations that can quickly get out of control, just like bamboo's rapid growth. Your group may also enjoy talking about ways that people could creatively use bamboo and make the most of its natural characteristics to help people in need.

Story

Bountiful Bamboo

BOUNTIFUL BAMBOO

There once lived a man who grew very discouraged with life. He had worked hard, and yet it seemed he had failed at everything he tried. In frustration, he gave up and left everything behind. He chose to live in the woods, where he could be alone. No one would know about his failures there. In the woods he could cry quietly to himself.

But to his surprise, he *wasn't* alone. One day a hermit wandered by his little thatch house and sat down on the man's tree-stump chair. The hermit was a good listener. So the man shared his story of failure with him.

After hearing the man's tale, the hermit pointed and said, "Look at those two plants."

The man spied a fern and a bamboo plant. "I see them," he said.

The hermit went on, "I planted the fern and the bamboo seeds at the same time. I watered them and fertilized them, and the sun warmed them. The fern grew quickly."

The man began to wonder where this story was going.

"I took good care of that bamboo for a few years, but it did not grow as much as an inch," the hermit said. "It didn't grow at all in that first year. But I didn't give up on it. I kept watering and nurturing it and I waited patiently to see what would happen."

"And what did happen?" asked the man.

The hermit continued his story. "It was a big surprise. In the fifth year, a tiny sprout finally poked up through the earth. And within just six months, that tiny bamboo grew a hundred feet."

"A *hundred* feet?" the man wondered.

"That's what I said. That little tiny bamboo grew a hundred feet."

"But how did it grow so much?" The man looked at the giant bamboo towering above them.

The hermit smiled. "Once I looked at the question in another way, I understood what had happened. I had to see things from the perspective of the bamboo itself. That little bamboo shoot had big plans. It was growing underground *the whole time.* It was making very strong roots. It needed all that time to make a root system strong enough to hold up a magnificent, hundred-foot-tall plant."

The man was looking at the hermit in surprise.

"Don't you think that all the time you were struggling, you were growing strong roots?" asked the hermit. "Just like the bamboo?"

The man thought quietly about the question. He nodded his head. He took the hermit's hands and squeezed them. And then the man left his hiding place in the forest and walked out into the bright sun. From that day on, he worked hard to grow into a patient, confident, and successful person.

BAMBOO FACTS

- Bamboo has a higher tensile strength than many alloys of steel and a higher compressive strength than many mixtures of concrete. It has a better strength-to-weight ratio than graphite.

- In China, bamboo has long been used to treat infections.

- Flutes made from bamboo are traditional instruments in many Asian countries.

- Have you ever thought of building a house of grass? Bamboo is a type of grass. But it's very strong. People build homes from bamboo because they can even last through earthquakes and storms. These homes can stand for hundreds of years.

- Bamboo grows in Asia, Africa, Australia, and North and South America. In other words, much of the world is home to some kind of bamboo. Bamboo grows faster than almost any other plant. Some types of bamboo can grow more than 4 feet in a single day! Most trees take thirty to fifty years to grow from seeds to their full size. But some kinds of bamboo need just six months to grow up. Fast-growing bamboo can cause trouble too. Roots spread far and wide underground. Spiky young bamboo shoots pop up all over the place. They can even crack sidewalks or streets.

- Buildings are a good way to use bamboo. But this plant can do much more. Inventors have used tiny pieces of it to do big jobs. Thomas Edison used thin strings of bamboo in his first lightbulbs. Alexander Graham Bell used a sharp sliver of bamboo as the needle in his first record player.

- Have you ever eaten bamboo? Cooked bamboo shoots are tasty and tender. People in many countries eat it. Bamboo is also a giant panda's favorite food. Pandas eat up to 85 pounds of the plant each day. (They don't cook their bamboo, though!) Could bamboo help feed people around the world? Because it grows so fast, it might be able to help a lot of hungry people.

TALK IT OVER

Use these questions to guide your students in comparing the strength of bamboo (and its roots) to people who become aware of their inner strength. This awareness is a cornerstone of emotional growth. Also discuss problem-solving, confidence, and other traits and behaviors that people may have.

The strength of bamboo might surprise you. Have you ever found strength in a surprising place?

- Someone unexpected stepped forward as an inspiring leader.

- In an emergency, you found inner strength and courage that you didn't know you had.

Bamboo is a sturdy, reliable material for building homes. What are strong, reliable "building materials" that you can use to build your life? How can you work on having more of these materials in your life?

- Dedicated work, good family and friends, learning to cope with problems, education, and service to others can all be good "building materials" in your life.

- You can build a healthy life on a foundation of positive social and emotional skills and strengths, such as honesty, responsibility, empathy, fairness, forgiveness, cooperation, and hard work. Like building strong roots, learning these skills will pay off in time.

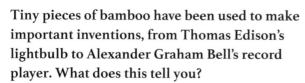

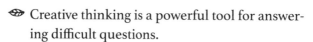

Tiny pieces of bamboo have been used to make important inventions, from Thomas Edison's lightbulb to Alexander Graham Bell's record player. What does this tell you?

- Every part of the whole is important, and even the smallest pieces have a function. Therefore, each small job is important for the proper functioning of the government, business, organization, school, team, and family.

- Every small part of the body has a purpose. Treat your body with care.

- When we are creative in solving problems, we can do amazing things.

Some kinds of bamboo grow very, very quickly. What else can grow quickly or spread out of control quickly? If appropriate for your group, encourage kids to consider, among other ideas, the way that a small mistake can sometimes lead to larger, more harmful mistakes. Luckily, good actions can grow quickly as well.

- Skipping homework or chores can quickly leave you far behind, making it hard to catch up.

- Rumors can spread quickly. They can cause hurt feelings and misunderstandings.

- Caring acts and friendly words can be contagious. So can laughter and smiles.

- Try to face smaller disagreements and talk them out before they destroy relationships.

- Take care of small health problems before they grow into more serious health issues.

- Debt can grow rapidly when we don't save and spend wisely. Before you know it, you might have no money to spend. Try to save up your money before you buy, so that you know you can afford the purchase.

You might not think of using bamboo to build your house. But bamboo is a common building material in many countries. People use bamboo in many other creative ways too. How can you connect this idea to problem-solving?

- Sometimes thinking about things in new ways can help you solve tough problems.

- Creative thinking is a powerful tool for answering difficult questions.

- Many people have hidden talents.

Bamboo's fast growth can be very useful to people. With careful planting, we can continue to have lots of bamboo. This could be important, especially if people are using bamboo for food and for building homes. How could this connect to human behavior?

- Sometimes the ideas that come to your head the fastest are the ideas that you should look at most carefully.

- Building a strong inner confidence can help you do better in all areas of your life—in school, family relationships and friendships, your homework, jobs, and so on.

ACTIVITIES

Activity 1: Characteristics of Bamboo

Materials

Small slips of paper (2 per student)
2 containers for slips (hats, jars, plastic cups)

Directions

In addition to being a building material, a food, and a material for inventors, bamboo was once used as a writing surface. Many hundreds of years ago in China, people used thin pieces of bamboo as paper.

Give each student a small slip of paper and ask them to write down a word or phrase that might make them think of bamboo. (*Examples: strong, tall, responsible, dependable, confident, hard worker.*) If necessary, you can help kids brainstorm ideas.

Next, invite children to say the name of someone in the group who demonstrates that word. Make a rule that only kind things can be said about anyone. This activity can be a positive self-confidence experience for those named. (If appropriate, it can also offer you a chance to name someone who might be overlooked.)

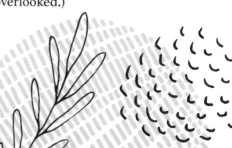

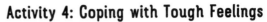

Activity 2: Growth of Bamboo

Materials

An unused compressed sponge

Bowl or jar

Water (with food coloring, if desired)

Directions

Bamboo's fast growth is sometimes helpful and sometimes harmful, depending on the situation. Demonstrate how a little bit of an outside factor or influence—whether positive or negative—can lead to big results.

Place the dry sponge in a bowl or jar and begin pouring a small amount of water on it to show how a relatively small amount of liquid—drip, drip, drip—can have a big effect. As the sponge grows and expands, talk with the group about comparisons to human behavior and character.

Activity 3: Bamboo Haiku

Materials

Optional: Bamboo Haiku handout (in digital content)

Directions

In Japan, one of the many countries where bamboo thrives, haiku is a traditional form of poetry, which usually explores the natural world and also human emotion. Have each student write a haiku about bamboo, connecting it to a relevant inner strength. For example:

Bamboo, reaching high *(5 syllables)*
Stretching to the skies above *(7 syllables)*
So strong—so silent *(5 syllables)*

For younger students, it may be helpful to use the Bamboo Haiku handout. Show kids how to fill in each space with one syllable.

After everyone has had time to write a poem, invite volunteers to share their poems with the group. You could also post poems on a bulletin board in class, or create a compilation for kids to take home and share with their families.

Activity 4: Coping with Tough Feelings

Materials

Materials will vary

Directions

Like the man in the story, children need help handling their feelings when they are frustrated, sad, or discouraged. Here are a few suggestions. Talk through these ideas and consider trying a few of them as a group to help students see how they work.

- Bake "cope-cakes," using a cupcake or muffin recipe. Decorate them and give them to someone who needs cheering up.
- Talk with someone you trust.
- Rub your arms or legs for five minutes.
- Read a book to someone.
- Write, draw, paint, take photos, or make something from clay.
- Play an instrument, sing, or listen to music.
- Take a shower or bath.
- Spend time outside.
- Take a nap.
- Walk, run, dance, go for a bike ride, skip through a sprinkler, or get your body moving in some other way.
- Read a book.
- Play a game or do a puzzle.
- Organize something, like your papers, binder, desk, or backpack.

Activity 5: Watch It Grow

Materials

2 small bamboo plants (available at a local nursery or an online nursery)

Directions

Purchase both a fast-growing tropical bamboo plant (not a seed) and a small, slower growing pygmy bamboo plant. Care for them in your classroom or space, monitoring their growth over time. See how quickly the fast-growing one gets bigger. Compare this to rapidly spreading rumors. Talk with kids about preventing or stopping rumors, lies, and other harmful talk that can sometimes get out of control.

LESSON 3
BOX JELLYFISH

Key Words
The behaviors, traits, and emotions below are just starting points for aligning SEL, character education, and this lesson's story. Most of these ideas can easily be connected with more than one competency or domain.

Self-Awareness: Courage and Boldness • Fear

Self-Management: Coping Skills and Stress Management • Healthy Habits • Planning and Preparation • Safety • Self-Regulation

Social Awareness: Acceptance of Others • Discernment • Perspective-Taking

Relationship Skills: Listening

Responsible Decision-Making: Analyzing and Evaluating • Discernment • Identifying Challenges • Positive and Ethical Choices • Understanding Consequences

Students will

- learn about the box jellyfish and its dangerous poison
- draw comparisons between the box jellyfish's enticing appearance and activities that seem fun but may be dangerous
- discuss the consequences of actions and behaviors and consider how things are not always what they seem
- discuss the value of exercising self-control and think about how to stay safe in potentially dangerous situations

Overview
The box jellyfish lesson is one of the more serious ones in this book. It takes a close look at temptation, danger, and other weighty ideas. Kids will be intrigued by the box jellyfish's beauty and by its deadly poison. The story might awaken emotions of fear or anxiety in some children. Both can be important emotions to recognize and learn to manage. As students learn about the box jellyfish—which is tempting in appearance—they will draw comparisons to human activities. Some experiences may seem fun and exciting, but they can quickly put kids in dangerous and harmful situations. Students will understand that they are free to choose what they do, but they may not always be able to choose the consequences. At the same time, kids will consider the pitfalls of judging people based on appearance.

Story
Box Jellyfish—Beautiful but Deadly

BOX JELLYFISH—BEAUTIFUL BUT DEADLY

You might not even see it at first. The box jellyfish is pale blue and transparent. It's almost invisible. It moves through the water with a dancer's gentle grace.

But beware! This delicate beauty is a dangerous beast. Even its other names sound scary. *Marine stinger. Sea wasp.* These names come from the jellyfish's deadly sting.

Most jellyfish drift wherever the ocean takes them. But not box jellies. They move themselves through the water as they hunt. They eat shrimp, fish, and other sea creatures. They have 24 eyes to help them find food.

Box jellyfish live in waters around Australia, Hawaii, and the Caribbean Islands. These delicate jellies are silent and hard to spot, even though they have up to 15 long tentacles. Each tentacle can be 10 feet long. And each one has about 5,000 stinging cells.

Box jellyfish stings are very, very painful. Even worse, the stinging cells carry deadly poison.

If a swimmer gets stung, acting quickly is important. The person needs medicine within 20 or 30 minutes. Otherwise, they may die. Swimmers who have been stung have died from heart attacks and from drowning.

Of course, the best way to stay safe is not to get stung at all. Many divers wear suits that protect them. Others avoid beaches where jellies live.

But here's some good news. There is a quick and simple way to help someone who has gotten stung. Put vinegar on the sting. It stops more poison from getting into the body. So be prepared. If you swim where the jellies prowl, take some vinegar with you. It may save a life. But sorry—vinegar won't take away the pain. Only time can do that.

BOX JELLYFISH FACTS

- The box jellyfish's sting and venom do not affect sea turtles, which eat the jellies.
- A group of jellyfish is called a smack.
- A box jellyfish can weigh up to 5 pounds.

TALK IT OVER

Use these questions to guide your students in considering comparisons between box jellyfish and safety, self-control, and other attitudes in people. Challenge children to try to remember each classmate's comment during the discussion. At the end of the conversation, ask children to list or write down comments made by other students. This can be good practice in developing better listening skills. But encourage children also to understand the meaning of what each child has said.

The box jellyfish is beautiful, but very dangerous. What are some things that may be tempting to people but can also be dangerous or unhealthful?

- Disobeying your parent or teacher
- Eating a lot of unhealthy food or not exercising enough
- Ignoring your beliefs or goals in order to be popular
- Hanging out in dangerous places that appear exciting
- Trying cigarettes or other smoking products, alcohol, or other harmful substances

The box jellyfish is not exactly what it appears to be. Can you think of ways to compare this to meeting new people or forming ideas about others?

- You might think that someone isn't very interesting or exciting when you first meet them. But often, when we get to know people better, we find out that we really like them.

- It's not a very good idea to judge people by the way they dress, the music they like, or the food they eat. It's what a person is like inside that is important.

The box jellyfish sometimes swims near beaches that are popular with people. To stay safe from these jellies, swimmers need to be careful and prepared. In your life, what are some good ways that you can be safe?

- Always let a parent, caregiver, or other trusted grown-up know where you are.
- Avoid talking with strangers when you are alone, online, or when you just don't feel safe around about them.
- Be home before it gets dark outside.
- Try to walk with friends rather than alone.
- Make sure to have permission before looking at websites. If you ever see or read something online that makes you uncomfortable, confused, or scared, talk to a grown-up you trust.

A box jellyfish sting can kill a person within twenty to thirty minutes. What are some other things that can quickly become very dangerous?

- Sometimes a disagreement or a fight can get very serious and even scary in a short amount of time. What might you say to calm people?
- A bad storm can get dangerous quickly. It's important to be aware of what's going on around you, and to know where to go to be safe.
- Sometimes people get addicted to drugs or alcohol even if they only try them once. It's important to think carefully about an activity's risks and dangers before making a decision.
- A situation that seems safe at first might not be. It's important to make careful choices about where you go and which people you spend time with.

It's very important to be aware and act quickly after being stung by a box jellyfish. Can you think of any other times when you might need to act quickly to keep yourself safe?

👁 Follow your good instincts. If you're in a situation where you feel uncomfortable or scared, find someone to help you.

👁 You need to be careful and aware when you're crossing streets.

👁 It's important to pay attention to your health. If you feel sick but ignore the signs, you might get sicker.

Using vinegar is a simple way to protect the body after a box jellyfish sting. What kind of protection do you have against harmful choices and dangerous situations?

👁 You can develop strength and confidence in yourself by thinking about, talking about, and making positive decisions.

👁 When you feel afraid or worried, talk to a grown-up you trust.

👁 Think before you act.

ACTIVITIES

Activity 1: Vinegar Words

Materials
Vinegar Words handout (in digital content)
Colored pencils (2 per student)

Directions
Pass out copies of the Vinegar Words handout and give each student two pencils of different colors. In the column marked Jellyfish Words, ask kids to use one color to write down some harmful character traits, behaviors, and ideas related to the box jellyfish. These descriptions might include: *not what it seems to be, tempting,* or *dangerous.* Then ask them to use the other pencils to write down Vinegar Words in the other column—positive character words and ideas that can counteract the harmful ones. For example:

Jellyfish Words—Vinegar Words
Tempting—Self-control

When kids have filled in the handouts, invite them to share some of their ideas. Talk about these as a group and discuss how positive character habits can act as vinegar against negative ones.

Activity 2: What If?

Materials
None

Directions
Sit in a circle. Describe a situation in which kids would need to make good choices. Emphasize safety, health, and self-control. Then go around the circle, giving each student a chance to describe a positive way to handle the situation.

For example, you could ask the group, **What if you were home alone and a stranger knocked on the door? What would you do?** A possible response might be, "I would call a neighbor or friend."

Or you could ask students, **What would you say if a friend offered you a cigarette?** Kids might answer, "No, thanks," or "Nah. I think smoking smells gross."

Acknowledge and discuss that making these choices is not always easy. But it is important to think about what choices you can make in a difficult situation *before* it happens.

Activity 3: Jellyfish Jargon

Materials
Crayons, colored pencils, and/or markers

Directions
Invite kids to draw pictures of the box jellyfish, but instead of using regular lines to make the shape of the jellyfish, have them "draw" with words related to the jellyfish and its characteristics. For example, each of the jellyfish's tentacles could be a sentence or phrase, such as "Beautiful but deadly" or "Don't judge someone based on appearances." (*Note:* If needed, draw an example on the board to show kids how this idea works. Additionally, younger kids could draw basic pictures of jellyfish and then write words inside their drawings.)

Invite students to share their work. Talk about why they chose the words they did.

LESSON 4
BRISTLECONE PINE TREES

Key Words

The behaviors, traits, and emotions below are just starting points for aligning SEL, character education, and this lesson's story. Most of these ideas can easily be connected with more than one competency or domain.

Self-Awareness: Courage and Boldness • Inner Strength • Mindfulness • Understanding Personal Strengths and Weaknesses

Self-Management: Adaptability • Coping Skills and Stress Management • Hard Work • Patience • Peacefulness • Perseverance

Social Awareness: Acceptance of Others • Perspective-Taking

Relationship Skills: Listening

Responsible Decision-Making: Conservation • Positive and Ethical Choices

Students will

- ☜ learn about the bristlecone pine, especially its ability to live hundreds or even thousands of years

- ☜ discuss how patience, perseverance, and hard work can bring good results and big rewards

- ☜ think about the importance of respecting and protecting our planet

Overview

The long lifespan of many bristlecone pine trees will amaze kids. The trees' fascinating longevity is an excellent starting point for conversations about patience and perseverance. The bristlecone pine's strength and resilience will also inspire discussions about dedication and hard work. The story of the bristlecone pine's difficult existence can lead students to understand that struggles and problems can sometimes help people grow stronger. And the trees' place in history offers a jumping-off point for talking about the value of environmental conservation and about the importance of respecting older people.

Story

Tough Bristlecone Pine Trees

TOUGH BRISTLECONE PINE TREES

What do you think the oldest living thing on Earth is?

A sea turtle?

An elephant?

That fuzzy stuff at the back of your fridge?

Nope. One of the oldest known living things on earth is the bristlecone pine tree. There are several kinds of bristlecone pines. They grow in Colorado, New Mexico, Arizona, Utah, Nevada, and California.

One of the oldest bristlecone pines is called Methuselah. Scientists think it is between 4,600 and 4,850 years old. It stands in eastern California's White Mountains. Don't go looking for it, though. Its exact spot is a secret to almost everybody. This is to keep the ancient tree safe.

Methuselah has been around for almost 5,000 years. That's a very long time. It can be a little hard to even imagine that many years. Think about it. That means:

- Methuselah was a young tree when the pyramids were built in ancient Egypt.

- It was already over 4,500 years old when the United States became a country.

- It was around way, way, way before your great-great-grandfather was born.

The bristlecone pine tree lives in harsh places. The trees have learned to adapt to their environment. Many of the trees are on high mountain slopes. Strong winds sweep past them. Icicles droop from their branches. Very little rain falls for their thirsty roots and needles to soak up.

Yet the pines thrive. Their branches twist and turn white. But they are strong.

Bristlecone pines are related to giant sequoia trees, but they are much smaller than their cousins. Sequoias tower dramatically. Being big isn't always better,

though. The small, dense bristlecone pines are strong and have very long lives. Why?

One reason bristlecone pines live so long is that they grow very slowly. In some years, they barely grow at all. If too little rain falls one season, these trees almost go to sleep. Maybe this sounds a bit boring to you. But growing slowly makes the pines' wood dense and strong. The trees can resist bugs and other threats.

Bristlecone pines have another secret too. They grow in places where very few plants can survive. That means that these trees don't have to share soil and water with many other plants.

Some bristlecone pines do grow lower on mountain slopes. They grow faster than the trees higher up. The weather is warmer. The wind doesn't bend down the trees' trunks. The soil is rich and wet. But these pines don't live to be nearly so old as the ones that struggle to survive on higher, harsher slopes. Methuselah's long life is the tree's reward for endurance and hard work. And the view is great from up there!

BRISTLECONE PINE TREE FACTS

- The tallest bristlecone pine is just 60 feet tall. The tallest known sequoia is almost 380 feet tall.

- Often, ancient bristlecone pines are part living and part dead. The living part of the tree continues to grow, often on the side of the tree away from the wind.

- In 1964, a bristlecone pine called Prometheus, which is estimated to have been close to 5,000 years old at the time, was cut down.

TALK IT OVER

Use these questions to guide your students in considering how bristlecone pine trees can inspire courage, patience, perseverance, inner strength, and other social and emotional traits and behaviors in people.

Bristlecone pine trees grow very slowly, which makes their wood very strong. How does this idea relate to people and the work they do? (You might also ask: Is it hard to be patient sometimes? Why? What are some values of patience?)

- If you take the time to do a job right, you'll probably make something better in the end.

- The faster way to do something isn't always the best way.

- Relationships take time to grow. The time that we spend with a person—facing challenges together, sharing experiences, and learning more about each other—builds a stronger and more lasting relationship.

Bristlecone pines that grow at lower altitudes don't live as long as the ones growing in harsher places. Can you think of ways to compare this idea to people's experiences?

- Challenges can build strong character. By working through problems and adapting to change, you can develop other strengths, such as courage, patience, endurance, understanding, sympathy, caring, and so on.

- The easier path can be very tempting, but it's not always the most rewarding or productive.

- A big accomplishment is often the result of a lot of struggle and hard work.

Some bristlecone pines that are alive now were around for a lot of big events in the past. Why is this important? How does the long life of bristlecone pines relate to people's lives?

- If we cut down or harmed these old trees, we'd be losing a piece of history.

- It's important to protect nature and make sure plants and animals are still around for future generations.

- Older people have seen and experienced many things during their lives. As people age, their hands may grow gnarled and faces become wrinkled. But a person's character can grow stronger and stronger, especially if they have been kind and helpful to others.

The bristlecone pine is related to the giant sequoia tree. Bristlecone pines are much smaller than the soaring sequoias, which are also called giant redwoods. But bristlecone pines can live much longer. Does being the biggest person mean that you are the best or the strongest? What kinds of characteristics make a person strong?

- Inner strength of character can make a person strong so that they can work through problems and hardships. Qualities such as patience, hard work, and perseverance can help you grow stronger, regardless of your size.

- Being kind and friendly to other people is a type of strength. You don't have to be the biggest or strongest person physically to show strong character.

ACTIVITIES

Activity 1: Methuselah Mobile

Materials

Printouts of bristlecone pine tree picture (in digital content)

Hole punch

String or yarn

Cardstock or construction paper

Kid-safe scissors

Colored pencils, crayons, or markers

Twigs, sticks, or dowels (2 or 3 per student)

Directions

Hand out copies of the bristlecone pine picture. Invite students to cut their pictures into a few pieces, however they like. Punch a hole at the top of each picture piece. Next, have students cut out a few pieces of cardstock or construction paper in any shapes they like and write a word describing bristlecone pine trees on each cutout. (*Examples: strong, sturdy, dependable, patient.*) Punch a hole in each cutout.

Assemble mobiles. Help kids use yarn or string to connect the twigs or dowels, and hang the tree pictures and characteristic cutouts from these supports. Attach a string to the top of the mobile so kids can hang them up in the classroom or at home.

As kids work, guide them in discussing the bristlecone pine's characteristics and compare them to qualities in people. How can these trees inspire us? Do the trees display any traits that we would *not* want to have?

Variation: If possible, take a short nature walk with students to gather the twigs for their mobiles. Remind kids only to pick up twigs and sticks that have already fallen. As you walk, talk about respecting and protecting nature.

Activity 2: Finding Inner Peace

Materials

None

Directions

Children can benefit enormously from learning ways to calm themselves down and find peace when they are struggling—a critical self-management skill. Here are a few ways to do this. Children may need practice to learn the skills, so offer them chances to try and try again. Also discuss with students how it felt to try these exercises, and how they can develop the habit of doing them.

- Practice patience by making yourself wait. For example, wait a minute before eating something you want, or let someone else get in front of you in a line.

- Try to identify things that take away your inner peace and calm. For example, if you notice that when you play video games a lot you feel jittery, work on turning off the electronics for a while.

- When you feel overwhelmed, find a quiet spot to rest, even if it's only for a few minutes.

- If you can't be somewhere peaceful in the moment, imagine it. Picture being in your favorite place, or simply somewhere safe and quiet.

- Close your eyes if you feel safe doing so. Take in slow, deep breaths and then slowly let them out. Focus on your breathing.

- Slowly count backwards from 25, 50, or 100—whatever number works for you.

- Take a mindful walk. Pay close attention to your senses. What do you see, smell, hear, taste, and feel? If you can't go on a walk when you feel the need for peace, visualize doing so. Imagine as much detail as you can.

LESSON 5
CATS

Key Words

The behaviors, traits, and emotions below are just starting points for aligning SEL, character education, and this lesson's story. Most of these ideas can easily be connected with more than one competency or domain.

Self-Awareness: Curiosity

Self-Management: Healthy Habits • Sadness • Safety • Self-Regulation

Social Awareness: Communication • Empathy • Perspective-Taking • Reading Social Cues • Understanding Others

Relationship Skills: Listening • Playfulness • Service to Others

Responsible Decision-Making: Analyzing and Evaluation • Identifying Challenges • Positive and Ethical Choices • Understanding Consequences

Students will

- make comparisons between cats' curiosity, intelligence, playfulness, and ways of communicating and human behaviors
- feel empathy or care for cats in trouble and compare it to the feelings cats might have for people
- explore the value and the potential drawbacks of curiosity
- think and talk about the ways we don't always have control of the consequences resulting from our choices

Overview

Cats are famous for their curiosity. Sometimes cats find themselves in dangerous places because of that. A cat that gets stuck high up in a tree is similar to a person who doesn't think through potential problems or risks before acting. The story of Blackie in "Curious Cats" is a sad one. Depending on your group, you don't need to emphasize or dwell on the sadness. But you *can* choose to discuss the idea that sadness is an important emotion for kids to recognize and understand, and the idea that everyone feels sad sometimes. Sad things happen. And sadness will diminish and pass in time.

But cats are also underestimated for their intelligence. Cats learn by observing and imitating, and through trial and error. Cats have also rescued humans and other animals from danger. And cats communicate their moods through use of their ears, fur, whiskers, eyes, and tails, and with sounds such as purring and hissing.

Story

Curious Cats

CURIOUS CATS

Did curiosity *really* kill the cat?

Cats are natural adventurers. They like to explore new places. Sometimes their curiosity gets them into tight spots. Long ago, a cat named Blackie lived in a New York City apartment with his owner, Mable. Blackie was a quiet cat who mostly preferred sitting by the fireplace. But one day he decided to explore the apartment's chimney. Cats love to snoop and are very curious. They are good at climbing up. But Blackie must not have understood that cats' claws curl the wrong way to head back down. He started up the chimney. Halfway up, Blackie got stuck. He couldn't get down. Blackie must have been afraid. He meowed for help. No one else was home, and Blackie meowed for a long time. Finally, Mable came home, but Blackie still couldn't come down. Instead he tried to climb higher. But his claws could not cling to the chimney, and Blackie fell clear down to the first floor. He was badly hurt. His owner called for help from everyone— the police, the fire department, and more. No one could get Blackie out. Finally, a plumber cut open the back of the chimney. He carefully lifted Blackie out. But Blackie was badly injured, and he didn't live for much longer. Mable surely cried, because she missed her cat. But she was happy that Blackie had lived a long, happy, curious life with her.

Cats can't always rescue themselves. They have helped rescue others, though. Here is a happier story. You might think cats and dogs are enemies. And it's true that they don't always get along. But a cat in Rhode Island saved the family's dog. The dog was outside, and it was getting dark. Suddenly, the cat started jumping at the door. She did it over and over.

The owner was curious. What was making his cat act so strangely? He went outside to find out. There the owner saw a coyote. The little black dog was in its jaws. The man charged at the coyote. The coyote looked scared, dropped the dog, and took off. The dog was scared too, but safe—thanks to her pal, the cat. Somehow, the cat seemed to sense that the dog was in trouble, and she saved the dog's life.

Cats make wonderful pets, devoted companions, and playful friends. Cats love to pounce on toy mice, play with string, or chase flashlight beams. But cats are also very independent, and they can be pretty stubborn. So if you call your cat's name, she probably won't come running. She may be exploring a hole in the wall or water dripping from a drainpipe. Or she might just be taking a catnap.

CAT FACTS

- Cats have excellent memories. Studies have shown that a cat's short-term memory lasts up to ten minutes, compared to less than a minute in humans. Another study showed that cats could remember a piece of information for up to sixteen hours.

- Some breeds of domesticated cats can run 30 miles per hour.

- A cat's taste buds cannot detect sweet flavors.

- Cats have rescued people in some cases. For example, they have warned their owners about fires and dangerous gas leaks.

- You can learn about animal communication by watching cats. If you look closely, you'll see that cats tell you how they feel. When your cat rubs against you, he is claiming you as his own. (You might think your cat belongs to *you*, but he probably has other ideas.) If he rolls over and shows his tummy, it means he really trusts you. If he swishes his tail quickly, presses back his ears, or hisses, be careful. That means he is angry, annoyed, upset, or afraid. But when his tail waves back and forth slowly, he is calm and happy.

TALK IT OVER

Use these questions to guide your students in considering the ways people can be as curious as cats. You can also discuss the idea that cats and people both communicate, but they do it differently.

Like cats, people are often curious. What are some positive ways of being curious? How is curiosity related to learning?

- Being curious about new ideas often leads to learning. Learning in school teaches you things that are interesting and useful.

- Learning new skills can be fun. And when you learn to do something new—like play basketball, ice skate, play the guitar, or paint pictures—you can share that skill or talent with others.

- You can use many new skills to help others. Learning how to be a good citizen lets you help your community. Skills such as first aid can be lifesaving. Learning to listen to others and understand how they feel will make you a great friend.

Curious cats sometimes get into dangerous spots. What are some ways that people can also run into trouble because of their curiosity?

- You can put yourself in danger when you explore an unsafe place, such as an old building or a construction site, or by going exploring in any unfamiliar place, especially by yourself.

- Kids can get in trouble when they go someplace with a stranger or open the door to a stranger.

- Exploring on the internet without a grown-up can be dangerous.

- You may be really curious to see movies or play video games that are for older kids or for adults. But afterward, you might feel confused or scared.

Cats can't know or control what will happen as a result of their curiosity or exploring. People are free to choose what they do but can't always control the consequences that follow. What kinds of things do people do that can have negative results?

- Sometimes kids don't do their homework. Then they may fall behind in class, or they might get poor grades.

- Eating a lot of junk food might make someone unhealthy.

- A kid might ice skate on thin ice and fall into the cold water.

- Someone might make friends with a stranger on the internet and then get into a scary or confusing situation.

- A person might steal something and then be in very serious trouble.

- If a person lies a lot, other people will probably stop trusting them.

- If you don't wear warm clothes when it's cold, or if you don't wash your hands when they're dirty, you might get sick.

Cats can communicate in many ways: with their tails, ears, whiskers, and more. How do people communicate without words?

- People can communicate with their eyes, mouths, voices, body language, and gestures. Sometimes people's facial expressions don't match what they're saying with words. Sometimes people can misunderstand others by not knowing how to read the many ways people communicate through social cues.

- Some people are very good at imagining and understanding how other people feel and think, even without any words. This is called empathy. You can build empathy by imagining how other people feel and being kind and respectful to them.

Cats are very playful. Is it good to play? Can playing ever lead to problems?

- Some kinds of playing can spark your creativity. But if you play so much that you ignore your homework, you might not learn the things you need to know.

- Playing is fun and can help you relax and feel happy. But if you only play, you can start to get bored.

- You can make good friends when you play. But it's also important to do your chores and help your family at home.

Cats might be smarter than people recognize. They learn and communicate. Do people sometimes have talents or knowledge that others ignore or don't notice at first? Why do you think people do this?

- Sometimes we ignore what other people can do because we don't want to feel like they are smarter or more talented than we are. But everyone has different gifts. We're all good at something—and no one is good at everything.

- Sometimes we might make assumptions about what other people can do based on how they dress, speak, or look. But these assumptions are not always right. If we don't look deeper, we might never find out what interesting things other people can really do.

- Everyone has wisdom to share. It's important to value and listen to what other people have to say.

Cats have helped people and animals. Can you think of ways that you can help care for someone who needs help?

- We can help people in need by donating clothes, food, blankets, and other items.

- Sometimes, just listening to a friend and understanding how she feels is a very kind thing to do.

- If we notice that someone at school seems lonely, we could be friendly to them and ask them to play with us.

- We can help our environment by recycling, turning off lights, and riding bikes instead of riding in cars.

- We can help animals in need by volunteering at animal shelters.

- We can raise money for people who need help in our own communities or around the world.

- We can offer to help people in our own families with chores, homework, or other tasks.

ACTIVITIES

Activity 1: Cat Tales

Materials

None

Directions

Divide your class into small groups of four or five students each. Explain that they'll be writing chain

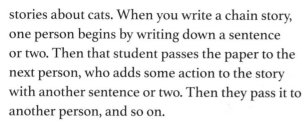

stories about cats. When you write a chain story, one person begins by writing down a sentence or two. Then that student passes the paper to the next person, who adds some action to the story with another sentence or two. Then they pass it to another person, and so on.

Have each group focus on a certain trait related to cats. One group could focus on a curious cat, while another could make up a story about a cat that helps someone. Another could write about a playful kitten.

Give the groups time to write, making sure that every student gets the chance to write at least twice. Then ask groups to read their stories to the class. As a big group, talk about the ideas that the stories address and any questions that they raise. And enjoy. The stories may be funny!

Activity 2: Cat Scenes

Materials

Cat Scenes handout (in digital content)
Scissors
Hat or other container for charades prompts

Directions

Before class, print out the handout and cut out the individual prompts. Mix the prompt slips together in a hat, bowl, or other container.

Explain the game of charades to the class. Rather than splitting up into teams, have all kids guess as a group, making the goal simply to figure out the behavior being pantomimed and to correctly identify what catlike traits it represents.

Ask for volunteers to be the actors. Have each actor show you the prompt before they begin pantomiming. If kids get stuck, help guide them toward the answer.

Play as many rounds as you have time for. Afterward, talk as a group about how difficult it is to communicate without words, and whether nonverbal communication can ever be better than using words. Why is communication important? What kinds of problems can come up without good communication?

Activity 3: Caring for Cats

Materials

Kitty Care handout (in digital content)
Colored pencils or markers
Optional:
Contact information of local animal shelter
Permission slips from parents or guardians (if visiting an animal shelter)
Digital camera
Computer and photo printer
Poster board

Directions

Cats seem to care for others, and we can also care for cats. Hold a brainstorming session with kids to generate a list of tips and ideas for taking care of a pet cat. Help students look up accurate information online or in print resources. You could also call a local shelter or vet and ask if they have any advice for new cat owners.

Pass out copies of the handout and have kids fill them in with the tips they think are most important or most interesting. Encourage them to add drawings or other decorations to the list if they like. Alternatively, choose as a group the tips that you most want to include on your list. Then enter these suggestions into the form on the computer and print out the completed form. However you create your list, make copies and distribute them to cat lovers, pet owners, local vets or shelters, and others who may be interested.

Variation: Take a class trip to visit a local no-kill animal shelter that has cats in need of homes.

Take a camera with you, and take pictures of each cat (or several of them, if there are too many). Back at school, print out the photos and help kids use them to make a poster (or posters) inviting people to adopt homeless cats. Encourage kids to include cats' names and other information, if you have it, under the photos. (*Examples:* "Adopt Fluffy!" "Mittens loves tuna fish.") Put the shelter's contact information at the bottom. Hang up copies of your posters at school. You also might ask for permission to put up these posters at the library, community center, and other locations as well. This activity can become a powerful leadership and team-building opportunity for kids.

LESSON 6
COCONUT CRABS

Key Words
The behaviors, traits, and emotions below are just starting points for aligning SEL, character education, and this lesson's story. Most of these ideas can easily be connected with more than one competency or domain.

Self-Awareness: Mindfulness • Peacefulness

Self-Management: Coping Skills and Stress Management • Courage and Boldness • Honesty • Perseverance • Safety

Social Awareness: Acceptance of Others • Perspective-Taking

Relationship Skills: Humor

Responsible Decision-Making: Positive and Ethical Choices • Problem-Solving

Students will
👁 learn some interesting information about coconut crabs, including their strong claws and their shyness during the daytime, and compare their characteristics to human behavior

👁 consider the coconut crab's perseverance in working to crack open tough coconuts, and think about perseverance in people when solving problems

👁 draw a comparison between the coconut crab's preference for nighttime and darkness and people who try to hide their actions from others or are too shy to let people see who they are

👁 compare the crab's sometimes daring behavior to the courage that people can show

Overview
The coconut crab is a mysterious creature. This story will bring out curiosity in children and maybe even a little bit of fear, so be prepared to discuss these feelings. This crab prefers the darkness of night to the bright daylight. It also seems to have a fondness for shiny objects, sometimes taking a chance and entering people's homes to take these treasures. But when the sun comes out, the crab disappears. Kids will find it interesting to compare this behavior to that of people who might lie or hide their actions to avoid blame or responsibility. On the other hand, some people just don't like being in the limelight. Nevertheless, many important contributions have been made by people who seek the shadows, not wanting the bright light of attention and fame.

Besides coconuts, fruits, and seeds, the crab will devour injured animals and even wounded people. These 3- to 4-foot-long crabs live in the Indo-Pacific islands. With their large size and fierce-looking claws, coconut crabs could be cast as monsters in a horror film. But coconut crabs are also problem-solvers. They work patiently and persistently to crack open coconuts for the sweet fruit.

Story
Creeping Coconut Crabs

CREEPING COCONUT CRABS

The coconut crab is a mysterious beast. It lives in the thick jungles of islands in the Indian and Pacific oceans. It is one of the biggest crabs in the world. Coconut crabs can grow to be 3 feet long or more. They have 10 legs. The back two legs are very small. The front two legs have big, strong claws. If you saw this crab, you might think it came from a scary movie.

But you probably *won't* see it. When the sun is out, the coconut crab likes to disappear. It prefers the shadows. It may come out if rain falls. But coconut crabs usually hide during the day. They dig into the sand or crawl between rocks.

The coconut crab also has other names, such as robber crab and palm thief. It earned these names by creeping into houses at night. Sometimes it eats food that it finds. Or it may steal shiny things like silverware or pans. The crab's raids are brave—and risky. When people find these big coconut crabs in their houses, they may hurt them.

Luckily, most of the time these crabs don't go into houses. Instead, they eat fruit and seeds in the jungle. Sometimes they climb coconut trees. They may use their claws to snip off the coconuts. When the fruit falls to the ground, sometimes it cracks open. But not always. The strong coconut crab can lift up to 60 pounds. So it might try to carry the coconut up the tree and drop it again. Or it may just use its claws to pound and pry open the shell. At last it gets to the sweet fruit inside.

The coconut crab has a great sense of smell. It can sniff out bananas and coconuts from far away. Sometimes the crabs eat dead animals or rotting plants. They have attacked rats and other small creatures. Some stories even say they have eaten people who were hurt or who had died.

But all creatures have weak spots. The coconut crab has rotten vision, and it can't swim. Plus, it seems to be ticklish—yes, ticklish! (Though it doesn't giggle.) So if you spot a coconut crab in your home, you could toss it into a full bathtub or other water. But be very careful picking it up. If its strong claws clamp onto you, it'll hurt—a lot. And it's almost impossible to pry open those claws. There's a trick for getting them to let go, though. Gently tickle the crab on its soft tummy. Pretty soon, the critter will lose its hold. Whew!

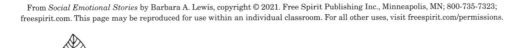

COCONUT CRAB FACTS

- Coconut crabs don't just eat coconuts. They also use the husks to line their burrows.

- Coconut crabs don't laugh, but they do loosen up when "tickled." For people, laughter is a healthy habit. Experts say that one minute of hearty laughter can provide heart rate benefits similar to a ten-minute workout.

- During Charles Darwin's voyage on the *Beagle* in the 1830s, he saw coconut crabs on islands in the Indian Ocean. He described them as growing "to a monstrous size."

TALK IT OVER

Use these questions to guide your students in connecting coconut crabs and their persevering habits, problem-solving, and other traits with behaviors in people.

Can you create an analogy between the coconut crab—which prefers to hunt in the darkness of night—and people who try to hide something?

- A person who fibs might try to cover up those lies with additional lies.

- During the day, coconut crabs sometimes hide under the sand. A person who has done something wrong might think that by hiding they can avoid responsibility or blame. They may try to hide their true personality.

- Sometimes someone might try to stay out of the light, just as the coconut crab that hides in the sand in the day. People may have many reasons for this. For example, they might not like the "limelight," they may be shy, or they might prefer to make contributions without the fame and attention.

Sometimes coconut crabs go into people's homes to take shiny things that are appealing or interesting to them. To the crab this is not being dishonest. In fact, it's probably more of an act of daring or even bravery. If people catch the crabs in their homes, they may hurt them. Can you compare this to times when people may do something daring or brave?

- It takes courage to speak out against injustice even when you're afraid.

- It can sometimes take courage to learn a new skill, or to perform in front of other people.

- It takes courage to tell the truth, especially if you know you might get in trouble for it.

- Many people stand up for what they believe in even when it's not popular. They have to be brave to stick to their values and be true to themselves.

The coconut crab is a good problem-solver. Coconuts are very hard to crack open, but the crab keeps trying. Sometimes it takes a long time. Compare this to challenges that people face.

- If you keep trying to solve a math problem, you will eventually understand it better.

- When you keep your mind focused on a problem and on learning—and when you can stop your mind from wandering—this can help you be "present." In turn, this focus can help you understand what to do.

- If you keep practicing a talent that you want to develop, you will improve that talent over time.

- If you keep going even when things are tough, you will eventually see the rewards. Even if you don't succeed in the way you hoped to, you'll be building strong character muscles and learning new things.

The coconut crab does have weaknesses. It doesn't see well and it can't swim. And while it has very strong claws, it will let go when its stomach is tickled. What comparisons can you make between these characteristics and human strengths or weaknesses?

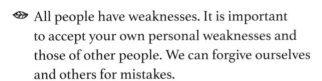

- All people have weaknesses. It is important to accept your own personal weaknesses and those of other people. We can forgive ourselves and others for mistakes.

- If you can imagine the results or consequences of a moment of weakness or of making a poor decision, you may be able to stop yourself or others from making that choice.

- Crabs let go when they are tickled, and laughter can also make people relax. Sometimes humor can lighten up a tense situation.

ACTIVITIES

Activity 1: Models of Perseverance

Materials

None

Directions

Learn about people who have persevered and overcome challenges. You could investigate as a group or ask students to write short individual reports and then share what they learn with the class. Talk about what it takes to persevere and what the rewards can be. The following subjects are examples of people kids might choose to study.

- Helen Keller lost her sight and hearing when she was nineteen months old. She became an educated woman and an author, and she spoke up for people with disabilities.

- Winston Churchill overcame a stuttering problem and poor performance in school to become Prime Minister of the United Kingdom and a renowned orator.

- Track star Jesse Owens won four gold medals at the 1936 Olympics in the face of racial prejudice.

- Bethany Hamilton, a surfer, lost her arm in a shark attack at the age of thirteen and went on to win a national surfing championship. Bethany's story was made into the movie *Soul Surfer.*

Activity 2: Why Lie?

Materials

Optional: Coconut crab picture (in digital content)

Directions

Ask your class this question: **Why do people lie?**

Before answering aloud, have students write down some answers to this question. If desired, they could write on copies of the crab picture. Ask kids to try to come up with one answer for each of the crab's ten legs. Talk about how sometimes, when we aren't honest, our lies seem to have "legs" of their own. A lie can run away from us and cause big problems.

After kids have had some time to work, ask them to share their answers. Talk about their ideas and thoughts. *Possible answers:* Fear of getting in trouble; to cover up an earlier lie; to impress someone; to damage someone else's reputation; because of insecurity; to pretend to be someone else; fear of the real truth; to get someone else in trouble; to embarrass someone; to avoid responsibility.

Then discuss why people tell the truth. What are the advantages of telling the truth? *Possible answers:* You don't have to remember lies; everyone can know what really happened; it can keep someone else from being blamed for something they didn't do; you usually get in less trouble with the truth; people will trust you more if you are always truthful; you can feel calm and peaceful inside when you know you've told the truth.

Activity 3: Words of Encouragement

Materials

Words of Encouragement handout (in digital content)
Colored pencils or crayons

Directions

Ask kids to think about the example of Jason Lester. At the age of twelve, Jason was riding his bike when a car hit him. He was very badly injured, and his right arm was partially paralyzed. But he went on to be a talented and dedicated athlete, competing in high school baseball and football. As an adult, Jason became an Ironman competitor. In 2009, he won an ESPY Award for Best Male Athlete with a Disability. Jason's message to everyone is, "If you don't stop, you can't be stopped."

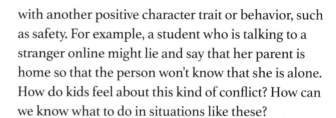

Pass out the handout. Invite kids to brainstorm messages and slogans that encourage perseverance. Here are some ideas to get kids started:

- When you are down, the only direction is up.
- I am happy being me.
- You can do it!
- You never lose until you quit.
- Hard work builds strong character muscles.

When kids have chosen their slogans, have them write these sayings neatly on their handouts. If they like, they can decorate with designs or drawings. Hang the slogans in your school. You could also ask permission to hang them in local stores, clubs, or faith communities. If you have budding musicians in your group, you could ask them to make one or more slogans into a song that your class could learn and perform.

Activity 4: Honesty Survey

Materials
None

Directions
Compose an honesty survey. Use the sample question below or brainstorm a question as a group.

How often do you tell the truth?
(circle your answer)
Always • Most of the time • Sometimes • Never

Write or print the survey question on small strips of paper and give one to each student. Ask kids to hand in their answers anonymously.

Complete the survey of your classroom. Count the number of responses from each of the four categories. If you'd like, older students can do a math exercise by calculating the percentage of responses in each category.

Variation: Kids could also survey another class or their family members and report back.

Share the results of the honesty survey with your group. Be careful to avoid blaming or criticizing anyone. Discuss why it's sometimes difficult to be honest. Then talk about how we can work on being honest more of the time. Ask kids if they think it's ever appropriate or okay to lie. Discuss the challenges that can come up when honesty comes in conflict

with another positive character trait or behavior, such as safety. For example, a student who is talking to a stranger online might lie and say that her parent is home so that the person won't know that she is alone. How do kids feel about this kind of conflict? How can we know what to do in situations like these?

Activity 5: Practice a Mindfulness Exercise

Materials
A quiet space

Directions
Mindfulness is the practice of being present where you are, without any judgment or criticism of yourself, which helps increase calm and reduce stress. Coconut crabs may not seem "mindful," but they must be acutely aware of where they are, especially since they may be in danger. Some of their senses are also very keen. Mindfulness is a good self-management activity to bring kids into focus and calm, especially in moments of stress or conflict. If you do this with a group of children, you may want to set a rule that everyone is silent through the exercise. After the experience, you might have a discussion. How did students feel before, during, and after the activity?

- Find your quiet and comfortable spot. You can do this alone or with other people around. If you are not in a quiet spot, think of one in your mind.
- Close your eyes if you feel safe doing so. Focus on relaxing your muscles. Start at your shoulders and move all the way down to your toes.
- Feel the air coming in and out of your lungs as you breathe. Take some deep, long breaths. Notice how good it feels.
- Switch your focus to outside your body and the things you see around you. What can you hear and smell? What do you feel at your fingertips? If you can touch something, notice the texture and how smooth or bumpy, warm or cool it is.
- Now switch your focus back to inside your body and notice your breath going in and out. Take some more big long breaths
- Go back and forth, from inside to outside, until you feel peaceful. Then try to carry that peace with you for as long as you can.

LESSON 7
CROWS

Key Words

The behaviors, traits, and emotions below are just starting points for aligning SEL, character education, and this lesson's story. Most of these ideas can easily be connected with more than one competency or domain.

Self-Awareness: Imagination • Inner Strength • Understanding Personal Strengths and Weaknesses

Self-Management: Assertiveness

Social Awareness: Acceptance of Others • Communication • Perspective-Taking • Respect

Relationship Skills: Bullying Prevention • Conflict Management and Resolution • Cooperation, Collaboration, and Teamwork • Listening

Responsible Decision-Making: Problem-Solving

Students will

👁 learn interesting facts about crows, including their problem-solving skills and high intelligence

👁 make a connection between the crow's negative reputation to the way people sometimes label or make assumptions about others and may even bully them

👁 relate the crow's cleanup activities to having respect for the different jobs that people do

Overview

In some cultures, crows are associated with death and bad news. And these birds *do* have some unnerving traits. They eat carrion, have eerie calls, and sometimes attack people. But students will learn that the crow is also intelligent, good at solving problems, and a great communicator. And while the job of eating carrion may seem distasteful to us, it's also important for the health of our planet and its ecosystems. This information will help kids appreciate the fact that work that may not seem pleasant is still necessary and beneficial.

In addition, students can make an important connection between the sometimes aggressive actions of crows and bullying behavior in people. You can help your group use the story as a starting point for productive discussion about bullying and how to address it through respect, assertiveness, and other behaviors. This discussion and exploration can help students think about their own feelings. Children sometimes do not recognize the feelings of anxiety, apprehension, and discomfort that may come from being bullied—or from bullying others. By recognizing that all people feel emotions, children can accept their own feelings as legitimate and gain self-confidence in their personal strengths, while also building empathy for others. This lesson can also help children develop social skills, as well as appreciation and respect for all people.

Story
Clever Crows

CLEVER CROWS

One day, a man named Shimshon heard squawking outside his home. A baby crow had fallen out of its nest. Shimshon was annoyed with its loud caws. So he picked up the chick and carried it outside his garden. "Problem solved," he thought.

Big mistake.

Suddenly a large mother crow swooped down. She attacked Shimshon's head over and over. He finally ran inside and was safe. But when he ventured out of the house again, guess what happened? The crow attacked him again, pecking at his head. It frightened Shimshon, and he tore right back into the house. And the crow wasn't done with him yet. Every time Shimshon left his house, the mother crow dived at him again.

Shimson thought to himself, "I need help. I don't have a life anymore!" He felt captive in his own house. He started wearing a helmet and carrying an umbrella whenever he went outside.

Then Shimshon noticed something odd. The crow never bothered his wife or kids. What was going on? Even the mayor of his city came and saw the crow attack Shimshon. But the mayor didn't have any answers. He said the only solution was to wait for the crow to move on and leave him alone. And after a few weeks, the crow attacks did stop.

Shimson was grateful that his ordeal was over. But he still didn't know *why* the crow had attacked him. (Do you have an idea?)

Bird experts have the answer. They have discovered something interesting. All crows look the same to most people. But we don't all look the same to crows. They can recognize human faces!

Like most animals, crows are very protective of their babies. They do not like people to touch their chicks. So Shimshon was in trouble when he moved the crow chick, even though he was trying to help the little crow. The mother crow recognized his face—and she took action!

CROW FACTS

- Crows are some of the brightest birds around. They're curious and playful. Some can mimic human voices. They communicate with other crows using more than two hundred different calls.

- Crows have tightly knit family systems. Young crows may stay with their parents for several years and even help care for younger siblings.

- Crows have good memories, and they communicate with each other. They warn each other about danger. If one crow is killed in a farmer's field, the whole flock may avoid the place for two years.

- Sometimes crows peck at windows and mirrors. This happens because male crows want to protect their nests and families. When a male crow sees his reflection, he gets confused. He thinks it's another bird on his turf. He can peck so hard at the reflection that he hurts himself.

- Crows are good at solving problems. They have made tools from leaves, grass, and sticks. Some crows have even been seeing dropping tough nuts on busy streets. Cars drive over the nuts and crack them open. Then, when the coast is clear, the crows swoop in and eat the tasty nuts out of the broken shells.

- As clever as they are, crows have a bad reputation with a lot of people. In some countries, crows are signs of bad luck. In other places, though, crows are more popular. In parts of Asia, they are a sign of good luck.

- Crows are good helpers for our planet. They carry seeds from place to place. This helps plants grow. Plus, crows eat thousands of pesky pests such as army worms. They also eat dead animals and other rotting material. Imagine what the earth would be like without the crow cleanup crew!

TALK IT OVER

Use these questions to guide your students in considering comparisons between human characteristics and traits that crows have, including their aggressive or assertive behaviors, their communication skills, and their problem-solving abilities.

Sometimes crows attack people they see as threats. Can you make a comparison with people who bully others?

- Crows usually attack because they think the person is an enemy. Maybe some people who bully see other people as enemies. Why might this be true? Why *wouldn't* it be true? Could these people sometimes really be their own enemies?

- Sometimes bullying happens because kids don't understand each other, or because they feel afraid.

- People who bully may pick on people who don't fight back. If you see bullying happen, be calm but assertive with the person who is bullying. You could say, "No bullying allowed." If you don't feel safe, get away from the situation. And always tell an adult if you are bullied or if someone else is being bullied.

Male crows sometimes attack their own reflections in windows or mirrors. What do people do that is similar to this behavior?

- Sometimes it's easier to blame others for our problems than it is to think that we might be partly responsible for them.

- When a crow attacks his image in a mirror, he can hurt his own beak. When we are unkind to others, we hurt ourselves as well. We feel bad later. We can damage friendships. And we can lessen the respect that other people have for us.

- We might not admit when we've made mistakes because we don't want other people to think that we aren't smart. But it's important to take responsibility for our own actions, even when we make mistakes.

Crows are great problem-solvers. Can you think of ways that people solve problems?

- Working together on a problem can make it easier. When people cooperate, their teammates can suggest solutions that other people might not have thought of.

- Some problems are really tough. But if we keep trying, we can make progress.

- Using your imagination is a big help when you're trying to solve a problem. It can spark new ideas and creative solutions.

Crows are good at communicating with each other. When they know of a danger, they warn other crows. How is communication important for people?

- Good communication makes relationships stronger. It brings people closer together.

- Sometimes people talk without truly communicating. Real communication requires good listening and understanding.

- When we see something that makes us nervous or afraid, it helps to tell someone about it. Telling someone can help us stay safe.

- Communication is necessary between groups of people, such as communities and countries. Good communication can help create understanding and peace.

People in some parts of the world believe that crows are bad luck, while others think they bring good fortune. Can you think of ways this idea relates to how people see each other?

- People have all kinds of different beliefs, traditions, and ideas. New ideas might seem strange to us at first, but different ideas make the world interesting.

- We should always respect other people's ideas, even if they're not the same as ours.

Crows are nature's cleanup crew. They eat dead animals, even when they're starting to rot. That might sound gross, but it's good for our planet. Can you make an analogy with this idea?

- People do many different jobs. Not all jobs sound good to everyone. But all of them are valuable to our community and our world in some way. It's important to see the perspective of others. It is important to appreciate and respect the jobs that people do.

- Sometimes we all have chores and other jobs that we'd rather not do. But doing these things—like cleaning your room, helping make dinner, or taking care of a sibling—makes our lives better and helps others.

- All animals play important roles in nature. All people are important too. Everyone's work has value.

ACTIVITIES

Activity 1: The Lemon Game

Materials
Tennis balls (4 or 5)
Permanent marker

Directions
Before playing the game, use a permanent marker to draw symbols—circle, square, star, and so forth—on several tennis balls. These symbols will remind you what each ball represents.

Have everyone stand or sit in a circle. Pass one tennis ball to the student on your right and say,

"This is a lemon." That first student then passes the tennis ball to the next student and repeats, "This is a lemon." This continues around the circle.

After two or three students have passed the first tennis ball, each making the above statement as they present the tennis ball to the next person on their right, introduce a second ball to the circle. This time, say, "This is a jelly bean." Continue to pass out the rest of the tennis balls, calling each one by a false name.

Then, once all the balls are being passed around the circle, say, "Reverse." Instruct kids to pass the balls in the opposite direction, each one restating the name that was given for each ball. You can reverse the direction as many times as you like. The game continues until most students are confused about what each tennis ball is supposed to be, and the laughter begins.

Follow the game with a conversation about open-mindedness, bullying behavior, and honest communication. Opening prompts might include the following:

- Just saying that a tennis ball is a lemon doesn't make it a lemon. And calling a person an unkind name doesn't make that name true.

- It's unfair to make assumptions about people or label them. Every person has many sides to their character.

- If you don't communicate honestly with others, you might start to feel confused about your true ideas and values. It's hard to remember a lie and keep it straight.

Activity 2: In Harmony

Materials
Optional: Sheet music for one or more songs
Optional: CD player, computer or tablet, or musical instrument(s)

Directions
Teach your students a song about assertiveness, conflict resolution, or ways to reduce bullying. If you are interested in purchasing music, you can find lyrics and music to songs such as "I Can Talk It Out," "Conflict Resolution Helps You Find the Very Best Solution," and "Bully-Proof Our School" at songsforteaching.com/charactereducationsongs .htm. You can also search YouTube for songs that fit your goals. Otherwise, write an original song with your class. If desired, you could provide simple instruments for students to play. Encourage kids to think about respectful and productive ways to resolve disagreements and address bullying. Talk about how conflict and bullying reduce harmony in your classroom.

Activity 3: All Mixed Up

Materials
All Mixed Up handout (in digital content)

Directions
Pass out copies of the All Mixed Up handout. (*Note:* There are two versions of this handout with different degrees of difficulty. Use one or both, depending on the needs of your group. The answers follow below.) Remind kids that crows are good at problem-solving. Explain how anagrams work and do an example together if desired.

Then give kids some time to work on the puzzles. Afterward, talk about what kids found challenging, fun, or surprising about this activity. Discuss how problem-solving can be a helpful skill, and brainstorm strategies for approaching a challenging problem.

All Mixed Up answers:
Simpler handout:
RWCO = CROW
PSREETC = RESPECT
VLOES = SOLVE
PEKE YRNIGT = KEEP TRYING

More difficult handout:
MICNEUOTMAC = COMMUNICATE
CENECCATPA = ACCEPTANCE
BPRLOME-LNOISVG = PROBLEM-SOLVING
ON BNLLUGIY EADWLLO = NO BULLYING ALLOWED

Activity 4: Problem-Solving to Prevent Bullying

Materials
Paper and pencils

Directions
Bullying is more likely to occur when kids don't have strong social skills. A lack of respect, poor communication, and a lack of understanding or empathy can all lead to bullying situations. Present this problem to students. Ask: **What are some positive ways to respond to bullying? How can we reduce bullying at our school?**

Remind children that they are great problem-solvers, and emphasize that you need their help in solving the problem of bullying. After you finish this activity, children will care deeply about the solutions they chose as a group. The following steps can help you structure this activity, which you may want to extend over multiple days.

- **Discuss the problem.** As a group, talk about the problem of bullying. Why is it a problem? How does it affect how people feel about school? If appropriate, remind children that there will be no finger-pointing or name-calling as part of this discussion.

- **Brainstorm solutions.** Pass out paper and pencils to all students. Ask them each to write down some ways to stop or reduce bullying. Give them a time limit that matches your age group. Offer individual help to students who might have a hard time writing ideas down. You could ask that child to tell you an idea that you quickly jot down.

- **Work in small groups to choose positive solutions.** Break the class into small groups. Assign (or have groups assign) one child from each group to write down their solutions and another to report them to the class. Have children read their individual ideas to team members. Then ask the small group to choose the best idea from each person's list.

- **Have each team report their top ideas to the whole group.** Write the ideas on the board as kids report. Make a chart showing the top ideas from all teams and place it on the wall.

- **As a class, vote on one solution to pursue.** Ask each student to vote for the two solution they think are best and use these results to select a winner.

- **Plan out how to put the solution into action.** Depending on which solution the group selects, write the necessary steps to do it. Then assign children to different roles to carry it out, and set a time to review how the plan is going.

- **Celebrate progress.** Set a later date to review how the solution is working and what still needs to be done. Celebrate any progress made along the way!

Variation: You could extend this problem-solving approach to other challenges or questions facing your group. For example, what might be the consequences if classroom rules are broken? What rewards could be established for students who show understanding and support for others?

LESSON 8
CUTTLEFISH

Key Words
The behaviors, traits, and emotions below are just starting points for aligning SEL, character education, and this lesson's story. Most of these ideas can easily be connected with more than one competency or domain.

Self-Awareness: Self-Confidence • Understanding Personal Strengths and Weaknesses

Self-Management: Adaptability • Healthy Habits • Honesty • Integrity • Trust and Trustworthiness

Social Awareness: Acceptance of Others • Discernment • Reading Social Cues • Respect

Relationship Skills: Resisting Social Pressure

Responsible Decision-Making: Discernment • Healthy Habits • Safety • Understanding Consequences

Students will

- ❧ learn interesting facts about the cuttlefish, including its amazing camouflaging skill

- ❧ compare the cuttlefish's ability to change its appearance to the way people sometimes change aspects of themselves—such as their language, behavior, or dress—depending on the people who are around them

- ❧ think about how staying true to yourself and being consistent in your behavior are part of integrity

- ❧ draw comparisons between the cuttlefish's adaptability and people who adapt to new situations

Overview
Your students face deception and dishonesty in many aspects of their lives, from false advertisements to people who hide their true character. Being able to think critically and to discern truth from falsehoods are important perception skills that will serve your students well as they grow. In addition, children need to be aware and confident of their own feelings, strengths, and challenges. Then they can grow in self-confidence, trustworthiness, and integrity. The cuttlefish lesson provides a starting point for conversation about these ideas, as well as an exploration of being true to oneself and developing personal integrity. (*Note:* Integrity can be a tricky concept for younger kids to grasp, so you may want to have a discussion about this character trait before you get into the details of this lesson. While honesty is mainly about telling the truth, integrity goes further. When a person has integrity, the things they say, think, value, and do are all in harmony.)

Story
The Not-So-Cuddly-Cuttlefish

THE NOT-SO-CUDDLY-CUTTLEFISH

Cuttlefish. The name sounds . . . well . . . cuddly! Maybe you think you'd like to have a cuttlefish as a pet. But what would happen if you put it in an aquarium with other fish? Chances are, your goldfish and guppies would begin to disappear. Cuttlefish eat little fish, crabs, and shrimp.

The cuttlefish's name is a little confusing. Cuttlefish aren't really fish at all. They're mollusks. Mollusks have soft bodies and no backbone. Many of them have hard outer shells. But not the cuttlefish. Its shell is inside and it's called the cuttlebone. This hollow bone has many little spaces in it. The cuttlefish moves up or down in the water by filling or emptying these spaces with gas.

And cuttlefish aren't cuddly. In fact, many of them are poisonous. They have toxins in their saliva and muscles. Cuttlefish don't have hard shells to protect them from predators, so their poison helps defend them against animals that want to eat them.

Cuttlefish also have other ways to stay safe. They're masters of disguise, like spies of the sea. When in danger, a cuttlefish sprays a cloud of black liquid into the water. This liquid is called ink. While the hungry predator fumbles in the darkness, the cuttlefish sneaks away.

And that's not all. Move over, chameleons! Many cuttlefish have an amazing ability. They can change their colors and patterns. They can even change texture and shape. When they sense danger, they quickly blend in with the background. They hide in plain sight.

The Pfeffer's flamboyant cuttlefish doesn't blend in. Instead, it puts on a wild display. It flashes quickly from one color to the next. One moment it's bright red. Suddenly it's neon yellow. This colorful show sends a message. *Don't you dare eat me. I'm poisonous. Stay back.*

Some cuttlefish use their camouflage skills to find partners. Small males sometimes disguise themselves as females. They change their color and pattern to match the way females look. Then they slip past bigger males and mate with females. Pretty sneaky!

CUTTLEFISH FACTS

- The cuttlefish has three hearts and blue-green blood.

- To move through the water, a cuttlefish uses a method similar to jet propulsion. It pulls water into its mantle cavity and then shoots it out with great force. The way cuttlefish control their buoyancy is similar to how submarines operate.

- Cuttlefish ink was the original source of the sepia (reddish brown) dye used by artists.

TALK IT OVER

Use these questions to guide your students in considering comparisons and connections between the deceptive behavior of cuttlefish with human qualities, such as honesty, adaptability, and integrity. Make sure children understand that the cuttlefish is not being dishonest when it changes its appearance. It changes colors for protection. But cuttlefish provide a great analogy to human behavior. Learning to be honest within yourself and others is a positive goal for self-management as well as social awareness and relationship skills.

Cuttlefish change color and texture to trick others—both predators and mates. Sometimes people also seem to change depending on where they are or what people they are with. Can you think of examples of this?

- People are not always exactly who they seem to be. For example, they might lie to make themselves seem important or to avoid trouble.

- A person might dress a certain way because they want to impress others.

- Some kids play violent video games or watch movies that are for grown-ups but tell their parents that they don't. You should always be trustworthy in the things that you do and claim to be.

The cuttlefish changes its appearance to stay safe. But when people pretend to be something they are not, it does not make them safe. Instead, it can damage their self-image and can lessen other people's trust in them. Showing integrity means that your actions and your values match. Why is it important to show integrity? When can it be hard to do this?

- When your actions and beliefs don't match, you might feel uncomfortable or unhappy inside. Integrity feels better.

- If you try to have too many different identities (acting differently with different people), you might start to get mixed up. You can feel like you forget who you really are and what you really care about.

- Sometimes people might tease you for standing up for your beliefs.

- Sometimes your friends might want you to do something that goes against your values. It can be hard to choose between being with your friends and staying true to yourself.

The cuttlefish can change its appearance to fool others. Can you think of things in people's lives that might fool them?

- Commercials and other ads might tell you something that is not true. For example, an ad might say, "It's the best product money can buy!" But is it really the best? It's important to think carefully about what you see, read, and hear, and to draw your own conclusions.

- Sometimes we are fooled by stereotypes. We think that all people from certain groups are alike. But instead, we should decide what people are like by getting to know them and by watching their behavior. It's not a good idea to assume all people are the same.

The cuttlefish uses poison, camouflage, and ink to keep predators at a distance. How do you think people sometimes keep others at a distance? Why do you think they might do this?

- A person might speak harshly or act unkindly to keep other people away. This could be because they are embarrassed about something or don't feel good about themselves.

- A person who seems unfriendly might actually just be shy or not know how to make friends.

- Some people who have had their feelings hurt in the past might be afraid of making close friends. They might be worried about being hurt again by people they care about.

The cuttlefish doesn't have a hard outside shell to protect it, though scientists believe its ancestors may have. Instead, it has other ways of surviving, such as changing color and spraying ink. Can you compare this to people who have to adapt to new or different situations?

- People who have health problems that prevent them from doing some activities can still do great things. For example, Stephen Hawking had a disease that made him unable to move or to talk. But he was one of the most famous scientists in the world.

- Kids who don't have the size or strength to do one sport can learn another one. For example, if you're not tall enough to play basketball, you might try swimming, golf, or some other sport.

- People who have allergies to certain foods must adapt to eating other foods instead. This can be hard, especially if they really like the foods they can't eat anymore. But they'll feel better if they stick to the foods that are good for them. People feel better when they make healthy choices.

ACTIVITIES

Activity 1: A Story of Deception

Materials

Chart paper, board, or other surface for composing the story

Markers or chalk

Directions

Write a group story about someone who lies or deceives others. Describe how one lie might lead to another. Try to guide the story to include a change of behavior when the character learns to be true to others and to themselves. It may take kids a while to get warmed up, so before the activity, compose a few prompts that you can use to get the storytelling started—and also, if necessary, to keep the story creation on track. For example: **What should we name our character? What does the character do next? How do you think this makes the character feel?**

Invite students to raise their hands to add different points and developments to the tale. The story could be funny or serious. Afterward, talk with kids about the story and how it developed. What ways could the story have gone differently? How can we write our own stories as we live our lives? Could deciding to lie—or not lie—in one situation have an effect on things that happen later on?

Activity 2: Master of Disguise

Materials

Drawing paper

Markers, pencils, crayons, paints

Optional: Printouts of cuttlefish picture (in digital content)

Directions

Have kids draw a cuttlefish in hiding. They might choose a cuttlefish that's pretending to look like sand, a plant, or some other background. (If you like, search the internet for images of cuttlefish in camouflage and show them to your students. Kids will be amazed by what cuttlefish can do.)

Variation: If younger students find it too challenging to draw their own cuttlefish, you can hand out copies of the cuttlefish picture and ask kids to color it with lots of bright colors like the Pfeffer's flamboyant cuttlefish.

When kids have finished their pictures, invite them to show the class. Talk about the ways people sometimes try to blend in with the background, like a hiding cuttlefish—or how they might try to stand out, like the colorful Pfeffer's flamboyant cuttlefish. Why do some people like to go unnoticed? Why do others prefer to be in the spotlight? (Be sure to guide this conversation carefully to keep it from getting personal about anyone in the class. And

point out that it is okay to be either way. Helping children accept themselves is a big step in positive self-image.)

Activity 3: Many Talents

Materials
Various

Directions
Hold a classroom talent showcase. Kids who want to perform can do so, while others can submit drawings, writings, or other work. If some kids' talents are sports or something else that can't be performed in class, ask them to share pictures of them doing these activities or to write stories about them. You could create a display space in your room for all of these contributions, or put together a booklet and make copies that kids can take home.

After the showcase, talk about how we all have different talents. No one is good at everything, and everyone is good at something. If some kids developed their talents because they were unable to do some other activity, invite them to share this information, but be clear that it's voluntary. Ask kids to think about what they would do instead of the talent they chose to showcase, if for some reason they couldn't have that talent anymore. Again, ask them to share their thoughts if they feel comfortable doing so. Compliment each child's skills.

Activity 4: Turning Off the Heat

Materials
Heat-resistant (tempered) glass flask with a
    narrow neck
Water
Balloon (8-inch round balloons work best)
Safety glasses
Hot plate or other heating unit
Hot pads or oven mitts
Optional: Shallow dish of ice water

Directions
Put a few tablespoons of water into the tempered-glass flask. Then place the balloon over the neck of the flask. Put on your safety glasses, and place the bottle on the hot plate. Slowly begin to heat the flask until the water boils and creates vapor. As the air and vapor heat up, their molecules spread out and bounce around more rapidly. The warming air takes up more space, moving and causing it to expand. Once the balloon has inflated a bit, turn off the hot plate.

Use a hot pad to remove the flask from the heating unit. Place the flask on a second hot pad.

As you do this experiment, talk with kids about the way dishonesty and deception can be like the balloon as the water heats up. Lies can grow and grow. Tell kids that if the air inside the bottle keeps heating up, the balloon could eventually pop. Similarly, when people find out that someone has been dishonest, their respect for and trust in that person can "pop." Ask kids to think about how to "turn off the heat" when they are being dishonest or pretending to be someone else. If they need help, you can prompt them to think about how correcting the lie "turns off the heat." Be honest about the fact that this can be difficult. Is it hard to be ourselves sometimes? Is it tempting to lie? Why is it better to tell the truth?

LESSON 9

DANDELIONS

Key Words

The behaviors, traits, and emotions below are just starting points for aligning SEL, character education, and this lesson's story. Most of these ideas can easily be connected with more than one competency or domain.

Self-Awareness: Frustration • Happiness and Joy • Mindfulness

Self-Management: Adaptability • Assertiveness • Goal-Setting • Hard Work • Healthy Habits • Organization and Self-Motivation

Social Awareness: Acceptance of Others • Perspective-Taking

Relationship Skills: Citizenship • Humor

Responsible Decision-Making: Problem-Solving

Students will

- 🍃 learn some facts about dandelions, including their rapid growth and their different uses throughout history and around the world

- 🍃 discuss the importance of problem-solving and hard work in finding solutions, as well as the idea that frustration can sometimes interfere with happiness

- 🍃 consider how looking at a situation in a new way or from a different perspective can change your ideas about it and can lead to greater acceptance and appreciation of others

- 🍃 compare dandelions' quick spread with human behavior that can grow out of control

- 🍃 draw comparisons between the dandelion's deep roots and the roots of citizenship

Overview

Dandelions have a pretty bad reputation in most parts of the United States. Their aggressive spread across lawns and their ability to adapt have made them Public Enemy Number 1 for many gardeners. They appear to be assertive, tenacious, and able to grow anywhere. But in many parts of the world, they are valued as a food crop and a source of medicine. Through the story, you can help kids understand that sometimes we have false perceptions of a problem or of other people, and that our views vary depending on where we live and what information we have. Learning more about something or someone can help us understand situations better and from a new point of view.

Your students can also explore the idea that, like the dandelion's rapid growth, certain behaviors can spread very quickly, such as telling rumors. The results can be damaging and hard to undo. On the other hand, kindness, good manners, honesty, dependability, and other positive traits can spread from person to person as well.

Story

Determined Dandelions

DETERMINED DANDELIONS

It's a beautiful springtime Saturday. You have plans with your friends. But your dad has a different idea. He says you're in charge of destroying dandelions in the yard. And, he adds, "Set a goal, get yourself organized with the right tools, and make a plan. Be sure to dig down to the root. Otherwise, those little yellow heads will be back before we know it."

So much for having fun. You crawl across the grass for hours. As you dig and pull, you pretend you're in a battle. You make explosion sounds as you rip out each dandelion. "Kaboom! Another one bites the dust." You toss the fluffy white heads onto the grass. You'll pick them up later. When you finish, there are no dandelions to be seen. You're proud of your work. But you also feel a little sad for the cheerful flowers.

Three days later, your dad sees a fluffy yellow blossom on the lawn. Then he spots another. And another. You remind your dad that you already did your job. But he just smiles and hands you the weed digger. He suggests you get a little *more* organized and drop the dandelions in a sack as you go. "You were helping them spread their seeds all over the lawn," he tells you. "You're just planting more of them." Your dad laughs.

You *don't* laugh. "My work will never be done!" You don't feel sorry for the dandelions anymore. You just want them gone. You attack the flowers with a growl and throw them in a sack. You have to get them before those white fluff balls appear. They look soft and harmless, but they are collections of tiny parachutes. As these parachutes float away, they spread dandelion seeds. And each dandelion head has 150 to 200 seeds. You decide you'll never again blow dandelion fluff across your yard.

Finally, you're sure you got them all. The grass will be safe from the dandelion invasion until your family gets back from your summer trip. Right?

Wrong. While you're gone, a few new yellow heads pop up. They draw bees like magnets. Bees just can't stay away from dandelion nectar. The bright,

beautiful yellow flowers burst into fluffy white balls. They scatter seeds all over your lawn.

You get home to a field of dandelions with tufts of grass growing between them. Your grassy yard has turned yellow with "lions." You decide this calls for all-out warfare. You grab a hammer from your dad's toolbox and stomp outside. You smash the flowers. "Take that! Bam!" But pretty soon your arm hurts. And you have a feeling the dandelions will still be back. You go in the house, sit down, and hang your head.

Next, your dad brings home an armful of library books. He says that there must be a way to beat the dandelions. Together, you read and plan your attack.

To your surprise, you learn that many people don't *want* to get rid of dandelions. In plenty of places around the world, dandelions are food. You read a legend about the island of Minorca, near Spain. Hundreds of years ago, the story goes, a huge swarm of locusts landed on the island. They ate up all the crops. But the islanders survived—thanks to dandelions. They dug up the roots and ate them until the locusts were gone.

You also find out that dandelions are good for you. The roots, leaves, and flowers have all kinds of healthful vitamins and minerals. People in Europe toss the greens into their salads. They eat the roots as veggies. Some people drink dandelion tea.

And that's not all. For centuries, Chinese people have used dandelions to treat sicknesses. So have some Native Americans. Dandelions might be one of nature's superfoods. You feel your frustration leave you. A feeling of peace settles in.

Your dad closes the book. He says, "I guess being wise means you know what you can change and accept what you can't. In the end, nature always wins." You remind your dad that you *told* him digging up dandelions wasn't a good goal! This time you both laugh. The war is over. Next spring, you won't bother fighting. You'll trade your garden fork for a salad fork. Then you'll relax and watch for a new crop of dandelions to eat and enjoy.

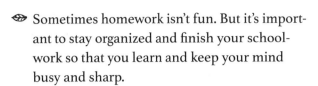

DANDELION FACTS

- Dandelion roots, leaves, and flowers have vitamins including A, C, and K, as well as many minerals.
- Dandelion root is a traditional ingredient in some kinds of root beer.
- The name *dandelion* comes from French for "lion's tooth."

TALK IT OVER

Use these questions to guide your students in considering analogies between dandelions and character traits and behaviors in people.

Dandelions spread very quickly if gardeners don't stop them early enough. Can you think of anything in your life that can get out of control if you're not organized and not careful?

- If you put off doing your homework for too long, or if you don't do some assignments, you can quickly fall way behind.
- If you lie a lot, things can get out of control.
- If you don't do your chores, they can pile up and get overwhelming.
- Rumors and gossip can spread very quickly.
- If you do kind things for others, that can spread fast too. People who are treated nicely often feel like doing nice things for others.
- Illness can spread fast. Washing your hands and staying home when you are sick can help slow down or even prevent the spread of colds and other illnesses.

The kid in "Determined Dandelions" felt that trying to get rid of the dandelions was a waste of time and energy. Are there some things that you do—or that other people do—that seem like wasted effort?

- Holding a grudge or staying mad for a long time wastes your energy. It can make you feel bad and keep you from having fun.

- Sometimes homework isn't fun. But it's important to stay organized and finish your schoolwork so that you learn and keep your mind busy and sharp.
- Some chores, like washing the dishes or cleaning your room, might seem pointless to you sometimes. After all, dishes just get dirty again, and your room probably will too. But helping with these jobs makes your home nicer for everybody.
- Sometimes practicing a skill seems like a waste of time. Progress can be very slow sometimes. But keep at it, and whatever skill you're working on will eventually improve.

The people in this story changed their minds about dandelions after learning more about them. Have you ever changed your mind about someone or something after getting more information? Have you had a problem that was really hard to solve until you looked at it in a different way? Did you feel happier and more peaceful when you figured it out?

- If you believe something is true, and then you get more information from someone who sees things differently, you might change your mind.
- When problems happen, you often have to learn to adapt to new situations and find new ways of working things out. When you discover new solutions to a problem, it can help you feel self-confident and empowered. You can feel happy about your ability to manage your own life, including your emotional response to facing a challenge.
- When you're doing homework, you may not understand it at first. But if you get help or look up more information, you might start to see the answers more clearly.
- Sometimes people think or say unkind things about people they don't know or who are different from them. But when people get to know other people, they understand them better. They might even become friends. It's best not to make assumptions about others.

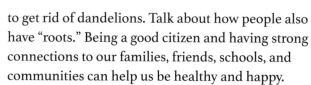

Dandelions' long roots make them strong. These roots are part of what makes them so difficult to get rid of. People have "roots" too. We have ties to our families, communities, schools, and other groups. Citizenship means being part of these groups. What are some ways to be a good citizen?

- Learning about how your government works

- Helping other people in the community

- Respecting and following the rules of your community, classroom, or family

- Helping keep your school, neighborhood, or town clean and safe

ACTIVITIES

Activity 1: How Does Your Garden Grow?

Materials

Long planter or several tall pots

Potting soil or dirt

Dandelion seeds (you can buy these or harvest them from fluffy dandelion heads)

Water

Directions

As a group, plan out your dandelion garden. Fill the planter or pots with potting soil or dirt, leaving about an inch at the top of the container. Bury the seeds about ¼- to ½-inch deep.

Put the planter or pots somewhere in your room that gets as much sunlight as possible. If you don't have a sunny spot, see if you can put the plants elsewhere in your school. Keep the soil moist. Invite kids to take turns watering the growing dandelions.

Over the next couple of weeks, check on your dandelion plants regularly. Talk with students about what plants need to grow, such as light, water, and soil. Discuss how people also need certain things to grow and be healthy. For example, exercise and nutritious food are important for keeping our bodies healthy. Learning and curiosity help our minds stay sharp and active.

Once you have a crop of dandelions, pull up one of the flowers. Show kids the taproot and explain that it can be more than a foot long in a full-grown plant. This is part of what makes it so hard

to get rid of dandelions. Talk about how people also have "roots." Being a good citizen and having strong connections to our families, friends, schools, and communities can help us be healthy and happy.

Variation: Get parents' permission to send some dandelion greens home with kids for their families to try in a dish. Make sure to choose young, tender greens. Dandelion greens get bitter as they age.

Activity 2: Dandelion Words

Materials

None

Directions

Have students write articles, stories, or poems about dandelions. Ask them to compare or contrast dandelions and their characteristics to human traits and behaviors, such as determination, problem-solving, acceptance, and hard work. If you like, hold an in-class workshop to help kids revise and polish their writing. Then encourage them to submit their pieces to the school paper or literary journal, or to a community newsletter. Or, compile the writings in a booklet and send it home with kids to share with their friends and families.

Activity 3: Survey Says . . .

Materials

Dandelion Survey handout (in digital content)

Directions

Conduct a survey to find out how people feel about dandelions. How popular—or unpopular—are they? As a group, come up with two to five questions, depending on the age of your group. Sample questions might include:

- Do your families dig up dandelions, or do they ignore them?

- Have you ever tasted a dandelion green?

- Do you think dandelions are pretty or just pesky?

Enter your chosen questions on the customizable Dandelion Survey handout and give every student two copies of the survey form. Then pair up kids and have them survey each other. In addition, ask them each to survey one person outside of school.

When kids have gathered all the answers, help them use the data to calculate fractions or percentages reflecting the information they collected. *Example:* Three-fourths (or 75 percent) of the people surveyed have never eaten a dandelion green. (Younger students can phrase these values as "Three out of four people . . .")

Talk with your class about what they learned. How hard or easy is it to change people's opinions? Did students' own opinions change at all in the course of the survey?

Activity 4: Let's Get Organized

Materials
This will vary, depending on what you are organizing.

Directions
You can use this list as a starting point for making goals, talking about the importance of organization, and building and strengthening habits of organization. This will help develop and improve self-management skills.

- Begin the day with a mindfulness exercise. While mindfulness is often associated with focusing on the present, mindfulness activities also improve attention and boost the ability to focus on tasks one by one, instead of feeling overwhelmed by the big picture. Warm up with a mindful posing activity, asking children to strike a superhero pose—feet planted just wider than hips, stretching the body upward, fists clenched, and arms reached out to the sky or with fists placed firmly on hips. (You can modify these poses as needed for individual children.) Ask kids to hold the pose for a moment, focusing on how they feel, and then relax. Repeat this several times. Talk with children about how they can be strong and focused, and how they can do what is needed. For example, they can be strong enough to organize, plan, and complete tasks.

- Ask kids to write or say their goals for the day.

- Set an example in the classroom by keeping your own desk or other space neat and organized.

- Have children practice organizing and ordering their activities and responsibilities. Children decide which assignment, chore, or activity needs to be done first, second, and so on, and write a corresponding number next to each task. Have them include after-school activities too, such as homework, soccer practice, shopping with mom, or helping dad make dinner. Children's lists will naturally differ. Find a place to keep the list, and always keep it there. Make changes as needed.

- Within the classroom, provide containers for organizing pencils, paper, erasers, markers, and other items for each child or group of children. Verbally reward good organization. If a child has difficulty doing a certain skill, you might ask another child to show how to do it. Then reward both children. You might have your own reward system of stickers, marks on the board, marbles, or whatever else you choose.

- Suggest that children adopt a "homework first" habit. Talk about how they could implement this rule at home. What might help them develop and practice this habit?

- Provide a monthly paper planner for each child, perhaps inviting kids to decorate or personalize their planners in some way. Talk about using these planners every day to keep track of assignments and other responsibilities.

- At the end of the school day, leave a few minutes for children to clean up their areas. Follow a "nothing left on the floor" rule. Make the classroom is all cleaned up before students leave.

- End the day with a mindfulness activity. Ask children to shut their eyes and breathe deeply, be aware of air going into their lungs and to every part of their bodies and returning out. Do this three times. Pause. Ask them to be mindful of what they are going to do next. Have they handed in assignments? Do they have their homework and activity list with them? Are they taking home the homework they need? Are all their things put away? This can also be done at home before bed.

LESSON 10
DOGS

Key Words

The behaviors, traits, and emotions below are just starting points for aligning SEL, character education, and this lesson's story. Most of these ideas can easily be connected with more than one competency or domain.

Self-Awareness: Courage and Boldness • Love

Self-Management: Goal-Setting • Hard Work • Healthy Habits • Responsibility • Sadness • Trust and Trustworthiness

Social Awareness: Caring and Kindness • Communication • Empathy • Helpfulness • Reading Social Cues

Relationship Skills: Forgiveness • Friendship • Leadership • Loyalty • Service to Others

Responsible Decision-Making: Problem-Solving • Safety

Students will

- learn some interesting characteristics about dogs, including their courage, service and helpfulness, loyalty, love, and caring
- discuss what we can learn from dogs about loyalty
- think about the friendship, love, and forgiveness that dogs seem to show toward people and make analogies to similar traits or qualities in people
- consider the many jobs dogs do for humans, and compare this to ideas of service and responsibility among people

Overview

The friendship that connects dogs and people provides an example of loyalty, unconditional love, caring, helpfulness, and dedication. When children take care of a dog or other pet, they grow in self-confidence as well as empathy. That empathy can extend to people and is a big step in social and emotional development.

The story in this lesson tells of two brave and dedicated dogs. The stories end sadly. But it is important for children to understand that humans feel many emotions, including sadness. Openly discussing sadness with children can also help them see that it usually doesn't last forever.

Many of your students may have dogs, or have friends or neighbors who do. They will probably be eager to share stories about the dogs they know. You might discuss how the way people treat their dogs can affect these pets' loyalty or friendship. You can compare this to how our treatment of other people affects our relationships with them.

Story
Dedicated Dogs

DEDICATED DOGS

Every morning, Hachiko wagged his tail good-bye as his owner left for work. Hachiko was a fluffy brown Akita dog. His owner was a professor at the University of Tokyo in Japan. The professor took the train to his job. Each afternoon, when the professor got off the train, Hachiko was waiting at the station.

One day, the professor didn't come home. He had died suddenly. But Hachiko was still waiting for the professor at the train. A new owner adopted Hachiko. Yet the dog continued to love and miss the professor. For nine years, loyal Hachiko kept going to the train station. He didn't understand that his beloved master was gone. So he waited and waited.

People at the station noticed Hachiko. His faithfulness impressed them. They fed him. They patted him and said hello when they passed. Although Hachiko would wag his tail and lick their hands, the faithful dog did not seem interested in a new owner. He just could not forget the professor.

Years later, when Hachiko died, people couldn't forget him, either. Today, if you go to the Shibuya train station in Tokyo, you'll see a statue of Hachiko. People pat the statue and touch its paws. They use the statue as a meeting spot. Sometimes they put flowers, blankets, or other little gifts on it. Every year, a ceremony is held for Hachiko, in memory of his honorable loyalty and love.

Many people also honor another loyal dog: a rescue dog named Trakr. Rescue dogs have saved people from all kinds of dangers. Trakr is remembered because he was especially brave.

On September 11, 2001, terrorists attacked the World Trade Center in New York City. The two towers fell in piles of rubble. Many people were trapped. Their families and friends didn't know where their loved ones were. The dust was so thick, people could hardly see, and they were terrified. Brave men, women, and animals rushed to help find those who were trapped in the rubble.

A Canadian police officer saw the destruction, and came to search with Trakr, his loyal police dog. Trakr was a brave German shepherd and a friend to anyone in trouble. Dogs can often sense how humans feel. Trakr may have sensed from his owner's emotions that this was an important mission. Trakr had been trained to hunt down criminals and to find missing persons. He seemed to know there was still someone buried in the rubble. He helped dig through 30 feet of dangerous debris to find a woman who had been trapped in the debris for 26 hours. He saved her life, and she was the last person found alive. Trakr could have died while digging through the dangerous rubble. But he was the right dog to find this last survivor of the attack.

Sadly, Trakr later got sick. He couldn't use his back legs anymore. Some people think the smoke from the World Trade Center made him sick. Doctors tried to save the heroic dog, but they could not. Even after Trakr died, people remembered his courage, devotion, and service. Scientists wanted to clone a dog. Cloning is like making a copy. Scientists have learned how to clone animals by using some of their cells. People decided that brave Trakr was a great dog to clone. Even though Trakr was gone, there were five young dogs born that looked just like him. They had his brave heart. They learned to be rescue dogs like he was.

With their loyalty and courage, dogs have earned the friendship of people around the world. Most dogs don't lead lives as dramatic as those of Hachiko or Trakr. But their love and warmth are still important. Dogs don't care what you look like. They accept you as you are. Maybe you had a bad day at school. Or you got into an argument with a friend. Maybe you made a mistake. Your dog puts his paws on your chest. He licks the tears from your face. He nuzzles your hand. And suddenly, you feel a little bit better. Your dog really might be your best friend.

DOG FACTS

- The dog name *Fido* comes from Latin and means "to trust" or "to believe in." Sometimes it is also translated as "I am faithful." Before he became president, Abraham Lincoln had a dog named Fido.
- Experts believe that the relationship between dogs and humans goes back at least ten thousand years.
- Dogs have about 220 million scent receptors in their noses. Humans have between 5 and 10 million.

TALK IT OVER

The two stories in this lesson can evoke empathy in children. Some children may even feel tearful in response. (For more information on how stories can spark feelings of empathy, see the introduction.) After feeling empathy, children will be more likely to want to help and share with others. Use these questions to guide your students in considering comparisons between dogs and their loyalty, love, courage, and service with behaviors in people.

Hachiko stayed dedicated and loyal to his owner long after the professor died. Sometimes people are sad for a very long time over the loss of someone or something they loved. Can this be helpful? Can it ever be harmful?

- Losing someone or something can cause you to think carefully about the way you feel and the things you think are important. Sometimes hard times and sadness can help us become stronger people. We can learn from what we've gone through.

- Different kinds of loss can make us sad. Sometimes when we move to a new home, switch schools, or go through another big change, we feel like we've lost something. These changes can be hard at first, but usually, over time, we begin to feel better.

- Mourning the loss of someone or something can help you be more understanding of other people in similar situations. Your own experience can make you better able to comfort others.

- It's normal and healthy to feel sad when we lose someone or something we love. But sometimes, being very sad for a very long time can keep people from moving on with their lives.

Dogs seem to like helping people and working with them. They seem to sense how we feel. When people understand how other people feel, we call it empathy. Do people gain happiness from serving other people or causes? Do you think service can be good for the people *doing* the service? In what ways might that happen?

- Doing service for others can make their lives better. At the same time, it can make the person doing the service feel needed and valued.

- Doing service feels good. Helping others makes us happy.

- Service can get you more involved and interested in your community. It can also help you meet people and make new friends.

- Serving others can give you a better understanding of what is important to you. It can help you learn how you want to live your life.

- *Note:* If desired, you can share this information with students and talk about it with them: Many students who get involved in service projects end up with better attitudes, higher self-esteem, improved grades and ability to use higher-level thinking skills, and increased school attendance. Serving others and volunteering can also result in health benefits. Researchers have found that it can lead to longer lives and lower rates of depression.

Dogs often appear to understand people's emotions or needs. Therapy dogs learn to be especially good at interpreting people's needs. Compare this to how important it might be for people to develop skills at understanding how other people might feel or what they might need.

👁 We can learn to read social and emotional cues by interpreting another person's tone of voice, facial expressions, gestures, and other nonverbal types of communication. When we do this, we can understand other people better.

👁 If we don't understand when another person is annoyed or angry, we might continue to anger them. The same can happen to us when other people don't understand our feelings.

👁 If a person does not understand social cues, they might tease or joke with other people in a way that is meant to be fun but isn't. They might not notice that the other person doesn't like what's happening, and this can be very hurtful.

👁 Learning to read social cues is an SEL skill that helps us succeed in interactions and relationships with others throughout our lives.

Dogs are usually very loyal to their owners. People can be loyal to each other too. How is loyalty helpful?

👁 When people feel loyal to their friends, school, neighborhoods, faith communities, or other groups, they are more likely to help. They will feel involved and cared about.

👁 When people are loyal to a group, they often grow to care about the other members of that group. They want to help each other. In return, they get support and help from other people in the group.

👁 When a person is loyal to you, that loyalty can help you feel safe and secure.

Dogs seem to show forgiving behaviors. A dog will usually love an owner even if the owner is not always kind. How does it feel when you forgive others? What about when you don't forgive?

👁 Holding a grudge against someone can make you feel miserable. It can even make you sick. But when you forgive, you can move on. You feel better and happier.

👁 Forgiving other people can sometimes change their behavior. They may think about what they did to hurt someone else and decide to be kinder in the future. And if they've been feeling bad about themselves, being forgiven by the people they hurt can help them forgive themselves too.

👁 If you don't forgive, your anger and hurt can get worse. Your feelings can grow into a bigger problem.

Sometimes dogs rescue people. The have even helped other species, including cats, which are often thought of as rivals of dogs. People naturally help people they love and those with common goals. What might you learn from the example of a dog's caring?

👁 As humans, we are all more alike than we are different, even if on the surface we don't seem to have much in common.

👁 All people who have needs deserve to be helped by others who can offer assistance and care.

👁 Helping others can help you find out new things about yourself. You might learn more about what you value, what you care about, or what you like to do with your time.

ACTIVITIES

Activity 1: Lend a Helping Hand

Materials
Various

Directions
Accounts of loyal dogs like those in "Dedicated Dogs" will spark empathy in kids and motivate them to plan a service project to help others. It could be as simple as writing letters to kids who are in the hospital, fundraising for supplies for dogs in animal shelters, or making welcome kits for kids who are new to your school. You could begin by having the group brainstorm a list of causes, charities, and service opportunities that they are interested in, and then hold a vote to choose one. (Expect several ideas to center around helping dogs.) Once the class has picked a cause, you could help them organize a fundraiser to support it. (If desired, you could narrow the field of possibilities by creating a list of ideas to choose from. but

it can also be powerful for children to generate ideas themselves.) Or, spend a day helping out as a group. Set up a visit to a local food shelf, community kitchen, animal shelter, or other organization that needs and welcomes volunteers. You could also choose to do a project that allows you to serve someone or something in your school.

Help students set goals for how they will carry out their plan, such as:

- Contact the people or organization that you've chosen to see if they want the help.

- Get support from families, as well as from your school's principal.

- Identify and gather the resources and supplies you'll need, including funds, support, transportation, and materials.

- Set a timeline for doing the project with the organization or people you want to help.

Whatever service you decide to do, talk with students afterward about empathy and other feelings this project may have sparked in them. What did they enjoy about the experience? Was performing this service different than they expected, and if so, how? What did they learn? What might they do differently next time? What kind of service would they choose in the future?

Activity 2: What Makes a Hero?

Materials
None

Directions
Tell the class some stories about real dogs that showed courage and rescued people from danger. If you like, you could show the group pictures of the dogs you choose to talk about. Use these dog stories as a starting point for a conversation with students about what it means to be a hero. How can we spot a hero? Is it always easy to know who might step up and be a hero in a time of need? What traits do heroes have?

Also ask kids who some of their heroes are. Invite them to write short essays or stories, talking about who their personal heroes are and why.

Remind them that not all heroes are famous. Some of their biggest heroes might be in their own families or communities.

Activity 3: Furry Friends

Materials
Furry Friend handout (in digital content)

Directions
Make a Furry Friends display. Talk with kids about how dogs are often described as people's "best friends," and ask them to think about their own animal friends. Pass out copies of the Furry Friend handout and ask kids to draw pictures of their dogs or other pets. If they don't have pets of their own, they can depict pets belonging to friends or neighbors. Or they could imagine "dream pets" and draw pictures of these imaginary furry friends. (If you like, a few days before this activity, you could invite kids who have pets to bring photos of them from home and attach them to their handouts.)

Next, have kids write words describing their furry friends on their handouts. Encourage them to think about more than physical characteristics and to consider ideas related to character traits. Ask kids to share what dogs or other animals have taught them about friendship, caring, or loyalty. Talk about ways that we can show these same traits to animals and to people.

When all handouts are complete, hang the pictures in your classroom or hallway.

Activity 4: Taking Care of a Pet

Materials
Pet to care for, *or* person to interview

Directions
Invite kids to spend a few days helping take care of dogs—their own, or those of friends or neighbors. (Make sure that the dogs are familiar and friendly to kids and their families.) Discuss with children what goals they need to set to take care of a dog. If the children are not allergic to or afraid of dogs, you might even have one visit the classroom. Beforehand, talk with students about what they'll need to do. For example, they need to think about

the goals of caring for a pet: food, water, exercise, companionship, and keeping the dog and its living space clean. Afterward, have a conversation about what it was like for kids to have this responsibility. Did they enjoy it? Did they ever feel overwhelmed by the job? Were some things fun at first and not so much fun after a few days? *Note:* If some kids have allergies, ask them if there's another pet they could care for, or have them interview someone who cares for a dog and ask what it's like.

Variation: If none of your students have allergies, you might get a class pet, such as a hamster, parakeet, frog, or fish. Students can take turns caring for the pet. You can talk with them about the ways that taking care of another creature helps them develop responsibility.

LESSON 11
DOLPHINS

Key Words

The behaviors, traits, and emotions below are just starting points for aligning SEL, character education, and this lesson's story. Most of these ideas can easily be connected with more than one competency or domain.

Self-Awareness: Happiness and Joy • Self-Confidence

Self-Management: Goal-Setting

Social Awareness: Caring and Kindness • Empathy • Helpfulness • Reading Social Cues • Respect • Understanding Others

Relationship Skills: Communication • Cooperation, Collaboration, and Teamwork • Friendship • Helpfulness • Playfulness

Responsible Decision-Making: Analyzing and Evaluating • Problem-Solving

Students will

- learn how dolphins behave, with each other as well as with humans, and make comparisons to the ways people treat each other
- connect cooperation between dolphins and people to the idea of cooperation among people, and learn why it's valuable
- talk about the helpfulness that dolphins show and how it affects their relationship with people, and compare that with how we can be helpful to others
- consider the respect that many people have for dolphins, and compare that with our respect for each other, for other species, and for the environment

Overview

People have felt friendly toward dolphins for thousands of years. From ancient Greek sailors who saw them as good luck to modern tourists and moviegoers, people have been charmed by dolphins' playfulness and their often-friendly nature, along with their ability to learn skills.

Kids will be fascinated by the ways dolphins interact with people. When dolphins are respected and treated in a caring and friendly manner, they appear to enjoy the company of humans. This fact can spark comparisons to the ways people treat each other, and why it's important to be respectful and friendly to others and to understand how others feel. In addition, dolphins seem to help fellow animals, as well as people. They've even worked together with people to catch fish. You can use these scenarios to spark productive discussions on cooperation, problem-solving, empathy, and helpfulness.

Story

Friendly Dolphins

FRIENDLY DOLPHINS

In the 1900s, many ships crashed on the rocks along New Zealand's shore. Sailors had to be very careful. But they found an unexpected friend. When sailors were near the dangerous Cook Strait, they would slow down their ships and wait. Looking through spyglasses, they watched for Pelorus Jack. He was a friendly dolphin. Pelorus Jack knew these waters better than people did. He swam next to ships and guided them safely through narrow, rocky channels. Some people say that the ships Pelorus Jack guided never wrecked. Pelorus Jack grew famous. Postcards with his picture were popular.

Many other dolphins have also swum alongside ships. Dolphins probably do this to save their energy. A ship makes a wave in the water as it moves. Dolphins use this wave to help them swim faster or more easily. But for thousands of years, sailors have considered these dolphins to be good luck.

Pelorus Jack was only one of many well-known dolphins. Everyone in New Zealand seemed to know Moko. He was a bottlenose dolphin. For years, he charmed locals and tourists. Moko seemed to enjoy playing with people at Mahia Beach. He tossed beach balls with waders. He pushed kayaks with his nose. He made people laugh and feel happy. He jumped out of the water and did flips. Local people and tourists loved Moko.

But Moko was more than a playmate. He was also a lifesaver. In 2008, a mother sperm whale and her calf got trapped near the beach. They swam into a narrow space near the shore and couldn't find their way back to the sea past the sandbar. People tried to help the whales. But they couldn't guide them through the narrow escape route. The whales were too big for the people to push back out. It looked like the whales might die.

Then Moko showed up. He sped through the water and pushed himself between the people and the whales. Somehow, he seemed to understand the problem and sense what to do. Amazingly, Moko could communicate with the whales. He made strange little grunts and whistles. The whales seemed to understand. They wiggled and squirmed and followed Moko. He led them to the end of the sandbar. Then he turned to the right and led the whales through a narrow channel and out into open water. The whales swam away, safe and sound, arching their backs as they moved through the water. The people watching were astonished. It appeared to everyone that it didn't matter to Moko that he was a dolphin and the other creatures were whales. He simply saw that the whales were in danger, and he took action to help.

DOLPHIN FACTS

- Dolphins can jump 20 feet out of the water.

- Dolphins use a type of sonar called echo-location to find and track their prey, which includes fish and shrimp.

- A group of dolphins is called a pod. Sometimes several pods join together in a herd.

- Dolphins sometimes help each other. Sometimes when they are hurt or sick, they can't get up to the water's surface to breathe. Some dolphins have lifted others to the surface to help them get air.

- The playful, helpful behavior of dolphins has made them popular with people. Dolphins have been in many movies and TV shows. They're natural stars. They even look like they're smiling!

- Dolphins are very smart animals. They communicate with clicks, whistles, and grunts. They learn fast and can be trained to understand human words and commands. They even help people do their work. In a town in Brazil, dolphins herd fish toward people waiting near shore. Then the dolphins do quick little dives in the water. This tells the fishers where to throw in their nets. The fishers respect these dolphins and are grateful for their help. The fishers get a big catch. And the dolphins eat fish that try to swim away from the nets. Working together, the dolphins and people all get more fish than they would alone.

TALK IT OVER

Use these questions to guide your students in considering analogies between the behavior of dolphins and behaviors and emotions in people.

Sometimes dolphins swim next to ships. They probably do this to save energy. How can people save energy by "swimming in the same direction"? (*Note:* **Kids may need a little extra help understanding this analogy. Explain that, for people, "swimming in the same direction" means working together and having a common purpose.)**

- A group of people with a shared goal will reach that goal more quickly by working together.

- It can take time to agree on a shared goal and a common direction. But once you've decided on a plan, if you cooperate and focus on the same thing, you'll waste less time disagreeing.

- Whether you're on a team, doing a group project at school, or trying to get along with a sibling, working together can help everyone experience more fun and greater joy.

Dolphins always seem like they're smiling. They aren't *really* smiling. It's just the way they look. But it helps people feel friendlier toward them. How can smiling also affect relationships that people have with each other? Help children recognize how their smile affects others and how a grouchy look might also affect someone. Invite children to show different emotions in front of the class and discuss how the group reacts or feels in response. Children can learn to read and use social cues to help them develop more successful social relationships with others throughout life.

- You meet more new people and win more friends when you smile. It is okay to feel grouchy sometimes—we all do. But it's helpful to know that a grouchy or angry expression will often turn people away. It is also important to understand your own feelings. You might consider *why* you feel grouchy. Then you can think of ways to try to work through your grouchy feelings. Sometimes smiling can help!

- If you smile at someone, sometimes it can encourage them to be friendlier to you in return—even if they don't know you well or haven't been friendly to you in the past.

- Smiling is a social cue that can help tell others how a you're feeling. It helps you show that you are happy, friendly, and nice to be with.

The people in Brazil who fish with dolphins respect their dolphin helpers. How is respect important? How can it be helpful?

- When you respect other people, they can learn to respect and trust you in return.

- People feel safer when they are around people who respect them.

- Respect can create loyalty and friendships among people.

- People will usually work harder toward a shared goal if they have respect for each other.

- When we respect animals and the environment, we work to care for them. Keeping our planet healthy is good for everyone.

Moko seemed to show problem-solving skills when he led the trapped whales to safety. Have you ever had to solve a hard problem? How did you do it? (Encourage kids to share stories about challenges they faced and overcame.)

- It can be hard to see the answer to a problem right away. We might need to sleep on it. Sometimes the best solutions come to us when we're thinking about something else.

- Sometimes two heads are better than one. Talking to someone else about a problem can help us see the situation more clearly. The other person might have ideas about how to solve the problem.

- When we're facing a tough problem, learning more about the situation can often help us find a solution. Finding a solution can help us feel positive about our problem-solving skills and have confidence that we can overcome the challenges we encounter.

By helping the whales, Moko reached out to animals that were a different species from him. How do people also help others who may be different from them? Why is this important?

- One important thing that can cause people to help someone in need is *empathy*. Empathy allows us to sense how others feel and to care about them. Sometimes people send help, supplies, or money to faraway places when people there are facing natural disasters or other problems.

- Just as Moko helped the whales, sometimes people who are very different share a common goal. They may help each other and work together even though they don't agree on everything.

- Everyone needs help sometimes. It's important to care for and help others no matter what beliefs they have or what cultures they come from. Everyone deserves compassion.

ACTIVITIES

Activity 1: To the Rescue

Materials
None

Directions
Role-play scenes in which students show someone helping or rescuing someone else. Some scenes can involve dolphins, while others may feature people only. You might also do this as a game of charades. You can write the scenarios on pieces of paper and let the children draw them out. Possible scenarios include:

- Moko rescuing the whales

- Pelorus Jack helping sailors

- rescuing someone from a fire

- helping someone who is being bullied

- dolphins helping people catch fish

- offering help to someone who is lost

Note: Some situations may be too frightening for younger kids. Choose whatever feels appropriate for your group.

After each role play, talk about what happened. How did the person doing the rescuing or helping feel? What about the kids who were being helped? If you like, extend the conversation to talk about what steps kids can take to keep themselves safe, as well as ways to help others.

Activity 2: Dolphin Stars

Materials
DVD player, VHS player, or streaming subscription
    TV, computer, or projector and screen
Dolphin movie

Directions
Watch a movie about dolphins in nature. Options include the documentary IMAX film *Dolphins* (2000) or the fictional movie *Dolphin Tale* (2011). After watching the film, talk about the challenges facing dolphins in the wild. Ask kids whether they think it's important for people to respect animals and nature. What might happen if we don't treat our planet well? How can we help take care of dolphins and other wild animals?

Variation: If you live near an aquarium or zoo that has dolphins, take a field trip to see these animals in action. If possible, have a zookeeper or aquarium worker talk to the group about dolphins and their lives in the wild. Afterward, talk with kids about conservation and respect for nature and its animals.

Activity 3: Swimming in the Same Direction

Materials
Masking tape
Paper clips (1 per team)
Rulers (1 per team)
Balls (1 per team)

Preparation
This activity works best on a playground or in a large multipurpose room. Before playing the game with your group, use tape to mark out a starting line and a finish line, about 10 to 20 feet apart.

Directions
This is a game of problem-solving and teamwork. Divide your group into teams of four. (If your group doesn't divide into fours, simply make sure that each team has one object fewer than they have team members.) Ask teams to line up behind the starting line. Then hand one paper clip, ruler, and ball to the first kid in line for each team. Tell the group that the object of this game is to get all three items across the finish line. The first team to do so wins. But there's a catch: Every player on the team must carry at least one object all the way to the finish line, and no one can ever move toward the finish line without an object.

A little confusion will follow as kids figure out how best to accomplish this goal and realize that they must cooperate to make it work. For example, Team 2 is made up of Danielle, Hector, Sara, and Asad. Hector, Sara, and Asad could each carry an object to the finish line. Then Hector could return to the starting line carrying the ball and the paper clip. Finally, Danielle and Hector could each carry one of these two objects to the finish line. Or, Asad and Danielle could each carry one object, and Sara and Hector could work together to carry the third object at the same time. (For example, each of them could hold one end of the ruler.)

After the game, invite kids to describe how they figured out their plan. Did they choose team leaders? If so, how? Did they have trouble agreeing on a plan? How did they eventually make a decision? Focus on how cooperation made it easier and faster to accomplish their goal.

LESSON 12
ELEPHANTS

Key Words

The behaviors, traits, and emotions below are just starting points for aligning SEL, character education, and this lesson's story. Most of these ideas can easily be connected with more than one competency or domain.

Self-Awareness: Love • Peacefulness

Self-Management: Anger and Impulse Management • Peacefulness • Sadness • Trust and Trustworthiness

Social Awareness: Accepting Others • Caring and Kindness • Empathy • Helpfulness • Respect

Relationship Skills: Conflict Management and Resolution • Friendship

Responsible Decision-Making: Positive and Ethical Choices

Students will

- learn about elephants and their friendship and love for each other, as well as their relationship to humans, and compare this to relationships among people

- think about the unusual friendship between Tarra the elephant and Bella the dog, and make analogies to friendships among people who might be different from each other

- consider the aggression shown by some elephants and make a comparison to people who show angry or hostile behavior

- compare the behavior of orphaned elephants to the way people without positive role models might act

Overview

Elephants are sometimes said to never forget. And in fact, they do have long memories. They have recognized each other even after years of separation. Many scientists place them among the most intelligent animals on the planet. In addition, they form firm and sometimes unexpected friendships. They've also been observed helping other animals. Kids will draw natural connections between elephant friendships and behaviors of caring, love, trust, and open-mindedness among people.

The story in this lesson is an emotional and sometimes sad one. Most children are naturally attached to their mothers, and this story tells of a sort of adoptive relationship between two elephants who are later separated. It is therefore likely to spark empathy in your listeners. (It also refers to abuse and mistreatment of the elephant, but it is not graphic.) Feeling empathy for the elephants in the story can help children develop and grow emotionally, expanding into empathy not only for the elephants but for any animals or people who have been mistreated, lonely, or hurt in other ways.

Story

Amazing Elephants

AMAZING ELEPHANTS

"Elephants never forget."

Have you heard this saying? Really, elephants probably forget lots of things. But they *do* seem to have long memories.

Jenny and Shirley were two elephants that had worked together at a circus. Jenny was brought there as a baby. Shirley was older and took care of her almost like a mother. They held trunks like people hold hands. They followed each other and loved to be together. But one sad day, they were separated.

Jenny's life was not happy after that. She ran away from circus performances many times. Maybe she missed Shirley. The circus people chained her for hours every day. Later she was sent to Illinois to have babies. There she was attacked by a large bull (a male elephant) who seriously injured her leg and left her with a limp. She ended up in another circus, and when the owners no longer wanted to use her in their shows, they dumped Jenny at a shelter for cats and dogs. Fortunately, a kind person found her outside the shelter and helped her. He called the Elephant Sanctuary in Tennessee, and they agreed to let her come to live there. Jenny was weak and sick when she arrived at the sanctuary.

Shirley's life had not been happy either. At one circus, a rogue elephant had broken her leg as well. After that she was sold to a zoo in Louisiana. She was the only elephant there. She would not see another elephant for more than 20 years. She spent those years in chains. It was a very lonely and sad life. At last, Shirley was also sent to the Elephant Sanctuary in Tennessee. Her years there would become the happiest time she had known.

More than 20 years had passed since Shirley had been separated from Jenny. When Jenny saw the old friend who had been like a mother to her, she called out with loud trumpets. The two elephants wrapped their trunks lovingly around each other through the iron fence and even bent the bars trying to be near each other. A kind person at the sanctuary opened the gate between them. Jenny rushed right into Shirley's space. With deep, roaring, emotional calls, they rubbed against each other. They bumped their trunks together. They were inseparable once again. Jenny and Shirley were finally happy together and roamed freely through the peaceful sanctuary forest.

Sadly, Jenny never completely recovered from the unkind treatment she had received when she was younger. Many years later, when Jenny was sick and dying, Shirley went into the woods. She didn't eat for two days. But another elephant friend named Bunny came and took care of Shirley, cheering her up. Shirley came out of the woods with Bunny. Shirley would probably always remember Jenny fondly, like a daughter. But she grew happy again with her other elephant friends.

ELEPHANT FACTS

- Elephants live in hot parts of the world. An elephant's big ears radiate heat from the body to help keep the animal cool.

- When bathing, elephants use their trunks to suck up water and spray it on their bodies. (An elephant trunk contains about 100,000 muscles!) Then they spray dirt and mud on their wet bodies. This mud dries and acts as sunscreen.

- Elephants are the world's largest land animals.

- Many elephants seem to form close friendships. Sometimes these friendships are unusual. Tarra is another elephant at the Tennessee home. Her best buddy was a dog named Bella. Tarra and Bella explored the woods. They played in fields and splashed in ponds. They ran through the snow in the winter and enjoyed the warm sun in the summer. Tarra's big gray body was over 8 feet tall. She weighed almost 9,000 pounds. Bella was a small yellow dog with big brown eyes. Bella and Tarra didn't seem to care that they were so different. They just liked being together.

- Elephants have reached out and helped other animals. For example, a group of elephants in South Africa came to the rescue of antelopes. People had captured the antelopes and locked them up. The elephants could see the unhappy antelopes running in circles. Eleven elephants quietly surrounded the fence. Then the elephants' leader walked up to the gate. She unlocked the metal latches with end of her trunk and swung the gate open. The antelopes quickly ran off into the night.

TALK IT OVER

Use these questions to guide your students in considering comparisons and connection between elephants and humans, including traits like respect, friendship, love, and other feelings and behaviors.

Elephants appear to have good memories. Some have even recognized each other after twenty years apart. How can you compare this to human behavior?

- Strong friendships can last for a lifetime. Sometimes close friends still feel connected even after not seeing each other for a long time.

- Both good memories and bad memories can stay with people for a long time. It's natural for people who survive dangerous or scary events such as hurricanes or wars to continue to feel sad and afraid long after these experiences. It is important to accept emotions like sorrow, fear, anger, and loneliness for what they are. Everyone feels these emotions at different times. And it takes time to work them out. It is good to talk about them and what they mean with a trusted adult. But there's good news too—happy memories can also last a long time. Sometimes if you're feeling sad, it helps to think about a cheerful memory. Jenny and Shirley were very unhappy for a long time. But they survived it and became happy together later.

Shirley and Jenny showed love for each other without using words. They showed affection through body language, such as wrapping their trunks around each other, and in other nonverbal ways like roaring and trumpeting happily. How can you connect this to human behavior?

- Friends have many ways of showing their caring for each other. They might hug or hold hands. They could do nice things for each other without expecting anything in return. They smile and laugh together.

- When people deeply care, they understand and share the feelings of another person. They have empathy. They will usually want to help each other. And when people learn to have empathy for one person, they can extend this feeling to other people who need help.

Tarra the elephant and Bella the dog were very different in appearance, but they were good friends. Can you think of ways this is similar to friendships between people?

- Even people who seem very different on the surface can become close friends.

- When you get to know someone better, you may learn that you are more alike than you are different.

- True friends don't care what you look like. They care about you because of what you are like on the inside.

Elephants seem to have rituals related to death and mourning. They sometimes cover a loved elephant that died with leaves and continue to visit the place for years. How is this similar to people?

- People have rituals to mourn people who die. These rituals vary from culture to culture. But all of these different traditions are important and valuable.

- It's important to take the time to mourn a loss in some way. It helps us start to heal and feel better.

At a time when there were too many elephants at Kruger National Park in South Africa, park officials decided to relocate some of the young males to another South African game reserve, at Pilanesberg National Park. But these young elephant males formed a gang that attacked and killed other animals in the preserve. Rangers brought in some large adult male bull elephants to the preserve. Until that point, the young elephants had been left without older elephants to teach them. Within weeks of the bulls arriving, the violent behavior of the young elephants stopped completely. The older bulls had taught them how an elephant should behave. Can you compare this to human behavior?

- Kids whose parents or other role models don't model positive traits might show negative behaviors.

- We all need people to look up to, no matter how old we are. We all need someone to help us learn how to behave. And almost everyone can learn

to manage their emotions. Stop and think before you act. Recognize your emotions. Take deep breaths and think about what you could do to make a situation better.

- Kids who gain good role models can change their behavior and can learn positive character traits.

ACTIVITIES

Activity 1: The Kindness Project

Materials
Slips of paper
Box or other container

Directions
Invite each kid to make a secret plan to do something nice for someone they know. This is a great activity to develop social awareness and relationship skills. It encourages children to notice the reactions of others and can motivate making friendships. If you choose to keep this activity inside the classroom, write each student's name on a slip of paper and put these slips in a box or other container. Then have kids draw one name each from the box, ensuring that all kids are included.

Alternatively, you could have kids choose to show kindness to people outside of your classroom. If you take this route, ask kids to try to choose people who are not already their close friends. For example, a student might select a different teacher, a new kid in a club, or a neighbor.

Suggest that kids do three nice things over the course of a week for the person they've chosen. For example, someone might make a special effort to include their person in games; write a nice anonymous note to them; or ask about their day. Encourage kids to pay attention to how people respond to their kind actions.

After the week is over, talk with kids about how the kindness project went. How did they feel when they did these nice things? Did they want to tell the people about what they were doing, or did they enjoy keeping it a secret? How did the people respond? Did they seem friendlier, happier, or more peaceful? Did kids notice the people acting kinder to other people in turn?

Activity 2: Act and React

Materials
8-inch balloon
Optional: Roller skates or in-line skates
Optional: Ball

Directions
Demonstrate Newton's Third Law of Motion: For every action, there is an equal and opposite reaction. Use this principle to demonstrate how acts of kindness or unkindness have an effect on the people around them.

Inflate the balloon but don't tie off the end. Then let go of the balloon and watch it shoot around the room. Explain that the *action* was forcing air into the balloon. The *reaction* was the air quickly leaving the balloon. (Blowing up the balloon represents the *action* of kindness. The balloon shooting around the room represents the *reaction* of passing kindness to other people.)

Variation: If you have a student who is comfortable and competent on roller skates or in-line skates, ask them to put them on and stand at the front of the room holding the ball. Ask the student to toss the ball to you. What happens? As the student throws the ball forward, they will roll backward. (In this case, throwing the ball represents the *action* of doing a kindness. The *reaction* of the person rolling backward represents the way an act of kindness can have a larger effect than we might expect.)

Talk with kids about how these actions and reactions are similar to the way unkind or violent actions can sometimes cause unkind or violent reactions. Compare it also to acts of kindness encouraging acts of kindness in return. Discuss ways that we can be careful that our actions result in positive reactions rather than negative ones.

Activity 3: Sadness to Sunshine

Materials
Various

Directions
When children struggle with sadness or other difficult feelings, it helps to know some coping activities. Read through the activities that follow, choose a few to do with your group (or one-on-one if that is needed or appropriate). Remind children that they can use these same strategies anytime they face a challenging feeling.

- Discuss how emotions can be more understandable and easier to manage when we know how to describe them. Practice labeling emotions and allow children to talk about how they feel. Do not judge or minimize their feelings. Do not tell them it's not a big deal.

- Talk about how everyone feels sad sometimes. Sadness is part of life, and it will pass. But it's okay to feel sad and to not rush ourselves through that feeling.

- Discuss the importance of empathy, and also acknowledge that it can be difficult. Feeling sad for another person or animal can be uncomfortable, but it shows caring and understanding. It can help to remind ourselves of this when empathy feels painful.

- Blow bubbles. Take a deep breath and slowly release the breath into the bubble for a restful slowing-down of emotions. Repeat several times.

- Read a story from this book or elsewhere and talk about the emotions from the story—both the emotions felt by characters, and the emotions the story sparked in the listeners.

- Crying sometimes helps. It can diminish tension and ease strong emotions.

- Move your body! Walk. Wiggle. Play ball. Have a race.

- Meditate, pray, or practice mindful breathing.

- Care for a pet or other animal, whether in the classroom or at home.

- Care for plants in a school garden, in windowsill pots, or elsewhere.

- Volunteer to help someone or something.

- Play, sing, or listen to peaceful music.

- Wind up a ball of yarn or make a ball out of elastic bands.

- Go to a quiet, peaceful spot to draw or read.

Activity 4: Anger Management Skills

Materials
None

Directions
Sometimes people are treated unkindly, just as Shirley and Jenny were. Talk with kids about how they feel when others are mean to them. How do they handle their anger? Helping kids learn to cope with and manage angry feelings that arise for any reason is a big part of social and emotional development. You may have your own list of strategies to teach and practice with your students, but some suggestions follow below. And remember, if a situation escalates and you believe that you or anyone else is in danger, always seek help.

Discuss feelings versus behavior, considering the differences and the connections between the two.

- It is okay to be angry. We all feel anger sometimes.
- When we can manage strong emotions, we're less likely to act on them in ways that might be damaging or counterproductive.
- Attacking or hitting someone is never acceptable behavior, even when we're in the grip of difficult feelings.

Talk about and practice skills for handling anger.

- Walk away when you feel angry and want to hit.
- Make a time-out place where you can go to calm down.
- Calm yourself by focusing on each of your five senses, one at a time. What do you see, hear, smell, taste, and feel?

- Practice deep breathing. You could try what's called four-square breathing: Breathe in slowly and deeply through your nose while counting to four. Then hold that breath for another count of four. Exhale through your mouth, counting to four. Hold your breath once more for a count of four. You can repeat this as many times as you like.

As a group, agree on a set of rules about angry behaviors that are not okay.

- Name-calling or saying mean things
- Hitting or attacking someone else
- Throwing or damaging things
- Refusing to cooperate

Talk about what to do when the rules are broken. As a group, agree to specific consequences.

- You might choose loss of certain privileges that are valued in the classroom.
- Be consistent when applying the consequences. If the consequences seem to become unfair, discuss the problem with children and make any necessary changes.
- Offer *positive* consequences for managing behavior and controlling angry outbursts. Positive rewards could include stickers, free time, skipping a chore, or having extra time to do an assignment.
- When needing to correct a behavior, try to balance one correction with five supportive or positive comments.

LESSON 13
FIREFLIES

Key Words
The behaviors, traits, and emotions below are just starting points for aligning SEL, character education, and this lesson's story. Most of these ideas can easily be connected with more than one competency or domain.

Self-Awareness: Happiness and Joy • Inner Strength • Self-Confidence

Self-Management: Honesty • Integrity

Social Awareness: Service to Others • Understanding Others

Relationship Skills: Service to Others

Responsible Decision-Making: Analyzing and Evaluating • Healthy Habits • Positive and Ethical Choices • Understanding Consequences

Students will

- learn interesting facts about fireflies, such as the purposes of their flashing lights
- compare the male fireflies that are tricked and eaten to people who are tricked with poor choices and find that they can't control the consequences
- contrast the behavior of some fireflies that trick their predators and their prey with people of integrity who do *not* trick others but are true to what they say
- make analogies between fireflies' energy-efficient light and people who save their energy in various ways
- learn that fireflies share their light, just as people may happily share their "light" through talents, caring, and skills

Overview
Children familiar with fireflies may remember the happiness they have while felt watching or chasing these tiny lights. The experience can create wonder and curiosity. If your students live in an area where fireflies are common, you will have special fun with this story. Many of them will have chased fireflies and captured them in bottles. They may have wondered how fireflies make their light, or why. They will be intrigued by the answers.

You can compare the firefly's special talent of creating light—and its various ways of using that light—to human behaviors that involve the light of integrity and honesty. This lesson can also help students consider the value of thinking carefully and using good judgment when making decisions. They can learn that they are free to make choices, but that they can't always know or control the consequences of those choices.

Story
Flickering Fireflies

FLICKERING FIREFLIES

It's a warm summer night. It's almost time to go inside. But you're having so much fun happily chasing those tiny lights that mysteriously appear and then dart out of reach. Just five more minutes . . .

Wait. What's that?

Another light flashes. You see a glowing, greenish-yellow dot. It darts across the grass—and disappears. You spin around searching for it. Then you spot the light again, and again. Suddenly, dozens of lights are dancing in the dark. What are they?

These flickering lights are fireflies. Sometimes they are called lightning bugs. Have you ever caught one in a jar and watched it flash?

People have loved the firefly's beautiful glow for hundreds of years. These bugs like to live where it's warm. They especially like damp, humid places. They flutter around ponds, marshes, and trees. They flicker and flash in long grass.

Fireflies use their light to attract mates. A flashing male will fly toward a female firefly. If she's interested, she returns the flash. They flash back and forth to communicate. There are about 2,000 different kinds of fireflies. Each type has its own flash pattern. This special pattern is like a secret language. It helps fireflies find the right mates.

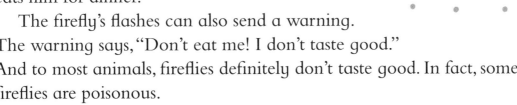

But some female fireflies play a trick. They copy the flashes of other lightning bugs. This can fool a male firefly. He thinks he sees a friend. But when the confused male firefly lands near the female, she pounces on him and eats him for dinner.

The firefly's flashes can also send a warning. The warning says, "Don't eat me! I don't taste good." And to most animals, fireflies definitely don't taste good. In fact, some fireflies are poisonous.

How do fireflies make their special light? Chemicals inside the firefly's body create its glow. A firefly's light can be yellow, green, or pale red. Even baby fireflies make light. These young fireflies are called glowworms.

Fireflies may look a bit like tiny lamps, but they have a special skill. When you turn on a lamp, the bulb gets warm. Most lightbulbs lose 90 percent of their energy on heat. That's a big waste of energy. If a firefly heated up like a lightbulb, it would burn itself up. Poof! But the firefly wastes almost no energy on heat. Almost all of its energy turns into light.

Imagine how much energy we could save if we used firefly light in our homes, schools, and shops. Saving energy is good for the earth and the environment. We can't *really* light the world with fireflies. But scientists are trying to learn how fireflies make cold light. Maybe someday someone will discover it. Maybe it will be you. The firefly's secret could light up the dark and save energy too.

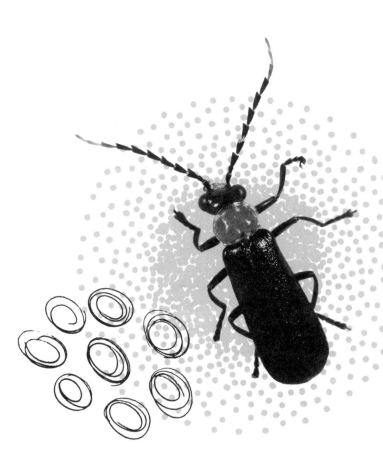

FIREFLY FACTS

- Fireflies produce their light using cells near their abdomens. This natural light is called bioluminescence.

- Some adult fireflies feed on pollen and nectar. Others do not eat at all during their short lives.

- Firefly larvae can live up to a year. Once a larva becomes a firefly, it lives only about two months.

- Scientists have used the firefly enzyme luciferase and its glowing properties to find blood clots and certain kinds of cells.

TALK IT OVER

Use these questions to guide your students in considering analogies between the flashing lights of fireflies and the social behavior of people. That flashing light could be compared to friendliness and cheerfulness or to integrity and good judgment in people. What else could you compare it with?

Fireflies use their light to attract mates and as a warning signal to predators. Some fireflies also use their light to trick prey into coming close. Fireflies are not being dishonest when they do this. However, we can think about how these behaviors might be similar to intentional dishonesty or deception. Can you make a comparison with people who use lies or deception to gain something?

- People sometimes make false promises because they want to gain popularity, power, or admiration.

- Sometimes people cheat on tests or homework because they want good grades but don't want to do the work.

- People may lie about themselves and their lives because they want to impress others.

- On the flip side, people can also be shining lights of integrity, honesty, good judgment, and positive choices.

Sometimes fireflies get tricked into making choices that land them near other fireflies that will eat them. It's not always easy to tell when a choice will have serious results. What can people do to protect themselves from making dangerous mistakes or poor choices?

- When you feel scared or worried, talk to someone you trust. Usually making the right choice feels good emotionally, even if it's a difficult decision.

- Make a list of good and bad things that might happen as the result of a choice. Ask yourself if your choice will harm or help you or others. Use this information to make the best choice.

- Avoid making choices that cause you to lie, or that conflict with your beliefs. Always try to stay true to your inner self and your positive values.

- Remember that everyone makes poor decisions sometimes. That doesn't make them bad people. You can always learn from a bad choice and have the confidence to make a better decision the next time.

Lightbulbs lose a lot of energy in the form of heat when they are on. But fireflies have the amazing ability to make light without losing much energy. What are some ways that people can save their emotional energy and use it wisely?

- When you have a problem, you can save energy if you talk about it calmly instead of getting upset. Stop and think about what triggered you to become upset.

- If you get good sleep at night, you will be able to work and play better during the day. It also helps you be healthier.

- If you tell the truth, you won't have to waste energy making up lies and trying to remember them.

- If you get your homework, chores, or other duties done on time, you won't waste energy being frustrated when you fall behind.

👁 Do your most important jobs first. It's easy and tempting to get sidetracked playing games, watching TV, or hanging out with friends. But then you might run out of time or get too tired to do the jobs you need to do. Instead, write down a list of goals that you need to do. Write down the most important jobs, and do them first. It can help you feel self-confident when you make a plan and carry it out. It is often empowering, helping you feel more in charge of your life.

ACTIVITIES

Activity 1: Firefly Poems

Materials
Firefly Poem handouts (in digital content)

Directions
Hand out copies of the Firefly Poem handouts. Depending on your group's ages, interests, and abilities, you may choose not to use all of them. Distribute roughly equal numbers of each handout that you choose. Invite kids to fill in the forms with acrostic poems about fireflies, and ask them to focus on emotions and behaviors of people. If kids aren't familiar with acrostic poems, model one on the board to show them how they work. For example:

> Caring
>
> Happy
>
> Open
>
> Integrity
>
> Character
>
> Example

If desired, younger kids can work in small groups, or the class can compose poems together as a big group.

When students have written their poems, invite kids to share them if they feel comfortable doing so. Talk about the poems as a group. Did they cause anyone to think about fireflies and character in new ways? What did kids find fun about writing the poems? What was challenging? How did people's ideas differ?

Activity 2: The Good Decisions Toolbox

Materials
None

Directions
Talk with kids about specific ways they can make positive choices or decisions. Brainstorm a list of ideas and write them on the board. For example:

👁 Take time to think about a decision carefully.

👁 Ask the advice of someone you respect.

👁 Learn all you can about your choice before making it.

👁 Think about whether you would feel comfortable sharing your choice with your mom or dad, best friend, older sister or brother, coach, or teacher.

👁 Brainstorm the possible results—positive and negative—of your choice. How will it affect you and others? If your choice is likely to hurt other people, modify your plan.

👁 Listen to the voice inside you. If you have to talk yourself into it, and it doesn't feel right, it probably isn't.

👁 Get a good night's sleep before making your choice.

Discuss each idea and how it might be helpful. Also consider the ways it might be hard to follow these suggestions at times. Be clear that children are probably not going to work through all these ideas each time they need to make a choice. But they *can* learn to be more aware of how their choices affect themselves and others and they can develop the skill of managing their emotions when making decisions.

When you have a list that the group is happy with, make copies and hand them out or ask kids to copy the list into their notebooks. Tell them that this list is like a toolbox. When they have big decisions to make, they can use these tools to help them succeed. Remind kids that making one positive choice makes it easier to make another. Over time, they can make a habit of good judgment and decision-making.

Activity 3: Decision-Making Role Plays

Materials

Slips of paper with scenarios written on them
Box, hat, or other container

Preparation

Role playing is a great activity for developing social and emotional skills in children, and this activity can involve all the social and emotional domains. On small slips of paper, write short situations that present dilemmas requiring a decision. These will serve as the starting points for role-playing. Fold the slips in half and put them in a box or other container.

Example situations:

👁 You are at the checkout counter at a store, and the salesperson gives you back too much change. What should you do and say?

👁 You have a friend who is telling lies about you, and you are afraid people will believe those lies. What should you do?

👁 You see a student taking money from another kid's desk at school. You don't want to be a tattler, but you also want to be honest. What will you do?

👁 You choose to go to a party. At the party, the kids start watching a violent movie. You want these kids to be your friends, but you know it's not a good choice for you to watch the movie. What could you do?

👁 Your mom tells you to be home at a certain time. But you're having so much fun with your friend that you get home late. Luckily, your mom isn't home yet either. She won't know that you were late. What should you do?

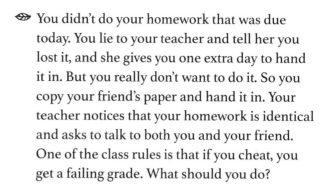

👁 You didn't do your homework that was due today. You lie to your teacher and tell her you lost it, and she gives you one extra day to hand it in. But you really don't want to do it. So you copy your friend's paper and hand it in. Your teacher notices that your homework is identical and asks to talk to both you and your friend. One of the class rules is that if you cheat, you get a failing grade. What should you do?

👁 You find out that your big brother is taking drugs. You're worried about him. But he says you'll be in big trouble if you tell anyone. What should you do?

Directions

Put kids in pairs or small groups and have each group draw a slip from the container. As groups role-play the situations they've drawn, circulate around the room to observe and guide as needed. Afterward, bring everyone back together in a large group and discuss the situations they role-played. Was it difficult to decide what to do? How did children choose?

Variation: Spontaneous Speeches

Have students give spontaneous speeches about honesty and integrity. Allow two or three students to each draw one slip of paper from the box. Ask them to read the character situations on their slips to themselves first. Then give them about five minutes to think of something to say about the situations they've drawn. Explain that spontaneous speeches don't need to be long (especially if you're working with younger kids), but that they should be more than a sentence or two. If desired, you can model an example of a short speech yourself.

You can do this activity periodically, doing only one or two speeches at a time. It will help kids develop their speaking ability as well as encourage them to think about choices, honesty, emotions, and needs of themselves and others.

LESSON 14
HORSES

Key Words

The behaviors, traits, and emotions below are just starting points for aligning SEL, character education, and this lesson's story. Most of these ideas can easily be connected with more than one competency or domain.

Self-Awareness: Frustration • Inner Strength • Love

Self-Management: Adaptability • Coping Skills and Stress Management • Courage and Boldness • Hard Work • Patience • Perseverance • Responsibility

Social Awareness: Empathy • Helpfulness • Service to Others

Relationship Skills: Cooperation, Collaboration, and Teamwork • Helpfulness • Loyalty • Resisting Social Pressure • Service to Others

Responsible Decision-Making: Positive and Ethical Choices • Problem-Solving

Students will

- 👁 learn interesting facts about horses, including their important role in human history
- 👁 consider the ways horses show dedication, responsibility, helpfulness, hard work, loyalty, love, and cooperation, and make connections between those characteristics and human behavior
- 👁 compare horses' deep connections to humans—including their ability to care for, protect, and sense the needs of their owners—to the empathy that people feel when they care for others
- 👁 learn that most horses manage to adapt to and handle difficult situations and see ways that people can adapt to doing hard tasks and handle the frustration that may accompany these changes

Overview

Stories about horses can deepen understanding of social and emotional skills in children, particularly as the lives of horses and people have been intertwined for many centuries. It might even be said that human history has been built on the backs of horses. Horses have served people in many ways, from building roads to harvesting crops to saving the lives of their riders. They have also carried people on their strong backs, helping spread cultures and share new ideas. Most horses usually can adapt to whatever their owners require of them. Horses have also held starring roles in many movies and books. And these faithful animals have shown great perseverance, dedication, loyalty, love, and an uncanny ability to understand their owners' needs. All of these traits will provide a good starting point for having a conversation with your students about similar traits and behaviors in people.

Story

Heroic Horses

HEROIC HORSES

Maybe you've heard that dogs are people's best friends. Dogs *are* great friends. But sometimes people say that history has been written on the backs of horses. Thousands of years ago, people learned that horses are good workers. They are strong and loyal. They work together well in teams. Horses have pulled carts, carried food, and worked on farms. They have helped build roads. They have even pulled trains.

People also learned to ride horses. On horseback, people could travel faster and farther. This helped spread and share ideas between different countries and cultures.

Soldiers found that horses were helpful in battle too. One famous American warhorse was named Comanche. In one battle, Comanche was wounded in the hindquarters by an arrow but still carried his master through the fight. He would be wounded many more times but never quit or left his rider. He carried a US army captain in the Battle of the Little Bighorn in 1876. This battle was between the US Army and a group of Native Americans. The battle was terrible, with gunpowder and dust clouding the air. The army was outnumbered and lost badly. Comanche's rider was shot right off his back. Comanche himself was shot seven times in all. Many people died, as did many horses.

After the battle ended and the dust settled down, soldiers searched the battlefield to help anyone who was still alive. To their surprise they found Comanche badly wounded, but alive. He had been lying on the battlefield for two days. Because Comanche had been so loyal and brave, he was given special honor and medical care. Kind people took good care of him. The rest of his life was calm and peaceful. When he died, he was one of the only horses ever honored with a military funeral.

Most horses are not famous. But that doesn't matter to their human friends. What really matters is the love and respect that people feel for their horses.

Sometimes horses seem to sense when people need them. Think about this story: A man and woman owned a refuge for abandoned horses. One day a car drove up to the farm. A woman leaned out the window and spoke to the man who owned the refuge. "Do you allow children to help you with your horses?" she asked. The man nodded.

The mother in the car went on, "Our daughter Sophie is 13 years old, and she has stopped talking. She hasn't spoken a word for two years. She likes reading books about horses, and we heard about you."

The man kindly told the woman that she could bring her daughter to help at the barn. When Sophie stepped out of the car, she looked sad and hung her head.

The man and woman who owned the farm had just rescued a horse named Darcy from an owner who didn't take care of her. The horse also looked sad. She was boney and neglected. Her hind legs were swollen. But something strange happened when Sophie went to the barn to meet Darcy. Darcy came right over to Sophie, making a soft whickering sound. She nuzzled Sophie's hand. Darcy hadn't done this with anyone else. The man and woman were surprised. They thought that Darcy somehow sensed something sad in Sophie—that she needed help too. Not all horses are patient, but Darcy seemed to care for Sophie, and was patient with her. Sophie was patient with Darcy as well and took care of the horse in return.

Sophie and Darcy slowly began to heal together. One day near the end of the summer, the barn owner heard a surprising sound. She listened closely. Sophie was talking. She had been helped by the love of an abandoned horse.

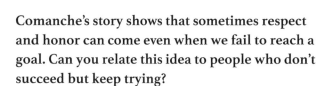

HORSE FACTS

- Historians think that nomads living on the Asian steppe first domesticated horses about four thousand years ago.

- Horses can sleep standing up or lying down. But in a group of horses, at least one will stay awake to watch out for the others.

- A newborn horse, called a foal, can stand up within about one hour of being born.

TALK IT OVER

Use these questions to guide your students in considering analogies between horses and empathy, responsibility, service, and other traits and behaviors in people.

Horses can help people who face mental and physical health challenges of many kinds. Scientists think that just being near horses changes how the human brain works. Horses can help us feel calmer. Some people learn to communicate better after spending time with these special animals. How can you compare this to the way some people provide care and comfort to others?

- Sometimes a person who has been hurt or sad can understand another person who has been hurt. This is called empathy—sensing and understanding how another person feels. This skill is very valuable and can be a great comfort to people who are hurting.

- When we take care of people or animals (including horses), it can help us develop social and emotional skills better, including love and empathy.

- People who seem to sense and understand our feelings can often provide comfort just by being near us or listening to us.

Comanche's story shows that sometimes respect and honor can come even when we fail to reach a goal. Can you relate this idea to people who don't succeed but keep trying?

- Sometimes not succeeding at something the first time makes us try harder the next time.

- You can learn a lot about patience, hard work, dedication, and courage if you persevere even when you face big challenges.

- The only real failure is giving up or quitting. Continuing to try, even when it's hard, is something to be proud of.

Many dedicated horses have protected their riders and stayed faithful to them even in dangerous situations. Can you think of people who help and protect each other and ways that this is helpful and positive?

- When we are dedicated to people, groups, or ideas, we are likely to work hard for them, and we often learn to care about them. This builds our connections to others and to our community.

- Many people in our lives help others, such as firefighters, nurses, teachers, doctors, and veterinarians. We all benefit from the work these people do.

- Sometimes we feel dedicated to friends who have negative behaviors. They may put social pressure on us. This can be confusing. When those friends or those behaviors start to make us feel uncomfortable, it's a good idea to talk to someone we trust about what to do. Friendship is important, but inner strength can help us to make positive decisions and avoid negative choices despite pressure from other friends.

Horses have a calming effect on some people. Can you see a relationship between this and human behavior?

- People who are patient and caring can help other people feel calm. When people are calm, they learn how to cope with their problems better. They can think more clearly and make better decisions.

- Gentle people often make others feel comfortable and safe.
- Sometimes just listening when someone is upset or sad can be a big help and can aid that person in calming down and feeling better.

ACTIVITIES

Activity 1: Growing and Changing

Materials

Growing and Changing handout (in digital content)

Directions

The contributions and responsibilities of horses have changed over time. A person's activities and responsibilities also change during their life. Kids will enjoy thinking about what they used to do (and not do) as babies and toddlers and imagining what they might do in the future. As they consider these ideas, you can guide them to think about the bigger ideas of caring for others and having new and changing responsibilities.

Pass out copies of the Growing and Changing handout and have kids fill it out individually, or project the handout on a screen or board and complete it as a group. For example, in the "When I was a baby" section, kids might answer, "I drank milk" or "I slept a lot." As you move through the other sections of the handout, remind kids to think about what other people have done and will do for them at each period in their lives, and also what they can do for themselves and for others.

Encourage kids to think about how they can contribute more and care for others more as they get older. What are the benefits and drawbacks of each stage in their lives? Do they miss anything about being younger? What are they most excited about as they grow older? How can responsibility be rewarding? Is it ever scary or difficult? Discuss their answers as a group.

Activity 2: Cooperative Catch

Materials

Blankets or pieces of cloth about 3 or 4 feet across (1 per team)

Foam balls (1 per team)

Directions

Note: This activity works best on a playground or in a large multipurpose room.

Divide kids into groups of four. Have each member of each team hold one corner of the team's blanket, holding it flat and parallel to the floor. Place a ball in the center of each team's blanket. Tell kids that they need to use only the blanket to toss the ball up into the air and catch it. The team that successfully catches the ball the most times in five minutes wins.

After playing, discuss the importance of cooperation and working together as a team. What happened if kids worked against each other? Horses that work in teams are more successful than ones that fight against their harnesses. People who work cooperatively in teams will also be more successful in what they do. Plus, the work will probably be more fun.

Activity 3: "I Think I Can"

Materials

Story of perseverance (such as *The Little Engine That Could, The Tortoise and the Hare,* or the story of Comanche in *Heroic Horses*)

Directions

Read the story about perseverance aloud to the class. Discuss what kept the main character trying. How would the story have been different if the character had given up? Talk about the idea of perseverance, and make sure that kids understand what it means. You might also remind kids of how much horses have accomplished throughout history through their perseverance. Ask kids to think about perseverance in their own lives. When have they been in situations that required them to keep trying even when it was very difficult? How did they handle these challenges?

Next, ask each student to make two lists. The first list is of things that are hard for them to do. The second list is of things the student finds pretty easy to do. Discuss why some things are harder than others. Talk with kids about how everyone has different talents, and how this makes the world a fun and interesting place. Also discuss how, if you practice a skill long enough and if you have patience, you will improve at it. Invite kids to share examples of skills or talents that they have already practiced and gotten better at, as well as ones they still want to work on. Ask why these things interest them. Explore the rewards of perseverance. How does it feel to reach a goal after working hard? What can we do to keep motivating ourselves even when things get tough?

Activity 4: Star Breathing to Calm Down and Cope

Materials
Star Breathing handout (in digital content)

Directions
Children sometimes need to take a breath to calm down from frustrations, anger, fear, and other emotions. Star breathing is a strategy they can learn and practice so that they can use it when the need arises.

Distribute individual copies of the Star Breathing handout. Teach kids the skill as a group first. Have the children keep their own copies of the star in a place near them, where they can grab the handout quickly and refer to it. Once children have a handle on the skill, you can invite a child to work with the star individually when facing a difficult emotion or other challenge.

To use the technique, touch a finger to any "breathe in" line on the star, and take a slow, deep breath in through your nose while slowly moving your finger along the line to a "hold" point. At the point, hold your breath for a moment. Then move your finger along a "breathe out" line while slowly letting out your breath through your mouth. Keep going—following the lines and points with a finger or just with your eyes—and continue around the whole star. Sometimes it may take several trips around the star to calm down. This can be a great calming and coping activity that has a hands-on element, one that many kids enjoy. Adults like it too. Try it!

LESSON 15
METALMARK MOTHS

Key Words
The behaviors, traits, and emotions below are just starting points for aligning SEL, character education, and this lesson's story. Most of these ideas can easily be connected with more than one competency or domain.

Self-Awareness: Inner Strength

Self-Management: Assertiveness • Courage and Boldness • Honesty • Integrity

Social Awareness: Fairness and Equality • Reading Social Cues

Relationship Skills: Bullying Prevention • Cooperation, Collaboration, and Teamwork • Resisting Social Pressure

Responsible Decision-Making: Analyzing and Evaluating • Positive and Ethical Choices • Understanding Consequences

Students will
- 👁 learn about the metalmark moth's ability to mimic the jumping spider, its main predator
- 👁 make connections between the metalmark moth's mimicking ability and the way people sometimes copy others
- 👁 compare the metalmark moth's bold faceoff with the jumping spider to the courage shown by a person who stands up to someone who bullies others
- 👁 talk about what it means to stand up for what you believe, and what the positive and negative results can be

Overview
Metalmark moths mimic the appearance and behavior of the jumping spiders that prey on them. For a moment, this mimicry confuses the spider. Usually, this gives the moth time to escape. The moth's behavior provides an opportunity for you and your students to make comparisons to inner strength, assertiveness, integrity, and standing up for others. Additionally, like the moths, everyone needs to make decisions—sometimes quickly, and sometimes over a long time. Decisions can be challenging. But if we don't make them, someone else likely will make them for us.

The metalmark moth story also provides a jumping-off point for discussing the ways that mimicking poor behavior can lead to poor choices. On the other hand, modeling behavior after the positive traits of others can sometimes result in developing the self-confidence and the emotional muscles necessary to resist unwanted social pressure. And self-awareness—understanding and accepting both our strengths and weaknesses—can bring confidence and inner peace.

Story
Mighty Metalmark Moths

MIGHTY METALMARK MOTHS

The jumping spider likes making a meal out of moths. It's pretty easy to understand why most moths panic when they see these spiders. The scared moths try to fly away. But the jumping spider is quick. Most of the time, the moths end up as the spider's lunch.

The metalmark moth is different. Instead of taking off, it usually stays put. It is small but gutsy. The metalmark moth makes a fast decision and stands its ground. It flares out its back wings and holds its front wings above its body at an angle. Sometimes the metalmark moth even dances *toward* the spider.

Do you think the moth's actions sound like bravery? Or do they just sound dangerous? Maybe it's a bit of both. But the metalmark moth has a secret. It's one of nature's most skillful copycats.

The metalmark moth's colors are similar to the jumping spider's markings. When the moth holds up its wings, it imitates the shape of the jumping spider. And when the moth dances toward the spider in a jumping, jerking way, it is copying the way a jumping spider moves. It's a tricky moth in spider's clothing.

These tricks confuse most spiders. Jumping spiders have good eyesight. But it's not good enough to spot the moth's trick right away. For a few seconds, the spider isn't sure if it's looking at a friend, a foe, or food.

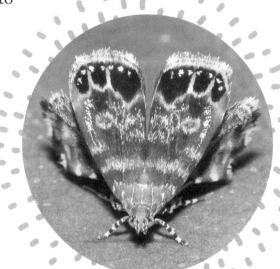

The spider isn't confused for long. It soon catches on to the moth's disguise. But usually, the spider hesitates long enough for the moth to flit away. The spider misses out on a tasty lunch. And the metalmark moth sheds its disguise—until it meets another jumping spider.

METALMARK MOTH FACTS

- Unlike many other moths, metalmark moths are active during the day.
- Metalmark moths get their name from the iridescent patches that many have on their wings, which are metallic in appearance.
- One study found that the jumping spider catches and eats only 6 percent of the metalmark moths it encounters, compared to more than 60 percent of all moths.

TALK IT OVER

Metalmark moths do not have identical behavior or emotions to humans. But we can compare their behavior to people's actions. Use these questions to guide students in considering analogies between metalmark moths and positive behaviors in people, such as courage, fairness, and decision-making.

Compare the metalmark moth's ability to copy a jumping spider to people who copy others.

- If you copy negative behaviors such as lying, cheating, or being rude, you might not feel good about yourself. These traits might become habits. You might get in trouble.

- If you copy positive character traits such as honesty, integrity, respect, and courage, you can learn to have greater inner strength. This can help you manage your behavior, feel good about yourself, and build strong relationships.

What might happen if you copy another person even when it goes against the voice inside you?

- Showing integrity means acting according to your positive beliefs. Your actions, words, and behavior match your beliefs. If you are *not* true to your own best values and to yourself, you might make poor decisions. You could also start to get confused about who you really are.

- Mimicking good behavior can help you strengthen positive character traits. But it's still important to stay true to yourself and to be genuine. You don't have to change the person you are to improve your character habits.

- Copying good behavior is not the same as copying another person's homework, test, or ideas. It's never the right decision to take credit for someone else's work. It is not fair to that person or to other people who are doing the work.

The metalmark moth stands up to the jumping spider. Can you make a comparison to a person standing up to someone who is bullying others?

- The moth is small, but it makes itself look big to the spider. Sometimes people can do that by showing confidence and strength.

- It takes courage to stand up for someone else when you see a person being treated unfairly.

- Sometimes you need to get help from an adult. It's not always safe to confront someone who is bullying. Use your good judgment, and remember that getting help is still a positive step.

The spider misinterprets the metalmark moth's behavior. Similarly, people sometimes have trouble interpreting social cues such as facial expressions, gestures, or tone of voice. It can help to practice recognizing these cues. What do you think the experiences are of people who need some extra practice in social skills?

- Sometimes people stay away from, ignore, or even tease people who have trouble reading social cues and who behave in different ways. But when we interact respectfully and kindly with people who are different from us, we grow in empathy and understanding.

- People who have trouble understanding social cues might become isolated and lonely. We can reach out to these people and help them feel more comfortable. However, we must always respect the wishes of others. If someone prefers to be alone some of the time, that's okay. We all have different needs.

- All people have their own special gifts to share, whether they have strong social skills or not. If we ignore people who interact differently, we may miss out on what they have to share.

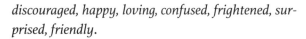

The metalmark moth doesn't immediately fly away when it faces danger. Can you compare this bold behavior to standing up for your own values and what you believe?

👁 It can take courage to stand up for what you believe, especially if others might make fun of you for doing so. But each time you do it, you get a little stronger inside. It may be easier next time.

👁 When you choose not to steal, lie, or cheat even when others are pressuring you to do so, you become a stronger person. It takes a lot of courage to stand up to peer pressure, especially if it is coming from people you think of as your friends.

👁 When you don't use hurtful language around people who do talk that way, you are standing up for what you believe.

Sometimes, the moth *does* get eaten by the spider. Can you make an analogy between the risk the moths take and dangerous situations that people might be in?

👁 It's important to protect yourself in dangerous situations. Being careful doesn't mean you're not brave. Making positive choices is likely to influence your future in positive ways.

👁 Sometimes people get away with risky behavior. But that doesn't mean they will always be safe if they continue that behavior. For example, someone might cheat on a test once without anyone knowing. But the next time, they might get caught and be in big trouble. Even worse, they've damaged their integrity.

ACTIVITIES

Activity 1: Feelings Charades

Materials
Slips of paper with feelings words written on them
Hat, box, or other container

Preparation
Before doing this activity, write feelings words on slips of paper, fold them in half, and put them in a container. Suggestions for feelings words include: discouraged, happy, loving, confused, frightened, surprised, friendly.

Directions
Play Feelings Charades. Have kids take turns drawing slips and acting out emotions without using any words. Give the group a set amount of time (for example, two or three minutes) to guess the feeling. Like the metalmark moth tricks the jumping spider, can you trick people as to how you really feel?

Allow as many students to act as you have time for, while leaving time for discussion. Then talk about how easy or difficult students found it to guess the feelings correctly. Are some people easier to read than others? Are some types of feelings harder to identify than others?

Extend the discussion to consider whether it's a good idea to hide our emotions. Should we always show people how we really feel? Why or why not? What if expressing our feelings fully would be harmful to another person? Explore ideas of honesty and integrity.

Activity 2: Creative Cartoons

Materials
Paper
Crayons, colored pencils, markers, or paints

Directions
Ask kids to write and illustrate cartoon drawings about metalmark moths standing up to jumping spiders. Then ask them to write down a comparison to a story about bullying, courage, or being true to oneself. Assure them that they don't need to create timeless works of art; the main thing is to creatively explore some of the lesson's ideas. If desired, allow them to exercise teamwork by pairing up and cooperating on these cartoons. Invite them to title their finished works with slogans related to the cartoon's theme. For example, "It isn't big to make others feel small." After kids are finished, invite volunteers to share their cartoons with the group.

Activity 3: Copycats

Materials
Copycats handout (in digital content)
Kid-safe scissors

Glue sticks, school glue, or tape
Colored pencils, crayons, or markers
Small strips of paper

Directions

This activity helps strengthen self-management skills. Pass out the Copycats handout and help kids make their envelopes. Ask them to write their names on their envelopes and give them some time to decorate them. Place all the envelopes on a shelf, table, or other space in your room.

Next, hand out several strips of paper to each student. Ask kids to think of positive traits that children in the group have or have developed, and to consider how other kids could copy or mimic these traits to improve their own habits. Ask each child to write the name of the person they're describing on one side of a slip of paper, and the positive trait or behavior on the other side. For example, the student is caring, courageous, or honest. Remind students that only positive words are allowed. Insist on an atmosphere of respect and kindness.

Collect all the papers and put them in the correct envelopes. (As you do this, make sure the traits are all positive. Discard any that aren't.) Do this every day for a week, changing the system each time so that students aren't describing the same classmates as they did the day before. If someone in your group especially needs a boost, you could write a note for that child. At the end of the week, give kids their envelopes to open. If kids feel comfortable doing so, allow them to read some of the traits out loud. Ask kids if there are some traits they wish were stronger in themselves. Talk about how to choose positive role models. Then give the whole group a round of applause for all their good traits!

Activity 4: Making Positive Decisions

Materials

Pencils (optional)
Paper (optional)

Directions

When facing a tough decision, it can help to have a plan for considering options and making a positive choice. The following steps can fit into such a plan. Discuss these with your group and talk about times when they might use them, ways they could be helpful, when it might be difficult to follow these steps, and so on. If desired, students could write their responses to each step.

1. Identify what decision needs to be made.

2. Identify the timeline for making the decision. Does a choice need to be made quickly? Or can it wait for a while?

3. Gather information about the decision.

   - What do you need to know to understand the decision?

   - Look at all sides and see all perspectives.

   - Talk to people you trust and get their input.

4. List all the possible choices you could make.

5. Evaluate the choices.

   - How would each choice affect other people or things? How would each choice affect you?

   - Which one would probably make the most positive difference?

   - Which choices are the most possible to follow through on?

   - Think about how you feel. What seems right to you?

   - Think about how your feelings about the decision match up with the facts you have.

6. Using both your feelings and the facts about your choices, number the choices in order of which you think is best, second best, and so on.

7. Act upon your first choice.

8. Later, evaluate what happened.

   - Was the outcome of the decision positive? Do you feel satisfied with how things turned out?

   - What have you learned from your decision?

   - If you faced this decision again, what would you do differently, and why?

Remember: Every time you make a choice—no matter how it turns out—you're gathering information and experience that will help you in the future.

LESSON 16
OLEANDERS

Key Words

The behaviors, traits, and emotions below are just starting points for aligning SEL, character education, and this lesson's story. Most of these ideas can easily be connected with more than one competency or domain.

Self-Awareness: Inner Strength

Self-Management: Healthy Habits • Honesty • Integrity

Social Awareness: Discernment • Fairness and Equality • Perspective-Taking • Respect

Relationship Skills: Helpfulness • Loyalty

Responsible Decision-Making: Analyzing and Evaluating • Discernment • Positive and Ethical Choices • Problem-Solving • Safety

Students will

- learn about the beautiful but poisonous oleander plant and discover reasons to respect this flower's place in nature
- compare and contrast the beauty and poison of oleander blossoms to human qualities of honesty and deception (which are self-management skills)
- talk about how mixing apples and carrots with oleander leaves can be compared to mixing the truth with a few lies, or positive behavior with a little bit of negative behavior

Overview

The blossoms of the oleander plant are beautiful—and they contain a deadly poison. This contrast will give you and your students a good starting point for discussions about appearance and how looks can be deceiving. Discernment is an important skill for children to develop. Sometimes we call it intuition or perception. This skill can help children understand what may happen in a situation and make positive choices. You can extend this idea in the other direction by considering that, although oleander's poison makes it unsafe to eat, the plant also has disease-fighting properties that make it an important part of nature.

In the story, kids will learn that oleander leaves taste bitter, but that mixing them with something sweet can disguise the poison's flavor. This fact is good fodder for making a comparison to a person who mixes truth with small lies that may go undetected. In addition, some animals seem to have developed a resistance to oleander poison. Your students can consider how this resistance is similar to the way people can get used to negative behavior over time and may get out of the habit of making positive choices. Similarly, they can see that practicing positive behaviors can become a habit as well.

Story

Pretty, Poisonous Oleanders

PRETTY, POISONOUS OLEANDERS

The oleander doesn't *look* dangerous. Its bushes show off flashy blossoms in white, pink, red, purple, yellow, or orange. Its flowers smell fresh and sweet like spring. Their scent is used in some perfumes. But the beautiful plant can deceive you. It has a deadly secret.

Workers at a horse farm in San Diego learned that secret. They woke up one morning to an awful sight: 23 of their horses were very sick. How could they all get sick at once? Could it be something they all ate? The employees were very loyal to the horses, as the horses were to them. They needed a clue to help them save the horses. When the farm workers searched the horses' stalls, they were shocked to find bits of oleander leaves. Oleander leaves are very poisonous. How could the leaves have gotten inside the horse stalls? And why would these horses have eaten them? Horses' instincts tell them to steer clear of dangerous foods.

Then the ranch owner discovered something else. Each of the stalls had pieces of carrots and apples mixed in among the poisonous leaves. The sweet taste of apples and carrots had tricked the horses. They ate the leaves along with the apples and carrots.

What had happened became clear. Someone had secretly climbed over the farm's gate in the night and fed oleander leaves mixed with apples and carrots to the horses. Who would do such a thing?

The horses at the farm could have died from the oleander poison that scary day. But the farm's owners and employees were good problem-solvers. They moved fast. They got help right away. They sent three of the sickest horses to the hospital. With personal care, all the horses got better. The horses seemed grateful. They nuzzled the hands of the employees. Although the farm owners never found the person who had done this cruel act, they were very happy and relieved that their horses survived the attack. But as they had learned, it's best not to get too friendly with the oleander plant.

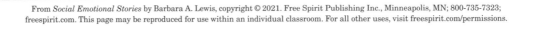

OLEANDER FACTS

- Oleander bushes can grow to be more than 20 feet tall.

- Every part of the oleander plant is poisonous, including its blossoms. Even breathing in the smoke from burning oleander can be dangerous.

- Not all animals seem to mind the oleander's poison. It doesn't hurt some caterpillars, butterflies, rodents, and birds. Maybe these creatures have built up a resistance to the plant. Maybe they don't eat enough to get sick. Or maybe their bodies change the poison into something safe.

- The oleander plant has a good side too. For about 1,500 years, people have used oleander to help fight sickness and treat injuries. Some doctors think the plant can treat snake bites. It might also help fight skin cancer and other diseases.

TALK IT OVER

Use these questions to guide your students in comparing the poisonous oleander plant to certain traits and behaviors in people. These discussions can become practice in developing emotional self-awareness and self-management of these behaviors.

Mixing apples and carrots with oleander can sweeten the bitter taste of the poisonous leaves. Can you make an analogy to people who are honest or dishonest? If someone mostly tells the truth but sometimes mixes in a few lies, it's easy to be fooled. The truth "sweetens" the lie, so that it becomes hard to tell what is true and what is false.

- If you let yourself be dishonest some of the time, you might eventually get used to it. You might lower your own standards.

- Half-truths, fibs, and "white lies" are still dishonest. Always try to tell the truth.

- If you watch movies or play games that have violent or scary parts, you might excuse those parts because you like the rest of the movie or game.

The farm owners in "Pretty, Poisonous Oleanders" acted quickly to save their horses. Can you think of other times when acting quickly might save something or someone?

- Sometimes when you have a disagreement with someone else, talking it through right away can keep it from becoming a bigger problem. Or if you realize that you've hurt someone, it's best to apologize as soon as you can. If you wait too long, anger, misunderstanding, and hurt feelings can grow stronger.

- If you are sick or hurt, the sooner you take care of it, the sooner you'll start to feel better.

- If you catch yourself cheating, lying, or making other poor choices, try to stop as soon as you can. If you don't stop early, it can get easier and easier to do these things.

- Speak up if you think you or someone else might be in danger. If you wait, it might be too late to help.

The oleander bush has beautiful blossoms and looks harmless. Are there situations that people might get into that seem safe at first but are actually dangerous?

- It's never a good idea to go anywhere with a stranger, even if they seem nice.

- You might go to a party that sounds fun and then find out that kids there are doing risky things, such as smoking, drinking alcohol, or using drugs. If that happens, call a parent or another grown-up to pick you up and take you home.

Caterpillars, moths, and some rodents and birds seem to be immune to the oleander's poison. Can you make an analogy to behaviors in people?

- It is possible to build up immunity to (get used to) disrespect, lying, mean language, and other

poor behavior by doing it over and over, or by seeing it over and over. Maybe at first you feel bad about doing or seeing these things. But after a while, they don't bother you as much as they used to. It's better to avoid these behaviors in the beginning. And if you do find yourself making poor character choices, you can try to stop right away.

👁 You can build up a tolerance for poor character patterns by taking part in them or watching them. But you can also build up a habit of good character by making small, positive choices each day.

The oleander's appearance is deceiving. It's beautiful, but also poisonous. At the same time, even though it's unsafe to eat, it might help us treat some sicknesses. Can you compare that to making judgments about people?

👁 No one is all bad or all good. Every person has positive *and* negative traits. And we can all work on making better choices and building our positive habits.

👁 It's best not to make assumptions about a person based on just one of their traits. Get to know someone before you draw conclusions about their character.

👁 Everyone deserves respect.

ACTIVITIES

Activity 1: Hidden in Plain Sight
Materials
Hidden in Plain Sight handout (in digital content)
Optional: Colored pencils

Directions
Pass out copies of the Hidden in Plain Sight handout and invite kids to spend some time hunting for the hidden objects. If desired, kids can color them in as they find them. As children work, talk about how easy or hard it is to spot the hidden pictures. Point out that it is easy to miss these pictures unless you are looking for them. Even then, you might not see some of them. Make an analogy to the oleander

leaves mixed with sweet foods. Is it also easy to overlook or stop noticing negative behavior if you are only looking at the big picture? You might teach children the word *discernment*, depending upon age of the group.

To further explain this idea, present the following hypothetical situation to students and talk with them about the questions it raises:

Your best friend often tells small lies. You care about your friend a lot, and the two of you have fun together. But you know that lying is wrong. What should you do? If you do nothing, will you eventually stop noticing the lies? Will your friend try to get away with bigger lies? How will you know whether your friend is telling *you* the truth or not?

Activity 2: Small Acts and Big Results
Materials
Milk (2% or whole)
Soup bowl or other broad, shallow dish
Red, yellow, green, and blue food coloring
Liquid dish soap
Cotton swabs

Directions
Connect this activity to how quickly the poison of the oleander plant can act. Pour enough milk into the dish to cover the bottom completely. The milk should be about ¼-inch deep. Near the center of the dish, add a drop of each food coloring: red, yellow, green, and blue.

Next, dab the end of a cotton swab into a little bit of dish soap. Put the soapy end into the middle of the milk and food coloring. Hold it there for about 10 to 15 seconds. Suddenly the colors in the milk will start moving, swirling together and outward.

Compare this phenomenon to the idea that a small act can have big consequences—bad or good. It is important to be aware of your choices and consequences. It is also important to manage your own behavior. A negative habit can soon become hard to break. A tiny lie can quickly spread. And a situation that seems safe can sometimes become dangerous in a hurry. Talk with kids about how they can deal with all of these situations. Discuss various related scenarios and brainstorm positive responses to them. Ask children to consider how kindness can spread out to other people in the same way as the experiment, and invite them to "pay it forward." Children could plan to do acts of kindness secretly and watch to see if their actions are paid forward. But even if they are not, remind children that doing nice acts and spreading kindness are worthwhile on their own.

Note: The secret behind this demonstration is in the tiny drop of soap. Dish soap weakens the chemical bonds holding the milk's proteins and fats together. The food coloring allows you to see this process. For more details see: stevespanglerscience .com/experiment/milk-color-explosion.

Activity 3: Seeds of Respect

Materials
Newspaper
Marigold seeds (4 to 6 per student)
Mini clay pots (1 per student)
Pebbles
Potting soil
Large tray(s) to hold pots
Construction paper, cut into pieces about 1 inch by 2 inches (1 per student)
Markers or crayons
Plastic straws (1 per student)
Tape or staples

Directions
Spread newspaper on your classroom floor or on a large work surface. Tell kids that you're going to plant marigolds and work on "growing" respect. Relate this activity to the idea that acting respectful can help us and others grow. Respect is an important part of social awareness and connection with those around us. Explain that oleander wouldn't be a good plant to grow in the classroom, but that marigolds are also pretty flowers that can remind us to show respect for others and ourselves.

Show kids how to plant their marigold seeds. First, place a few pebbles in the bottom of the pot to help the water drain from the soil. Then add enough potting soil to fill the pot up to about 2 inches from the top. Sprinkle the seeds on the soil and add another half inch of soil.

Note: Instead of clay pots, you can use 16-ounce biodegradable plastic cups or reuse clean food containers of similar size. If you use plastic, be sure to poke a few holes in the bottom of each container first. Whatever you plant the seeds in, start a couple of extra plants in case some kids' seeds don't germinate.

Assist any kids who need help planting their marigold seeds. While they work, talk about how respect can grow just like a flower. Discuss the ways that positive and negative behaviors and habits are related to respect, both for themselves and for others. For example, if you respect your teacher, you do your homework on time. If you respect your family, you help keep your home clean. If you respect others, you are polite to them. If you respect yourself, you take good care of your health. Help kids brainstorm other ways of growing respect, and invite them to talk about possible causes and effects of respectful (and disrespectful) actions.

When all kids have planted their seeds, have each kid write a way to be respectful on a piece of construction paper. (If some have trouble fitting their messages on the paper, you can write for them.) Then help each student tape or staple their piece of paper to one end of a plastic straw, resembling a flag. Kids can then plant these respect flags in their pots.

Finally, place all the pots in a tray near a window.

Talk about how kids will need to care for their plants by watering them. Compare this to the way being respectful is a habit and takes practice. If we work to care for it, respect can grow and grow.

LESSON 17
PARROTS

Key Words
The behaviors, traits, and emotions below are just starting points for aligning SEL, character education, and this lesson's story. Most of these ideas can easily be connected with more than one competency or domain.

Self-Awareness: Balance • Courage and Boldness • Inner Strength

Self-Management: Adaptability

Social Awareness: Empathy • Understanding Others

Relationship Skills: Bullying Prevention • Communication • Friendship • Humor • Playfulness

Responsible Decision-Making: Problem-Solving • Wisdom and Learning

Students will

- learn about parrots, including that they are highly intelligent, are good at mimicking human voices and words, and have a playful and sometimes bold nature
- compare parrots that mimic human voices to people who mimic the attributes of others as a form of bullying
- consider a comparison between the parrots' adaptability and skill in learning and saying words (despite the fact that they have no vocal cords) to people who develop new skills and adapt to new situations
- draw connections between Willie's rescue warning and people who discover inner strength and courage they didn't know they had

Overview
Parrots are well known for their ability to mimic human words. Some African gray parrots have learned to recognize up to a thousand words and to say over one hundred words. This talent is especially impressive because parrots do not have vocal cords. Parrots also amuse and entertain people, learning tricks and repeating words that get a laugh or a reaction.

Along with this adaptability and high intelligence comes an attitude. Parrots are playful and fun. They can also be very demanding, and they sometimes repeat annoying words endlessly. But they make popular pets. They seem to connect easily with humans, and often build strong and lasting relationships with their owners.

Story
Playful Parrots

PLAYFUL PARROTS

Have you ever seen a parrot at a soccer game? It's not a common sight. But a Senegalese parrot named Me-Tu is a great soccer fan. He and his owner go to soccer games in Northern Ireland. Me-Tu learned to copy the sound of the referee's whistle. But it got him into trouble. When Me-Tu whistled, everyone thought it was the referee. The game stopped. The players scratched their heads and looked confused. And Me-Tu just kept whistling. Each time, he stopped the game. Finally, the referee figured out the problem. He red-carded Me-Tu and kicked the pesky parrot and his owner right out of the stadium.

Alex was an African gray parrot who liked to talk instead of whistle. Alex was very good at learning words. His trainer taught him to say more than 150 words. Alex could name colors and pick out shapes. He learned to count up to six, and even to add up numbers. Alex's trainer said the parrot was as smart as a five- or six-year-old child. Not all experts agree. But everyone could see that Alex was definitely bird-brained—in a *good* way!

Some parrots even dance! Snowball is a cockatoo. He boogies to popular songs. Millions of people have watched Snowball strutting and swaying in videos online. Snowball stomps his feet. He bounces his head to the music's beat. He even ends his performance by bowing to the camera. Scientists were surprised to learn about Snowball's sense of rhythm. They had thought that only people could move to the beat of music. Snowball helped change their minds.

Another parrot star is a Quaker parrot named Willie. He isn't a performer like Snowball. But he sure earned his owner's love and admiration. One day Willie's owner was babysitting a two-year-old girl named Hannah. While Hannah was eating breakfast, the babysitter left Willie and the little girl alone for a moment. Suddenly, Hannah choked on some food. Willie screamed and rattled his cage. He yelled, "Mama, baby," again and again. Right away, the babysitter rushed back. She grabbed Hannah and got the food out of her throat. She saved her life. But if Willie hadn't made so much noise, Hannah might have died. The babysitter was surprised. She had never heard Willie use the word "baby" that way before. Other people admired Willie for his actions too. The local Red Cross gave him an award. They named him an Animal Lifesaver.

PARROT FACTS

- There are about 350 different kinds of parrots. Many kinds of parrots are endangered in the wild.

- Many parrots have long life spans. Some can live to be eighty years old. In that time, they can form close relationships with people.

- Parrots can copy a wide range of sounds. Many are great at mimicking human voices. But parrots don't have any vocal cords. So how do they talk? To make sound, parrots push air across a special part of their throat called a bifurcated trachea. They can make different sounds by changing the trachea's shape and depth.

- Parrots are also good at learning tricks, and have entertained many people. They swing on parrot-size swings. They hop through hoops and untie shoelaces, and make people laugh. They ride tiny tricycles.

- Along with high intelligence, parrots can have big attitudes. They are very loud. They love attention. They demand toys and snacks. Sometimes they keep repeating a bad behavior. It's almost as if they're *trying* to annoy you. And they seem to like getting a big reaction. So be careful what you say around a smart parrot. They often repeat naughty words over and over.

TALK IT OVER

Use these questions to guide your students in considering analogies between parrots and learning, adaptability, and other character traits and behaviors in people.

Although many examples of parrots mimicking human voices are funny, it's not always funny for us to mimic other people. Understanding others and not teasing them is a social awareness skill. It shows that a person understands how another person feels. It is also related to empathy. When is it not nice or not funny for people to copy others?

- If someone copies another person's gestures or voice in order to put them down, it can embarrass and hurt the other person.

- Mimicking another person's voice in a joking way can be a form of bullying. It may start out as a joke, but it can quickly grow into something much more hurtful and serious. For example, if you mimic another person's voice or actions in a mocking way, that behavior can spread to other people.

- If you copy someone else, it can hurt you too. After a while you might feel like you're forgetting who you really are. It's better to create your own voice and personality than to be a copy of someone else.

Can you make a comparison between parrots that learn to speak without vocal cords and people who learn new skills and adapt to new situations?

- People who are injured or who are born without certain abilities can learn new skills and lead very productive lives. For example, Stephen Hawking was a great scientist. He had a disease that made him unable to control his muscles. But Hawking adapted. He had a special wheelchair, and he communicated with a voice synthesizer. Another example of adaptability is Mike McNaughton. He stepped on a landmine in Afghanistan in 2002, losing his right leg. After recovering from his injuries, he became an avid runner and bicyclist. McNaughton has also worked to help other injured war veterans.

- Most kids have trouble with some subjects in school. Instead of giving up on those subjects, they can try to get extra help from the teacher or a tutor.

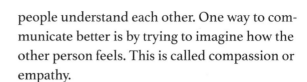

- Some people might love music, but not enjoy singing. They could learn to dance, play a musical instrument, or write songs instead.

- Moving to a new town or a new school can be difficult. Adapting to a different place and making new friends is harder for some people than it is for others. But everyone can practice and improve on these skills. And that will make it easier to adjust the next time there's a big change.

Parrots can be playful and mischievous. Their behavior can be funny, but sometimes they get in trouble too—like Me-Tu at the soccer game. Can you think of ways to compare this characteristic to people?

- Everyone needs to play. Playing helps us have fun, be creative, and make new friends. It can even make us healthier. Playing nicely with others helps you build and strengthen friendships.

- Sometimes too much playing can get in the way of doing homework, chores, or other necessary tasks. It's important to balance your work time and your play time. Sometimes learning how to reach this balance takes time and practice.

- People don't all think that the same things are fun or funny. Everyone is different. It's important to respect other people's feelings.

Parrots are very skilled at learning tricks. They seem to be good at solving puzzles too. Can you make an analogy to people learning new things?

- You can learn new skills and get better at them if you practice.

- Learning new ideas and facts is fun and interesting.

- Your brain is like a muscle. The more you use it, the stronger it gets.

Some kinds of parrots learn words, and Alex the gray parrot seemed to understand how to communicate with his trainer. How do people communicate?

- Learning to communicate well takes practice. True communication only happens when

people understand each other. One way to communicate better is by trying to imagine how the other person feels. This is called compassion or empathy.

- There are many ways to communicate. Talking is just one of them. People also communicate with their facial expressions and their gestures. You can communicate with other people through writing, drawing, touch, or music too.

- People in different places use different languages. People with hearing impairment use sign language. It can be challenging to learn another language. But it's fun and rewarding to be able to communicate with others.

Willie the parrot turned out to be an unlikely hero. Can you make a comparison between his story and people who become heroes?

- Heroes aren't always obvious. You probably can't look around in a classroom and say, "Oh, I see a hero over there." But that doesn't mean that heroes aren't around you. And you may be a hero yourself. Courage can come from unexpected people and show up in unexpected situations.

- People who become heroes are often ordinary people who stay brave just a little longer than others in a scary situation, or people who don't give up. Sometimes they discover courage and skills that they didn't know they had in order to rescue or help someone. Heroes are people who have inner strength and empathy that inspire them to help others.

ACTIVITIES

Activity 1: Switch It Up

Materials

Soccer ball or kickball

Directions

Invite students to switch it up and see how adaptable they are. First have them try writing with their nondominant hands. Give them some time to have fun with this. Next, have each kid kick a ball with the opposite foot from what they would usually use.

Variation: You could also give students other challenges in this activity, such as playing guitar with opposite hands.

Afterward, talk with kids about the experience of switching their hands and feet. Did they find that the tasks they were doing got any easier after a little while? How long do kids think they would have to practice before they felt just as comfortable and skilled using their nondominant hands or feet for the same tasks? Do they think they would *ever* get to this point?

Expand the conversation to talk about adaptability. Why do kids think it can be difficult to adapt to change and new situations? What are some ways to increase our adaptability? Why can it be helpful to develop this positive trait?

Activity 2: New Words

Materials
None

Directions
Parrots are great at learning new words—and so are people! Have each student learn a few words in another language (for example, how to count to ten, or how to say hello and good-bye). Help kids choose their languages. Some overlap is fine, but try to have as wide a range of languages as is possible and realistic for your group. Help kids find the words they want to say and learn how to pronounce them correctly. Then give them a week or so to practice and memorize their words. If desired, you can set aside a little bit of time each day to work with kids on this activity.

When the week is over, have every student say the words they've learned (along with the English meanings) in front of the class. Be sure to celebrate kids' efforts even if they don't get the pronunciation exactly right.

After kids share what they've learned, talk about their experience learning these new words. Was it fun? Challenging? Both? What did they like best about it? What did they find the most difficult? Why do they think it's important to be able to communicate with others, even if it takes some extra time or work? What are other skills that may be challenging but rewarding to learn?

Activity 3: What's It For?

Materials
What's It For? handout (in digital content)

Directions
Pass out copies of the What's It For? handout. Ask kids to imagine that they've never seen any of the items on the list before, and that they don't know what they are used for. Invite them to come up with a new use for each thing. For example, kids could imagine that a shovel is for cooking food over a campfire, or that a fork is used for combing hair.

Encourage kids to be really playful and creative with this activity. They can fill in the handout individually and then share their ideas with a partner, or you can brainstorm as a group. Either way, keep this activity fun, light, and full of laughter. Talk about how ideas that seem silly at first can turn out to be amazing. Some of the world's greatest inventions sounded nutty or impossible at the time. And many inventions have been created by changing the form or the use of an item that already exists. For example, one legend claims that potato chips were invented because a restaurant customer kept complaining that his French fries were too soggy. Popsicles were invented by an eleven-year-old boy who accidentally left some soda on a porch overnight in freezing temperatures. Velcro, penicillin, and a host of other inventions were also happy accidents. You might also discuss how people sometimes adapt their interests, hobbies, and talents by thinking of different ways to express themselves, interpret ideas, or use materials.

If you like, extend the conversation to encourage kids to consider what it would be like if they had *really* never seen a shovel or a fork, for example. What would they think when they first encountered one? Talk about how it can be hard to make sense of something new and unfamiliar. Everyone is confused or uncertain at times. We should never be afraid to ask questions. That's how we learn and strengthen our minds.

LESSON 18
PENGUINS

Key Words
The behaviors, traits, and emotions below are just starting points for aligning SEL, character education, and this lesson's story. Most of these ideas can easily be connected with more than one competency or domain.

Self-Awareness: Balance

Self-Management: Goal-Setting • Organization and Self-Motivation • Responsibility

Social Awareness: Acceptance of Others

Relationship Skills: Communication • Cooperation, Collaboration, and Teamwork • Leadership • Loyalty • Playfulness

Responsible Decision-Making: Analyzing and Evaluating • Problem-Solving

Students will
- learn about penguins, including the fact that there are many different species that have unique characteristics
- consider the responsibility and organization that penguins need to have in order to take care of their young, and compare this to the responsibility and organizational skills that people use to accomplish tasks
- make analogies between the cooperation that exists among penguins and cooperation among people

Overview
Movies and books about penguins have helped make them much-loved creatures, famous for their tuxedo-like feathers and waddling walks. But penguins are more than just celebrity birds. They have many interesting behaviors that can serve as starting points for analogies to human behaviors. For example, Adélie penguins mate for life, demonstrating lasting loyalty. Each penguin has a unique sound that makes them identifiable to others. Mother and father penguins can easily find their chicks in a huge crowd. They communicate with sounds and movements. And many penguins, including emperor penguins, share the responsibility of rearing their chicks. Penguin mates—and whole penguin communities—organize and cooperate to keep themselves, the eggs, and the chicks warm and safe in Antarctica's cold, windy conditions.

But it isn't all work and no play for penguins. They can also be curious, spirited, and playful.

Story
Penguin Partners

PENGUIN PARTNERS

Thanks to their tuxedo-like feathers, penguins already look like they're wearing little suits. But even penguins need special outfits sometimes!

Pierre was an African penguin who needed a new suit. He lived at an aquarium in San Francisco. Pierre was a very old penguin. He was an alpha male (or leader) in his group. His fellow penguins followed him around in the pool.

But Pierre developed a big problem. He had bald spots on his back and his chest, and his tail and head were nearly featherless. That's bad news for a penguin. Pierre needed his feathers to keep warm. Pierre didn't want to swim in the zoo pool anymore. It was too cold for him without all of his feathers. He no longer behaved as a leader or communicated much with the other penguins. They started to ignore him. They no longer accepted him. They didn't follow him. Pierre shivered by himself on the side of the pool—cold and lonely.

At the aquarium, a biologist named Pam felt sorry for Pierre. She was worried he might die. Pam set a goal to solve his problem. She analyzed the situation and looked for solutions. She tried to keep Pierre warm with a heat lamp. She gave him medicine to try to make his feathers grow. But those plans didn't work.

Then Pam had a great idea. She remembered that divers stay warm in wetsuits, even in very cold water. She gathered and organized her information to convince others that Pierre needed a wetsuit too. A special penguin-size wetsuit was made for Pierre. It was shaped like a vest so Pierre could still waddle and swim. It had Velcro in the front. If Pierre ate too many tasty dinners of fish and krill, the aquarium workers could loosen it. The flashy black vest would keep him warm until his feathers grew back. But there was still one big question. Would the other birds accept Pierre's new look?

When Pierre dived into the water, the other penguins swam around him. They nudged him with their beaks. They circled Pierre, as though sizing him up. Their decision? No problem! They didn't seem to care about his wetsuit. Soon enough, Pierre was splashing, playing, and swimming with the other penguins. He was once again accepted as their leader—and he was by far the best-dressed penguin at the aquarium.

PENGUIN FACTS

- Emperor penguins are the biggest penguins in the world. The parents share the job of raising their chicks and balance their responsibilities. These penguin partners take turns sitting on the egg to keep it warm. They also take turns hunting for food and taking care of their chick once the egg hatches. Families find each other among thousands of other penguins by making little trilling, honking noises. Each penguin in the family recognizes these sounds.

- Emperor penguins huddle together for warmth in a large group of up to several thousand. When they do this, they can temporarily increase the temperature within the huddle from sub-zero to over 90 degrees Fahrenheit.

- The world's smallest penguin is called the little penguin or little blue penguin. It stands just 13 inches high and weighs around 3 pounds.

- Adélie penguins sometimes swim more than 150 miles round-trip while hunting for food.

TALK IT OVER

Use these questions to guide your students in considering analogies between penguins and loyalty, cooperation, organization, acceptance, empathy, teamwork, and other character traits and behaviors in people.

The emperor penguin is the world's largest penguin. It can be up to 4 feet tall and weigh almost 100 pounds. Adélie penguins are some of the smallest penguins, at only about 27 inches tall and 8 to 12 pounds. But the Adélie are faster and nimbler than the big emperors. Can you make a comparison to people who have individual strengths and talents regardless of size or appearance?

- 👁 It isn't always the biggest or toughest-looking person who is the most athletic, the most skilled, or the best or most inspiring leader.

- 👁 It's best not to make assumptions about a person's character or talents based on what they look like.

- 👁 If you're willing to work hard and keep trying, you can reach almost any goal you set for yourself.

- 👁 It is the drive inside you—not the way you look—that makes you succeed.

Male and female penguins share the responsibility of hatching their eggs and raising their chicks. If both partners didn't do their share, the young penguins would not survive. They take turns in an organized way to handle responsibilities, like sitting with the egg while the partner seeks food. This helps keep penguin chicks safe, and also helps create balance and order in the life of the penguin family. Can you make a comparison between this and the responsibilities people have?

- 👁 Parents and family members share responsibilities in caring for children. They organize their time and their roles so that different family members may earn money, prepare meals, and so on. Kids also have responsibilities. They help their families with household chores and other tasks.

- 👁 In every area of life, people have different responsibilities. All of these different responsibilities are important. They help keep things running smoothly in families, homes, companies, communities, and countries.

- 👁 Everyone in a classroom has responsibilities. The classroom works better if everyone does their job.

Penguins cooperate to stay warm in Antarctica's bitter cold. Can you make a comparison with people who cooperate to do jobs or reach goals together?

👁 Families may cooperate by assigning different chores to different family members. That way, all the chores get done and no one has to do all the work.

👁 Cooperation is an important social skill and often helps a job get done faster and better. For example, students working together on a project might each be responsible for a different part of the project depending on their strengths. The student who loves drawing can make a poster, while the person who enjoys facts and figures can gather some of the research. Working in a team helps members grow in cooperation as they help one another.

Adélie penguins mate for life. They remain loyal to their partners as long as they live. And Pierre's fellow penguins accepted him again in his wetsuit, even though he still looked a little different from them. Can you compare this to acceptance and loyalty among people?

👁 If you are loyal to your family members, you stick together and support each other—no matter what happens. You help each other achieve goals.

👁 If you are loyal to your friends, you stick up for each other, no matter what anyone says. But loyalty can also mean having the courage to tell a friend that you're worried they are making a mistake or practicing a habit that might be harmful.

👁 You should always know what you are being loyal to. Before you promise your loyalty to people, groups, or causes, it's important to find out what they believe and what they stand for.

👁 Loyalty goes beyond appearances. You're loyal to your friends and family because of who they are inside, not what they look like or what they are wearing.

Penguins work hard to care for their eggs and their chicks, sometimes in very harsh conditions. But penguins also seem to have fun. They appear to enjoy playing and sliding on the ice and snow. Can you make a comparison to people?

👁 If you only work, you can feel stressed. If you only play, you don't learn and grow as much as you could. Everyone needs balance in their life.

👁 Part of the reason penguins are so popular with people is because they seem to be so fun and playful. If you have fun and have a positive attitude—both when you're working and when you're playing—people usually enjoy being around you.

ACTIVITIES

Activity 1: Organize a Responsibility Roster

Materials
Responsibility Roster handout (in digital content)
Stickers (penguins, gold stars, or other)

Directions
Create a classroom Responsibility Roster. As a group, brainstorm the jobs that need to be done each day in the classroom. (For example, watering plants or turning out the lights.) Decide who will do each job first, and then choose a fair way to rotate the jobs. Remind kids that not everyone will have a job every day, but that they all have responsibility in keeping the classroom a clean, safe, fun place where everyone can learn.

Fill out the Responsibility Roster with your classroom responsibilities and the names of the students assigned to carry out these jobs. If necessary, you can use more than one chart.

Tell kids that when a job is done on time, the student responsible for that job will get a sticker in their box on the Responsibility Roster. If the job is not done on time, the box will be left empty.

At the end of each week, look at your Responsibility Roster as a group. See how many stickers and how many empty spaces you have. Avoid placing blame on any individual. Instead, analyze the situation, keeping the focus on how responsibly you acted as a group, and how you could do even better. How does getting these jobs done help the whole class?

Activity 2: Good Guides

Materials

Masking tape or sidewalk chalk to mark 2 paths

Large open space for constructing the paths (inside or outside)

Bandanas or other blindfolds (1 for every 2 kids)

Preparation

Before beginning this activity, mark out two separate paths on the floor or the ground using tape or chalk. Depending on the ages and abilities of your group, you can make these paths as challenging as is appropriate, with zigzags and detours around simple (and safe) obstacles. However, try to make the paths of equal difficulty.

Directions

Divide your group into pairs. Then place the pairs in two teams, assigning each team to one of the paths. Blindfold one child from each pair. The partner who can see has to guide the blindfolded partner along the path. They must do this only with words, not by physically leading or moving the partner. Each pair gets one "freebie"—one chance to go outside the lines of the path. If they go outside a second time, they're eliminated. Each pair that reaches the end of the path wins one point for their team. After one round, switch partners so everyone has a chance to be guided and to guide. If you have time, you could also give each team a chance to try the other path. The team with the highest number of points wins.

Variation: You can also play this game without points and teams. Simply challenge the kids to try to reach the paths' ends.

Afterward, talk with kids about the activity. What was it like to be the guide? What was it like to be the person being guided? How did they need to work together to reach the end of the path? Did the blindfolded person have to trust their guide? How did that feel? Did the guides feel that they had a big responsibility as they kept their partners on track?

Activity 3: Find the Leader, Follow the Leader

Materials

None

Directions

Ask the kids to stand in a circle. For the first round, you be the leader. Let kids know that at some point you'll pass the leadership on to someone else—but that you'll do so without speaking. Maybe you'll nod your head in the direction of a student, or wink at them.

Start the game by demonstrating an action, such as nodding your head, clapping, or snapping your fingers. All the kids must follow what the leader is doing, repeating their actions. Each time the leader changes their action, everyone else changes their actions too.

At any time, the leader can choose another leader, but they must do so silently. The new leader models a new action, and the old leader follows.

When leadership changes, kids can cooperate to let each other know who the new leader is. They can signal others by nodding in the direction of the new leader. See how long it takes for everyone to recognize them.

As kids play this game, they will hone their skills in nonverbal communication and cooperation. After playing for a while, talk about what kids thought of the experience. Was it hard to spot the new leader? Did kids get better at it, or at signaling others, during the course of the game? Did they feel any responsibility to pay attention to the leader? Why or why not? Did they cooperate to let others know when the leadership changed? If so, how?

LESSON 19
PIGS

Key Words

The behaviors, traits, and emotions below are just starting points for aligning SEL, character education, and this lesson's story. Most of these ideas can easily be connected with more than one competency or domain.

Self-Awareness: Gratitude • Happiness and Joy • Inner Strength • Love

Self-Management: Courage and Boldness

Social Awareness: Acceptance of Others • Empathy • Perspective-Taking • Respect

Relationship Skills: Helpfulness • Leadership

Responsible Decision-Making: Identifying Challenges • Positive and Ethical Choices • Problem-Solving • Wisdom and Learning

Students will

- learn facts about pigs that may surprise them, including that pigs are very intelligent and that some kinds of pigs make good pets
- compare the courage shown by a pig named LuLu with people who show courage and inspiring leadership to help someone or something
- make an analogy between the false ideas that people sometimes have about pigs and the false assumptions that people might make about each other

Overview

Pigs have long had a bad reputation—but that reputation isn't true or fair. Many people don't realize, for instance, that pigs are highly intelligent. In fact, they seem to have an amazing ability to size up a situation and solve a problem. In addition, contrary to what many people believe, pigs are not naturally dirty or smelly. Since pigs have no sweat glands, their bodies don't give off sweaty odors. And their habit of wallowing in the mud is actually a way to stay cool and healthy.

Kids will enjoy learning more about pigs and dispelling the assumptions they may have had about these animals. Considering these misperceptions is a great starting point for discussion about how people sometimes misjudge each other and about the value of keeping an open mind and respecting all people. And the story of LuLu, a potbellied pig that saved her owner's life, will capture kids' imaginations and inspire lively and meaningful conversation about courage and the many ways it can be shown.

Story

Problem-Solving Pigs

PROBLEM-SOLVING PIGS

Unlike Wilbur, the "radiant" pig in the book *Charlotte's Web*, pigs don't really talk. But they *are* smart. And they're good problem-solvers. One farmer in Australia found out just how good pigs are at figuring out puzzles. He was having trouble keeping one clever pig in her pen. No matter how many different latches the farmer put on the gate, the pig always seemed to figure them out. She would open the latch and escape into the fields. But the farmer was tricky too. He made a latch that took two steps. To open it, the pig would need to press down a ring and also lift up a hook.

While the pig watched, the farmer put the latch on the gate. He tested it a few times. Then the farmer was curious to see what the pig would do. He decided to hide and watch her. When the farmer was out of her sight, the pig made her move. The farmer said that she opened the latch in thirty seconds. Then she trotted happily into the field.

Not all pigs live in pens. Some are pets and live with people inside their homes. LuLu, a potbellied pig, was a pet. She lived with a woman named Jo Ann. And LuLu showed that she was good at sizing up a problem. One day LuLu and Jo Ann were relaxing in Jo Ann's home in the north woods of Pennsylvania. Suddenly Jo Ann had a heart attack. She fell to the floor. Jo Ann was alone, except for her dog and LuLu. She was very scared.

The family dog didn't know what to do other than bark. But LuLu heard Jo Ann's cries. She seemed to sense that Jo Ann needed help. She shuffled over and sniffed out the situation. Then she took action. She crashed her 150-pound body right through the pet door of Jo Ann's home. She cut her tummy on the door's sharp edges. But she didn't stop. She charged out into the fenced-in yard. LuLu hardly ever set hoof outside the yard's gate. Sometimes she had taken walks on a leash. But on this day, she managed to push open the gate all by herself.

LuLu ran to a nearby road and laid down in front of the oncoming cars. Drivers swerved and honked, but LuLu didn't run away. Finally, a young man stopped. He followed LuLu to Jo Ann. Then the young man called an ambulance and saved Jo Ann's life. Jo Ann was so happy and grateful for Lulu.

LuLu's courage made her famous. She soon became the best-known pig in Pennsylvania and beyond. Reporters wrote stories about her. They took her picture. But LuLu didn't seem to care about fame. Her favorite reward? A gooey, jelly-filled doughnut. That made LuLu happy!

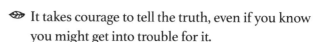

PIG FACTS

- Many scientists think pigs are in the top-ten list of the world's smartest animals. Some even believe that pigs can solve problems as well as a three-year-old child.

- Pigs communicate with each other using at least twenty different sounds.

- Pigs have a great sense of smell. They've been trained to sniff out targets from truffles to bombs.

- You may have heard that pigs roll around in the mud. And it *is* a pretty messy habit. But pigs have a good reason for rolling around in the muck. Pigs don't have sweat glands. Sweating keeps many animals cool. So on hot days, mud helps pigs cool down. It also protects their skin from bugs. The mud even acts as a sunscreen. Pigs can get sunburned, just like people.

- Pigs have a reputation for being smelly, but the animals themselves don't smell bad. The pigpens where they live can stink, *if* they get too dirty. But that's true of all animals—people too!

TALK IT OVER

Use these questions to guide your students in discussing characteristics of pigs and comparing them to human behaviors such as empathy, acceptance, courage, gratitude, and more.

LuLu showed courage and love for Jo Ann when she left her yard to help her owner. She instinctively put her own safety at risk, lying down in front of cars to get help. People also show courage by going outside of their comfort zones. What are some examples of people doing something courageous?

- It takes courage to tell the truth, even if you know you might get into trouble for it.

- If you know someone is telling a lie that might hurt someone else, it would take courage to report it to an adult in charge.

- Many people show courage in times of danger. Firefighters, soldiers, and police officers all risk their lives to protect others. We are grateful to those people for helping us or others during an emergency or another scary situation. We are grateful, too, for people who risk their safety even when it isn't their job.

- Trying something new can take courage. For example, it requires courage to start at a new school, audition for a talent show, try out for a team, or invite a new student to your home.

- We don't all need courage for the same things. Speaking in front of a group is easy for some people and takes courage for others.

Even though many people don't think of pigs as smart, scientists say pigs are very bright. People also think pigs smell bad, but that's not true. Can you compare this to the ways that people with false ideas might make false judgments about each other?

- If you get false information about someone, you might make the wrong judgments about them. You may develop prejudices against that person. It's best to make a decision for yourself based on what you know for sure is true, rather than what you've only heard from other people. Try to accept differences in others, see their perspectives, and understand how they might feel.

- All people deserve respect, regardless of their beliefs, lifestyles, cultures, appearances, or abilities.

- Rumors spread quickly, even (or especially) when they are not true. These rumors can hurt feelings and damage relationships. Sometimes false judgments can even lead to hatred or violence.

Inspiring leadership can come from unexpected places. You probably wouldn't expect a pig to show leadership and problem-solving. But LuLu's instinct nevertheless led her to understand that

her owner was in trouble, and her intelligence enabled her to figure out a way to help Jo Ann. In people we might call that *empathy*. Can you think of ways that people might show inspiring leadership and empathy in difficult moments?

- 👁 When someone is being made fun of, an inspired leader might stop the bullying by saying nice things about the person. Or they might understand how the victim feels and say, "Stop! We don't bully around here."

- 👁 An inspiring leader might be someone who sees another person or an animal in trouble and finds a way to help. Other people might then follow this leader.

- 👁 Parents are often seen as the leaders in a family. But another family leader could be a child who guides younger brothers and sisters and teaches them how to do what is right.

Pigs don't naturally smell bad. But when they live in dirty conditions—sometimes because the person who cares for them doesn't keep the pen clean—some people think the pigs themselves are dirty. Can you think of analogies between this idea and human behavior?

- 👁 It's risky to judge people based on where they come from or what they look like.

- 👁 Pigs in a dirty pen are in a bad situation that they cannot change by themselves. Sometimes people can get into bad situations too. If you ever need help getting out of a situation, don't be afraid to talk to someone you trust about what's going on.

Pigs show intelligence and problem-solving skills. They appear to enjoy learning new skills. They have even figured out how to open gates that have complicated latches. How can you compare this to human behavior?

- 👁 Pigs can't research problems, but they do have instincts that help them think about what to do. People solve problems by researching their options and looking at different solutions. This research can give people insights and information that help them find wisdom and discover solutions to their problems.

- 👁 Sometimes you might face a problem that seems too difficult or complicated to solve. But if you look at each piece of the problem separately, you might be able to figure out answers. Some problems have to be solved in several different steps, just as the pig in Australia had to learn to do two steps to open the latch on the gate.

- 👁 Solving problems can lead to gaining wisdom and feeling self-confident. And when we solve problems and help others at the same time, that can help us feel really happy. Helping equals happiness. It can also help us make new friendships.

ACTIVITIES

Activity 1: The Courage Box

Materials
Courage Box handout (in digital content)
Box with lid
Scissors
Pencil
String

Preparation
Make a class Courage Box. Cut a hole in the top of a shoebox or other lidded box, and attach a pencil to the box with string. Print several copies of the Courage Box handout and cut them in half. Place the box and a stack of Courage Box slips somewhere in your classroom.

Directions
Show kids the Courage Box and one of the slips as an example. Invite students to watch for acts of courage among their classmates and other people in their lives. Remind kids that courageous acts aren't always big or showy. Sometimes it takes courage to say hello to a new student, to try out for a play or a sports team, or to speak up for another person.

Explain to the group that when they notice other people showing courage, they can secretly fill out Courage Box slips and put them in the box. Then, depending on how quickly your Courage Box fills up, you can choose a slip once a week or once a month and read it aloud to the class. Invite students to talk about the story, what happened, and how the person showed courage.

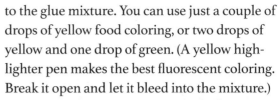

Activity 2: Saying Thanks

Materials

Notebook paper or construction paper
Pencils, crayons, and/or markers

Directions

Invite kids to write thank-you notes for gifts of caring, rather than for gifts of physical things. Ask students to think of people who have stood up for them, taken a chance for them, or said nice things to them. Then ask kids to write thank-you notes or cards to these people. They might be parents, friends, teachers, school principals, or others. Guide kids to include the following in their notes:

- a description of what the other person did

- an explanation of how this kind or caring action affected the note writer

- a "thank you" and the note writer's name

Allow kids to decorate their notes, if desired. Then encourage them to deliver these notes. Afterward, ask them how it felt to say thanks. What was it like to think of caring as a gift? Do they think people expect thanks for these kinds of acts?

Activity 3: Radioactive Slime!

Materials

2 bowls or measuring cups
Hot water
Borax
School glue gel (4 oz.)
Food coloring (yellow, green, or both)
Optional: Yellow highlighter pen
Optional: Plastic bag

Preparation

Before beginning this activity with your group, create slime ahead of time with a few simple ingredients and the following procedure:

- Measure out ½ cup of hot water in a bowl or measuring cup. Little by little, stir borax into the water. Continue adding and stirring until the borax stops dissolving.

- Measure out 1 cup of hot water in a second, larger bowl or measuring cup. Stir 4 ounces of glue gel into the water. Add a few drops of food coloring

to the glue mixture. You can use just a couple of drops of yellow food coloring, or two drops of yellow and one drop of green. (A yellow highlighter pen makes the best fluorescent coloring. Break it open and let it bleed into the mixture.)

- Mix ⅓ cup of the borax solution with 1 cup of the glue solution. When they combine, you'll create a gooey, slimy mixture. The food coloring will make it look slightly glow-y and radioactive. *Note:* When you mix the glue and borax solutions together, a chemical change happens in the glue. It causes the glue to stick to you less and to stick to itself more.

- If you don't plan to use the slime for a while, you can store it in a sealed plastic bag to keep it from drying out.

Directions

When you show the slime to your group, tell them that you have a great new product. It's a special glue that might even be used to hold together cars, planes, and rockets. The only trouble is that it's slightly radioactive. Explain that this means that if you touch it, you could get sick. (Depending on your group, you can elaborate on this idea as much or as little as desired.)

Variation: To reinforce the idea of the "radioactive" slime as dangerous, you could wear plastic gloves and safety glasses while you show your group the slime.

Invite a volunteer to touch the slime—but only briefly. You may or may not get any volunteers! If you do, urge them to wash their hands right away after touching the slime.

Carry this deception as far as you feel is appropriate for your group. Then let kids in on your secret. Tell them that, instead of being dangerous, the ingredients in the slime are actually harmless and even useful. Once kids have learned the truth, invite them to share how they felt about the slime before, and how they feel now. Use this as a starting point to talk about how an untruth or a misconception can sometimes lead people to shrink away from something or someone. Encourage kids to consider analogies to prejudice and discrimination, which often begin with false impressions and inaccurate information.

LESSON 20
QUAKING ASPEN TREES

Key Words

The behaviors, traits, and emotions below are just starting points for aligning SEL, character education, and this lesson's story. Most of these ideas can easily be connected with more than one competency or domain.

Self-Awareness: Inner Strength

Self-Management: Adaptability • Healthy Habits • Integrity • Self-Regulation

Social Awareness: Caring and Kindness

Relationship Skills: Bullying Prevention • Cooperation, Collaboration, and Teamwork

Responsible Decision-Making: Problem-Solving

Students will

- 👁 learn interesting facts about the quaking aspen tree, including about a huge, inter-connected grove of aspen called Pando, and make comparisons to human behavior
- 👁 draw connections between the aspen's connected roots and cooperation and adaptability among people
- 👁 compare aspen trees to people who may not be physically strong but who have self-control, integrity, and inner strength

Overview

Standing on the rolling hills of Utah's Fishlake National Forest is a colony of more than 45,000 aspen trees, their delicate leaves fluttering in the wind. The colony's massive root system dates back an estimated 80,000 years. Together, this huge aspen grove—known by names such as Pando and the Trembling Giant—is believed to be among the largest and oldest living organisms on the planet.

With their prolific growth and great longevity, aspen trees are models of survival and adaptability. They derive much of their success from the interconnectedness of their roots, all of which belong to a single plant. This underground root system continues to send up new shoots even as old ones die. The trees themselves are slender and delicate. But together, they have strength. Similarly, people gain strength from cooperation, teamwork, self-regulation, and integrity— whether in classrooms, families, or communities. These emotions and traits can make people stronger and healthier as a group than they would be as individuals.

Story

Quaking Aspen Trees

QUAKING ASPEN TREES

It is one of the world's largest living things. Experts think it weighs more than 13 million pounds. (No one knows for sure. There's no scale big enough to weigh it!) Any guesses? It's not a massive polar bear. It's not a blue whale. It's not a giant redwood. But it *is* a tree.

It's called Pando. Pando is a grove of quaking aspen trees in Fishlake National Forest in Utah. It covers more than 100 acres and has about 47,000 aspen tree trunks. Pando lives up to its name. The word *pando* means "I spread" in Latin. Sometimes people also call it the Trembling Giant. When the wind blows, it looks like the whole forest is trembling. Delicate aspen leaves flutter in the breeze. They make a beautiful rustling sound. In the fall, the leaves turn bright yellow. They float to the ground like golden coins.

How can a tree grow to be one of the world's largest living things? Aspen trees grow very fast. But that isn't the answer. Pando's real secret? Its thousands of trunks may look separate, but they all belong to one big plant. A huge underground root system connects them. Each trunk is like a branch on a giant tree. Scientists think this root system is at least 80,000 years old. That makes it one of the world's *oldest* living things too.

These ancient roots keep Pando alive. Sometimes windstorms or wildfires rip through the forest. Individual aspen trunks die. Yet below the surface, the roots survive. Soon they start sending up new shoots. They bring hope that the forest will live on.

But now Pando is in trouble. Many branches are dying. And not many new ones are growing.

Maybe the huge plant is just getting old. Another problem could be the trees' neighbors. Forest animals like the mule deer and

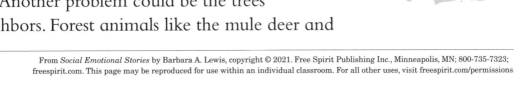

elk eat the tree's young shoots. Many new branches never get a chance to grow tall. Once, wolves roamed the forest. They kept down the number of deer and elk. But the area has few wolves now. Other animals gnaw on the aspens' white bark. Beetles and other insects sometimes harm the trees.

Experts have also found another culprit that could be harming Pando: cattle that roam right up to the plant's edges. The cows trample the aspen's roots and eat its vegetation. Scientists say that cattle should graze farther away for five years to see if this helps Pando recover.

Pando has adapted to changes and challenges many times during its long, long life. Can Pando save itself this time? Or does it need help? No one wants this natural wonder to fade away. So many people are thinking about how to rescue Pando. How do *you* think we could help Pando?

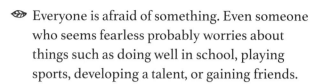

QUAKING ASPEN FACTS

- Several quaking aspen groves often grow in the same area. You can tell which trunks are in the same family by looking for similarities such as the shape of their trunks.

- Quaking aspen trees grow in all but thirteen of the US states and in all the provinces of Canada.

- Several different Native American tribes have traditionally used aspen bark to treat various injuries and sicknesses.

TALK IT OVER

Use these questions to guide your students in considering analogies between quaking aspen trees and cooperation, inner strength, and other emotions and behaviors in people.

The word *pando* means "I spread" in Latin. What connections can you draw between the spread of aspen trees across the hillsides and things that can spread among people?

- Rumors and name-calling can spread rapidly, and they can be very hurtful. The sooner they're stopped, the better.

- Friendliness and happiness can spread quickly too. If you're kind to people, they may pass along that kindness to others.

- Diseases and viruses can spread quickly if people are not careful.

Aspen trees have delicate leaves that tremble in the breeze. The trees may look delicate, but Pando is strong. Can you compare this to examples of how sometimes people or things might appear to be weak but are actually strong?

- Strength comes in many forms. Physical strength is only one. Self-control, integrity, and adaptability are all forms of inner strength.

- Everyone is afraid of something. Even someone who seems fearless probably worries about things such as doing well in school, playing sports, developing a talent, or gaining friends.

- Fear itself is not weakness. For example, sometimes fear helps us stay safe. If you are in a situation or place that is causing you to feel scared, get away or get help.

- A person's size does not determine how strong, brave, or kind they are.

Aspen trees face threats such as animals and insects that eat or damage the bark. Sometimes the trees rot inside. Can you make a comparison to habits and experiences that people have that might weaken their inner strength?

- People can damage their happiness and sense of peace by being filled with anger, hatred, or negative thoughts.

- Not eating nutritious foods, exercising regularly, or practicing other healthy habits can cause you to be sick inside, physically and mentally. When your body doesn't feel healthy, it is sometimes easier to become angry or fearful.

- If you use harmful substances—such as drugs, alcohol, or smoking products—you can become sick or addicted. It's important to have self-control to avoid these temptations.

The secret behind Pando's long life is the underground root system connecting all its trunks. How does this connectedness relate to people and their communities?

- A strong root system is like a family. When family members or close-knit groups support, help, and respect each other, the family or group is stronger as a whole.

- If you are grounded by managing your emotions and focusing on positive behavior, you will be stronger when you face challenges in life. You can also share your strength with others by helping them face challenges.

- When families, friends, classes, teams, and communities agree on shared goals, they reach them more easily. They help each other work toward these goals.

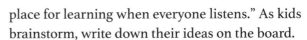

👁 Having integrity means that your actions are deeply connected with your values and beliefs. You don't change your behavior to please others. You have inner strength. You are trustworthy, consistent, and dependable.

The Pando aspen grove has adapted to many changes over the years. It may be able to rescue itself again, or it might need help. Can you compare this adaptability to the behavior of people?

👁 When you learn that you are doing something wrong, you need to be able to adapt. You can try to solve or minimize the problem by learning a new way to behave or a different way to approach a challenge.

👁 Times change. The world changes. Lives change. People often need to adapt to new conditions, such as moving to a new school, having new family members, and so on.

👁 Anytime you have a problem, you'll have more success solving the problem if you can be flexible and adaptable. Coping with change can be hard, but it's a good ability to have.

👁 Adaptability is a useful and positive skill. But everyone needs help sometimes too. Knowing when to ask others for help is also a good skill.

ACTIVITIES

Activity 1: The Cooperation Tree

Materials

Cooperation Tree handout (in digital content)
Optional: Aspen Leaf handout (in digital content)
Colored pencils
Optional: Chart paper or a bulletin board
Optional: Yarn or construction paper
Optional: Kid-safe scissors

Directions

Create a list of guidelines, goals, and rules for your class. Discuss with your group the kinds of rules that would help your classroom become an even better place to learn. Focus the conversation on cooperation, helpfulness, and mutual support and respect. For example, "Our classroom is a better

place for learning when everyone listens." As kids brainstorm, write down their ideas on the board.

Together, choose six to ten rules for your class to focus on. Pass out copies of the Cooperation Tree handout and have kids fill in the leaves with the guidelines and rules your group has chosen. Kids can also decorate the leaves or color them if they like.

Variation: Create a large Cooperation Tree in your space. On chart paper or a bulletin board, draw an outline of a bare tree or create one out of yarn or construction paper. Pass out copies of the Aspen Leaf handout and ask kids to decorate the leaves, write their names on them, and cut them out. Have some kids write the rules you've chosen on leaves, or write them yourself. Then attach all the leaves to the "tree."

Activity 2: Standing Strong

Materials

None

Directions

Have kids stand with their eyes closed (if they feel safe this way) and with their arms up in the air. If you can, have children all face away from each other so that even if some students keep their eyes open, no one can observe how the others respond during this activity. This is a nice introduction to self-awareness as an important social and emotional skill. It is not so much about "right or wrong" as it is about recognizing and accepting where they are in development.

Ask children to pretend that they are aspens in the Pando grove, and their fingers are their leaves. Next, make statements that address and test integrity. Some should be positive, and some negative. For example, *I have stood up for someone who was being bullied.* Or, *Sometimes I have told lies.* Tell kids to wiggle their fingers like Pando's trembling leaves if the statement is true for them. If the statement does not apply to them, they should hold their hands still. Remind them that no one will be watching how they answer, and assure them that you won't tell anyone, either.

After most kids have wiggled their fingers a few times, ask them all to open their eyes and sit in a circle. Without singling anyone out, ask kids to

think and talk about whether they would have felt afraid or embarrassed to answer honestly if their classmates could see them. Discuss the idea that integrity can be described as doing what you know is right, even if no one else sees or knows about it.

Pick a topic from one of the statements you made during the activity, such as honesty, and focus on this idea for a while. Ask kids if they think it would be easier to tell the truth if they knew the people around them were all truthful too. Discuss the way it can be easier to stick to our values when the people around us support our positive character traits and behaviors. Having support from the outside can strengthen our integrity. But we can also draw strength from ourselves, like Pando draws strength from its roots, by staying connected to our own values and beliefs, even when other people might disagree or make fun of us for doing so.

Activity 3: Connecting the Circuit

Materials
Flashlight bulb or small globe bulb
Size D battery
8–12 inches of copper wire
Wire cutters or scissors
Electrical or duct tape

Preparation
Make a simple circuit. First, cut the wire in half. Use scissors to scrape off about 1 inch of the plastic insulation at each end of both wires. Cut two small pieces of tape. Tape the end of one wire to the bottom (negative) terminal of the battery. Tape one end of the other wire to the top, or positive, terminal of the battery.

Test your circuit. Touch the end of the negative-terminal wire to the threading around the light bulb's base. (This is one of the bulb's terminals.) Finally, to complete the circuit, touch the other wire (connected to the battery's positive terminal) to the foot of the lightbulb. The light should come on.

Directions
Begin this demonstration with the wires attached to the battery but not the bulb. Show kids that when you connect all parts of the circuit by touching the wires to the right points on the bulb, the light comes on. Electricity is flowing through the wires between the battery and the bulb. But if any part is disconnected, the circuit is broken. The light goes out. Invite volunteers to try connecting and breaking the circuit for themselves.

Talk with the group about how these ideas apply to people. For example, when everyone in a family, classroom, or other group cooperates and works together, it's like the circuit is connected. Sometimes you have to adapt and use self-control to follow group goals. While it's not always easy to do this, it helps things go more smoothly. But if some people are not cooperating or doing their share of the work, it can break the "circuit" by disrupting the group.

Similarly, every person has their own set of values and beliefs. When we act according to those beliefs, we show integrity. We feel whole, as though our internal circuit is connected. But when we do things that go against our positive values, it's like we're breaking the circuit. We may feel uncomfortable or sad. Ask kids to talk about these ideas. When have they showed integrity and kept the circuit connected? How does it feel? Why is it hard to do this sometimes?

LESSON 21
SQUIRRELS

Key Words

The behaviors, traits, and emotions below are just starting points for aligning SEL, character education, and this lesson's story. Most of these ideas can easily be connected with more than one competency or domain.

Self-Awareness: Courage and Boldness • Curiosity

Self-Management: Goal-Setting • Hard Work • Organization and Self-Motivation • Planning and Preparation • Trust and Trustworthiness

Social Awareness: Empathy • Perspective-Taking • Service to Others

Relationship Skills: Communication • Helpfulness

Responsible Decision-Making: Conservation • Problem-Solving • Wisdom and Learning

Students will

- learn about squirrels and some of their characteristics, including their hardworking nature and their behavior of gathering and storing food
- analyze the value of being prepared for the future, and discuss the idea that even when people try to prepare, they may need help
- create an analogy between the squirrel's curiosity and people's desire to learn
- connect the squirrel's dependence on nature's abundance to the way people also depend on nature to support life

Overview

People seem either to love squirrels or loathe them. Squirrels' industry and energy set a great example. But their curiosity and boldness can sometimes cause headaches for gardeners, homeowners, and bird watchers. However, the planning, organizational skills, and hard-working behavior of squirrels provide a great segue to discussing SEL skills including self-management, hard work, curiosity, and preparation. The story will also spark empathy for the hungry little red squirrel that gets its food stolen and may inspire students to help or share with others.

The squirrel's story and habits connect to conservation as well. Gray squirrels bury thousands of nuts in a season. Their lives depend in large part upon nature's plenty. And they give back to the planet's natural resources. When they forget where to find or forget hidden caches of food, some of the buried nuts may grow into trees, helping replenish and maintain forests. Squirrels serve as a reminder that people need to respect nature and help preserve its diversity.

Story

Spirited Squirrels

SPIRITED SQUIRRELS

Once there was an old man who lived in a stone house in the mountains. His friends were the animals. He would call to them, "Klk, klk, klk. Come, my wild friends." Shy deer, bold moose, black-winged magpies, and a small red tree squirrel came to eat from his gnarled hands.

The red tree squirrel lived in a fir tree with branches that sagged over the old man's porch. The man scattered seeds for the birds, but he hid special peanuts behind a shovel for the little squirrel. The squirrel kept her biggest cache of seeds and nuts in a tall metal can on the old man's back porch. She worked very hard through the summer and filled the can to its brim.

"Klk, klk, klk," the man called, and the feisty squirrel jumped from a tree branch right into his arms. The old man chuckled as she ate nuts out of his pockets. Then she took a few more and scurried off to hide them in the metal can.

One autumn night raccoons rummaged noisily on the old man's back porch. When sunlight spilled through his window, the man heard the small squirrel's shrill cry. "Chchchchchchchchh!" She had discovered that the raccoons had tipped over her cache in the night and stolen all her food. She faced starvation in the snowy months ahead.

The man scooped her into his hands and whispered, "I'm sorry, little one. I know how hard you worked."

The small squirrel ignored his comforting words and wiggled to get away.

The man whispered again. "Don't you know that I am the one who put all those nuts behind the shovel in the first place? Trust me. I won't let you starve." The squirrel squirmed harder, screeched, and bit his finger, as though blaming him for not protecting her cache.

Surprised, the man gently put her down and wrapped a bandage around his finger. A big tear rolled down his cheek—partly because the squirrel's food had been stolen, but even more because she didn't trust him after all this time.

The little red squirrel kept right on screeching into the winter. The wind howled. Snow swirled and sifted down like powdered sugar over the stone house, and into the empty metal can on the porch. As icicles grew thicker from the eaves of the stone house, the red squirrel grew thinner in her nest.

She missed the man's soft voice. She wished that she hadn't bitten him. She called weakly for his help, "Chcht . . . chcht." But thunder suddenly crashed, smothering her faint cries.

But the wind picked up the squirrel's cries and carried her plea to the old man. He had sharp ears and knew the voice of his small friend. He smiled broadly. After the storm had passed, he placed fresh nuts in the metal can. Then he called her. "Klk . . . klk . . . klk."

The small squirrel pricked her ears. She gathered her strength and struggled through the snow to the metal can. The man stood there, holding peanuts in his gnarled hands. She rubbed her nose against his fingers.

Each day for the rest of the winter, she found the metal can filled with nuts again. She grew plump. In the spring she had two downy babies. Thanks to her cache, she was able to feed them and herself.

As aspen trees threw out light green leaves, the old man called his wild friends, "Klk, klk, klk." Shy deer, bold moose, black-winged magpies, and the small, red tree squirrel trusted his gentle voice and came again to eat from his hands. The old man scattered seeds for the birds, but he hid peanuts behind a shovel for the special little squirrel.

Sometimes the man put a peanut in his shirt pocket. The little squirrel scampered up his long white beard to snatch the nut. And sometimes she nestled in his pocket, next to his beating heart, and fell asleep.

SQUIRREL FACTS

- Squirrels live on every continent except Australia and Antarctica. There are more than 275 different species of squirrels.

- Squirrels communicate with body language such as stamping their feet or twitching their tails. They also communicate with sounds.

- In the summer and fall, squirrels spend lots of time busily gathering food. They work hard to store food for the winter. They bury nuts and other food in hundreds of different spots. That's a lot to remember! Scientists have learned that gray squirrels can't always find some of their stashed food. That's bad news for the squirrel. But it can be good for the planet. Some of the nuts that squirrels forget or lose can grow into trees.

- Squirrels can be sneaky with their food. If a squirrel notices that someone is watching, he may pretend to bury a nut. But he really keeps it in his cheek. Then he moves out of sight and buries it somewhere else.

TALK IT OVER

Use these questions to guide your students in considering analogies between squirrel behavior and curiosity, preparation, organization, empathy, and other traits and behaviors in people.

Squirrels work very hard to make their nests and to gather and store food for the winter. The little red squirrel needed help from the man when her cache was stolen. In turn, the man felt empathy for the squirrel's bad luck. Can you compare these behaviors and emotions to humans' actions and feelings?

- Family members often work hard to care for and support each other. Kids can help with chores at home and in the classroom. When everyone pitches in, tasks can get done more quickly.

- Like the little squirrel, sometimes people need help to get through tough times. We can help people and animals who might need food. It's also important to be sure we're providing people and animals with healthful, nutritious food.

- Planning and preparing for the future doesn't always mean saving money, food, or other supplies. It can mean studying hard and making other good decisions.

- Working to reach a goal can be difficult or tiring, but it's also rewarding. And even when we don't meet our goal, we can learn from our experience.

Squirrels bury so many nuts each season that they lose track of some of them. But that's not all bad. Some of these nuts grow into trees, which helps restore forests. Can you think of ways that you can help the environment too?

- You can use less paper, water, and electricity every day. You can also recycle paper, cans, plastic, and other materials from your classroom, lunchroom, and home.

- You can help animals by feeding them and caring for them. For example, you could volunteer at local animal shelters, or put out nuts and seeds for squirrels and birds in the winter. (*Note:* It's important to gather information before putting out food. Some areas have restrictions on feeding wild animals, and not all foods are healthy for those animals.)

- You can help animals that are endangered. You could raise money for organizations that help protect threatened animals. Also, you could learn about these animals and share that information with other people. Knowing more about a problem often inspires people to take action.

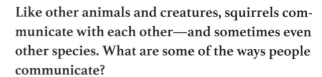

👁 You can help plant trees. Trees help clean the air, provide homes for animals, and prevent erosion.

👁 You can be sure never to litter. You can also help clean up trash in rivers, lakes, and other areas.

Squirrels are very good at remembering where they stored nuts and other food, but it can still be hard for them to keep track of all their hundreds of storage spots. Sometimes people have trouble remembering things too. How can we help ourselves organize, remember, and prepare for what we need to do?

👁 Write down homework assignments in a binder or notebook each day. Read your list when you get home to remind yourself of what you need to do.

👁 Before you leave for school in the morning, double-check that you have everything you need for the day.

👁 If there are tasks that are your responsibility at home, make a list of them each day or week.

👁 If you're working on a big paper, dance routine, or other project, sometimes it can feel overwhelming at first. You can try breaking down the big project into smaller steps. Then you can check off each step as you get it done and move on to the next one.

Squirrels are curious and persistent. They can get into chimneys, attics, walls, and even cars. Their curiosity also leads them to taste just about any sort of food they find. Can you compare this to people who are curious? Is curiosity positive, negative, or both? How so?

👁 Curiosity can often lead to discovery. When you're curious about something, your brain is active and learning.

👁 Curiosity has inspired people to discover cures for diseases, create inventions, and develop new ideas that change the world.

👁 Curiosity can be dangerous if it leads you to practice harmful habits or get involved in risky situations. Be careful that your curiosity doesn't cause you to go against your values or the behaviors you know are positive.

Like other animals and creatures, squirrels communicate with each other—and sometimes even other species. What are some of the ways people communicate?

👁 Like squirrels, people communicate with their voices. But we don't only do this with words. We also share meaning through the volume and inflection of our voices. For example, someone might be really mad and say something like, "Everything is fine." The words say one thing, but a tone of sarcasm or anger in the voice might communicate just the opposite.

👁 People also communicate with body language and facial expressions, including the way we move, stand, or gesture.

👁 People sometimes communicate through their emotions. Have you ever looked into someone's eyes and known they were sad? How do you think people can show and understand feelings without saying a word?

ACTIVITIES

Activity 1: Squirrel Snacks

Materials
Wooden boxes, tin cans, or other containers
Nuts and seeds

Directions
Even with all their preparation, sometimes squirrels don't have enough food to last them through the winter. Your class can help squirrels, birds, chipmunks, and other animals by making and setting out wildlife feeders. (Be sure to confirm that this is allowed in your area, and use raw food that is in the animals' natural diet.) In the course of this activity, your group can also talk about the importance of helping people in need.

You can find instructions for making a variety of simple wildlife feeders at the following website: birdsandblooms.com/Backyard-Projects /Bird-Feeders. Work together as a class to make and decorate the feeder (or more than one feeder, if you like). Finally, fill the feeder with raw seeds, nuts, or other wildlife-friendly food, and hang it up.

If possible, place it where you can see it from your classroom. If that's not an option, once a day or so, take kids to a spot where they can see the feeder. Kids will love watching animals visit the feeder to eat.

Talk with children about this experience. How did it feel to help some of the animals in your neighborhood? Would they like to take this action at home too? What are other ways they could help local wildlife? Discuss the idea that service does not have to be dramatic or have a wide scope to be important and helpful. Small actions can make a big difference too.

Note: Be sure to remind your group that squirrels, songbirds, chipmunks, and other wild animals are not pets. They can act unpredictably. It's better for wild animals and for us if we keep a safe distance from each other.

Activity 2: Planting Curiosity

Materials
Planting Curiosity handout (in digital content)

Directions
Kids are curious about many things, and curiosity can stimulate the brain and support learning. But kids don't always follow up these interests by looking into them more deeply. This activity encourages them to choose topics of curiosity and pursue them in a more focused and intentional way.

Pass out copies of the Planting Curiosity handout. Invite kids to brainstorm three things that they're curious about and about which they'd like to learn more. *Note:* If helpful, encourage them to phrase their ideas as questions. For example, "How do flying squirrels glide?" Or, "What more can I learn about Mars?"

Ask kids to write one curiosity starting point on each buried acorn, and then to choose one of these three ideas to serve as the basis for a research project. Tell them that a little seed of curiosity can be the start of something big. Just as squirrels help forests thrive by "planting" nuts, kids can use their curiosity questions to expand their knowledge and interests.

If desired, send notes home with kids to let families know about the project and encouraging them to help kids search for information about their topics. Set a due date for the research, and ask kids to report their findings to the class. But also remind them that this due date doesn't have to be the end of their exploration. It could be just the beginning. Maybe as kids answer some questions, they also might find new ones to wonder about. Curiosity can grow and grow.

Activity 3: A Plan to Help Out with Hunger

Materials
Various

Directions
Squirrels gather and organize as much food as they can, but sometimes they still go hungry during a long winter. When that happens, they need help. Talk with kids about how people around the world also struggle with hunger, and explain that they need help too. Discuss the problem of hunger in faraway places and also in your own community. Then brainstorm a list of ways that your group can help fight hunger, close to home and beyond. Ideas could include holding a fundraiser and sending the funds to an international organization fighting global hunger, volunteering at a food shelf, donating canned goods to a local shelter, or planting a community garden to help grow food for people who need it.

Choose one idea to put into action. Before getting started, talk with kids about the importance of planning and preparation in carrying out your project. As a group, create a plan with specific steps and goals. This project could extend over weeks or even months, depending on your group's age, interests, and resources. Whatever service you decide to undertake, create a detailed plan and recruit help from parents or other volunteers as needed. When you've completed your project, ask each student to write a short essay, story, or poem about the experience, or to draw a picture showing part of the action your group took. If desired, you could compile these pieces into a booklet that kids can share with family and friends.

LESSON 22
TURKEYS

Key Words

The behaviors, traits, and emotions below are just starting points for aligning SEL, character education, and this lesson's story. Most of these ideas can easily be connected with more than one competency or domain.

Self-Awareness: Inner Strength • Self-Confidence

Self-Management: Responsibility

Social Awareness: Acceptance of Others • Fairness and Equality • Perspective-Taking • Reading Social Cues • Respect

Relationship Skills: Bullying Prevention • Citizenship • Cooperation, Collaboration, and Teamwork • Leadership

Responsible Decision-Making: Positive and Ethical Choices

Students will

- learn interesting facts about turkeys, such as differences between farm turkeys and wild turkeys, and draw comparisons to human behaviors

- compare false stereotypes about turkeys to the way people sometimes stereotype each other, and draw comparisons between the lack of respect many people show for turkeys to people who display a lack of respect for others and who might bully people

- gain awareness of other people's perspectives, build respect for others, and learn to work together

- develop greater ability to interpret social cues from people who are different in order to better understand their feelings and needs

- examine the social habits of turkeys and their responsible care of their young, and compare these attributes to people who take civic responsibility to care for others

Overview

The word *turkey* refers to a species of birds, but it is also sometimes used as an insult. But while many people believe that turkeys are unintelligent, slow, and awkward, they are in fact quite bright. And while overfed farm turkeys are flightless and may live in very unpleasant conditions, wild turkeys are agile fliers and have interesting social habits and family structures. Turkeys share responsibilities in caring for their young and live in social groups. Exploring these traits can provide your group with opportunities to discuss the importance of responsibility, teamwork, citizenship, and leadership.

These contrasts between wild turkeys and farm turkeys may also give you and your students excellent starting points for learning to develop social skills, such as respect, acceptance, and fairness.

Story

Terrific Turkeys

TERRIFIC TURKEYS

"How can I soar with the eagles when I'm surrounded by turkeys?"

"What a turkey!"

"Oh, boy. I feel as dumb as a turkey."

Have you ever heard insults like these? It seems like turkeys get a bad rap. Even the thesaurus isn't very nice to them. *Birdbrain. Buffoon. Simpleton. Twerp.* These are just a few of the synonyms it gives for *turkey*.

But are turkeys *really* dumb?

Experts say turkeys are actually smart, social birds. Some of the false ideas people have about turkeys come from the way the birds are raised on farms. Farm turkeys are fed until they weigh twice as much as their wild cousins. These turkeys get too heavy to fly. But they still have the instinct to take flight. They may run and flap their wings hopelessly, never leaving the ground. These turkeys may appear awkward, comical, and not very bright.

In the wild, things are different. Wild turkeys can fly at speeds of 50 miles per hour. That's almost as fast as a car on the highway! And wild turkeys are fast on land too. They can run up to 25 miles per hour.

Maybe you've heard another story about turkeys. People say the birds look up while it's raining. Then they keep staring upward until they drown. That doesn't sound too smart, does it? But is it true? Turkeys *do* sometimes stare at the sky, even when it rains. But they aren't cuckoo. A medical condition causes some turkeys to do this. They can't help it. And most experts don't think that turkeys really drown this way.

Some people also think that turkeys aren't very bright because young farm turkeys sometimes starve, even when there's food nearby. How does this happen? In the wild, adult turkeys teach youngsters how to find and eat food. But on many farms, turkeys don't live with their families. Instead, they may be crowded into dark, smelly sheds. Young turkeys are separated from their parents. They don't learn by watching grown-up turkeys. So sometimes these young birds can't find food and water. They're not dumb. They're just alone and confused.

Wild turkeys are rarely alone. Before a turkey chick even hatches from its egg, it can hear its mother's voice. After hatching, the baby turkey can walk and leave the nest almost right away. But chicks stay with the flock. Young turkeys sleep on the ground, snuggled under their mothers' wings. Later, they fly to roost on low tree branches. Female turkeys, called hens, share the job of caring for chicks and showing them how to find food.

Sometimes, as a young turkey scampers around and hunts bugs, he might lose track of where his mother is. Then the young turkey raises his head high and calls out loudly. He listens for his mother's answer. They call until they find each other. Sometimes the whole flock may stop until mother and baby reunite.

As youngsters grow up, they stay in groups. Wild turkeys are very social. They feel safest when they're with other turkeys. During summer and fall, turkey hens that have chicks stick together. Older hens flock with each other. Older male gobblers hang out together too, while spirited, spunky young males form noisy groups of their own.

It seems like smart, social turkeys deserve more respect than people usually give them. And in the United States, people have an extra reason to care about turkeys. In the 1600s, Native Americans introduced turkeys to pilgrims in North America. Those were hard times for the new settlers. Eating turkeys helped people survive. Now, some people see the turkey as a traditional Thanksgiving symbol of family, love, and togetherness.

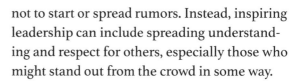

TURKEY FACTS

- A male turkey's distinctive gobbling call can be heard a mile away.

- The flap of skin under a turkey's chin is called a wattle. It changes color when the turkey is frightened, aggressive, or sick, or when he is courting a female.

- Benjamin Franklin once wrote that he wished the wild turkey would become the national bird of the United States instead of the bald eagle. He described the turkey as "a Bird of Courage."

TALK IT OVER

Use these questions to guide your students in considering social and emotional needs and in making connections between turkeys and character traits and behaviors in people, such as respect, fairness, and acceptance.

Sometimes people use the word *turkey* as an insult. But turkeys are smart, social birds. What connections can you draw between this false labeling of turkeys and ways that people might treat others?

- Name-calling is hurtful and unkind. If it happens over and over again, it can be a form of bullying. Bullying is never okay. If you are being bullied or you know someone who is, tell a grown-up.

- If someone calls you a turkey, it doesn't make you a turkey—any more than calling you a toad makes you a toad. It's hard to ignore mean and hurtful words. But if you can refuse to believe unkind things that someone says about you, you will get stronger and more confident over time.

- Rumors can spread faster than wildfire. If a lot of people believe a rumor, someone may end up with an unfairly charred reputation. It's best

not to start or spread rumors. Instead, inspiring leadership can include spreading understanding and respect for others, especially those who might stand out from the crowd in some way.

- Sometimes turkeys on farms flap their wings awkwardly in an instinctive attempt to fly. Similarly, sometimes people look unsure or awkward as they work toward difficult goals. We *all* make mistakes and we all look silly sometimes. But everyone deserves respect.

- We can't always know what challenges people have just by looking at them. It's important never to make assumptions about others, and to be kind and respectful to all people.

Turkeys are associated with negative stereotypes that are mostly untrue. On the flip side, sometimes people such as athletes and movie stars are associated with positive stereotypes. These aren't always true, either. What are some of the risks of stereotyping or labeling people in any way?

- Sometimes idolizing a person can lead to disappointment if you find out that your hero is not what they appear to be.

- A negative stereotype of a group of people transfers a bad reputation to everyone involved. It's important to have respect for every person as an individual. One example of poor behavior should not label a whole group. Everyone is different.

- If you stereotype a person and assume that they are a certain way, you might miss out on making a good friend or getting to know someone really interesting.

- In extreme situations, stereotyping and prejudice can lead to viewing an entire culture or group of people as less valuable than others. These negative and destructive ideas can lead to tragedies such as slavery and genocide (the attempt to destroy an entire group of people).

People who believe that turkeys are stupid are lacking accurate information. They make unfair assumptions about all turkeys. Do people have unfair ideas about each other too?

- 👁 Sometimes people use stereotypes to justify having false ideas about others. Stereotypes and prejudice are unfair.

- 👁 A person might dislike one person who has certain beliefs or a certain lifestyle. Sometimes they then transfer that dislike for this single person to *all* people who share those beliefs or lifestyle. But it isn't fair to lump everyone together like that. Just as all animals are different, so are people different, even when they might seem very similar. Everyone deserves respect as an individual.

Turkeys are very sociable and like to live in groups. Within these groups, they share some responsibilities. Can you compare this idea to the way people live in communities? How do people share responsibilities and show citizenship and membership in their communities?

- 👁 People have responsibilities in families to help each other. All members of a family have chores that need to be done. For example, small kids can put away toys. Older brothers and sisters may help take care of their younger siblings.

- 👁 Communities, states, and countries have organizations to help people who need homes, food, or other things.

- 👁 Within classrooms, students have different responsibilities that help keep the class running smoothly.

- 👁 People show responsibility and citizenship by following laws, taking part in the community, and understanding how the government works.

ACTIVITIES

Activity 1: Fair and Equal

Materials
None

Directions
Divide kids into two groups based on when their birthdays are. Place all kids with birthdays between January and May in one group and kids with birthdays between June and December in the other.

Declare that the kids born between January and May will have a leadership role in the class. Treat them a little bit specially for a period of time. For example:

- 👁 Seat them together in a certain section of your room.

- 👁 Tell them they'll be able to skip one of today's homework assignments.

- 👁 Ask them to line up first at lunchtime.

As the day progresses, keep a close eye on kids to see how they're reacting. End the exercise when you feel it's appropriate. Then gather your group in a circle and explain what was going on. Ask students in both groups to share how they felt about this experience. Discuss what it means to be fair and equal with everyone. Make sure that kids understand that everyone has unique skills and talents and that all people should be treated fairly. Brainstorm ways to be fair and equal in your class.

Activity 2: The Respect Report

Materials
None

Directions
Divide your group into pairs of students. Have each pair brainstorm a list of ways to show respect for different people, groups, and ideas. (For example: classmates, friends, parents, siblings, teachers, a school principal, coaches, laws, the environment.) Assign one person in each pair to write down their ideas and the other person to report to the big group.

When kids have had some time to work, ask the reporters to stand up and share their lists. Talk about the different ideas and the many ways we can show respect for others. Ask kids why respect is important. How does it feel when people respect us? What about when they show disrespect toward us? After the discussion, combine all the lists into one big list and create a classroom display.

Variation: To spread the message of respect beyond the classroom, you could send the list home to families in a newsletter. If your class has a website, you could post the list there.

Activity 3: Puppet Shows

Materials

Paper sacks (1 per student)

Crayons, markers, colored pencils

Yarn, buttons, colored paper, and other items for
  decorating puppets

School glue

Directions

Ask kids to make puppets out of paper sacks. Divide
the class into groups of two to four and ask kids to
create and perform short puppet shows acting out
situations in which characters show respect to each
other. For example, one group could show a student
or students being respectful to a teacher by speaking politely and following directions.

Activity 4: Links of Citizenship

Materials

Links of Citizenship handout (in digital content)

Kid-safe scissors

Tape

Optional: Colored pencils, markers, crayons

Directions

Turkeys take good care of their young. And within
their social groups, they share responsibilities. Talk
with kids about how this relates to ideas of citizenship and how people take care of each other and of
their communities too. For example, not littering is
one way to be a good citizen. As a group, brainstorm
acts of good citizenship.

Pass out copies of the Links of Citizenship
handout. Have each kid write one way to be a good
citizen on their link. (It's fine if there are duplicates.)
If desired, kids can color or decorate their links.
Then ask them to cut them out and help you make
a citizenship chain. Use tape to secure the links.

Explore the idea that, if everyone is a good citizen, we can build a strong community together. And
tell kids that the chain isn't complete yet. Whenever
they see someone being a good citizen, they can add
another link to the chain. Or, if they have new ideas
for acts of good citizenship, they can add those to
the chain too. Hang the chain somewhere in your
room and watch it grow and grow.

Activity 5: Respect and Connect

Materials

Chart paper and writing paper

Pencils and markers

Directions

Pass out writing paper and pencils. As a group, discuss the idea of "respect rules" that ensure everyone
in the classroom is treated with respect and that
no one is bullied. Next, ask children to individually
write down their ideas for respect rules. Then place
them in small groups and have them talk about
their ideas and decide which ones are the best
and would be most possible to enact. Come back
together as a full group and ask each small team
to read their "best of" list aloud. Write these top
ideas on a board or on chart paper. Here are some
important ideas you may want to include. If students don't make similar suggestions on their own,
you can guide them to consider these:

- We don't call people names.
- We don't scare other people.
- We include everyone who wants to join in a
  game or activity.
- We don't laugh at others' mistakes.
- We leave only kind messages online.
- We don't talk behind people's backs.

Finally, ask students to vote on three to five
rules that you'll all commit to following as a class.
Assign each small group one of the rules and have
them create a poster highlighting that rule and put
these posters up in your classroom. If you like, have
students talk to the school principal or other faculty
about placing their posters around the school.

LESSON 23
VENUS FLYTRAPS

Key Words

The behaviors, traits, and emotions below are just starting points for aligning SEL, character education, and this lesson's story. Most of these ideas can easily be connected with more than one competency or domain.

Self-Awareness: Curiosity • Fear • Imagination

Self-Management: Adaptability • Anger and Impulse Management • Responsibility • Self-Regulation

Social Awareness: Caring and Kindness • Perspective-Taking • Reading Social Cues

Relationship Skills: Conflict Management and Resolution • Friendship • Leadership • Resisting Social Pressure

Responsible Decision-Making: Positive and Ethical Choices • Problem-Solving • Safety • Understanding Consequences

Students will

- 👁 learn about the Venus flytrap and some of its characteristics, including the way it traps its prey
- 👁 draw comparisons between the Venus flytrap's adaptability and the need for people to adapt to new situations, which is a necessary skill for social and emotional growth
- 👁 create analogies between bugs that get caught by the Venus flytrap and the ways that self-management can protect people from dangerous situations or poor decisions, including negative social pressure
- 👁 consider the way the flytrap catches prey and draw connections to the need for people to have good decision-making skills and to take responsibility for their choices

Overview

Some writers and filmmakers have shown the Venus flytrap as a bloodthirsty monster because of its appetite for spiders and insects. But the Venus flytrap also presents a great opportunity for discussing social and emotional skills. Growing in the nutrient-poor soil of hot, humid bogs, the Venus flytrap developed its insectivorous diet as a way to obtain necessary nitrogen and other nutrients. Kids will be fascinated by this unusual plant and will enjoy making connections between flytraps—and their prey—and human behaviors such as self-control and accepting responsibility for the consequences of decisions.

Story

Snappy Venus Flytraps

SNAPPY VENUS FLYTRAPS

Have you ever heard of a movie star that's a plant?

Meet Audrey! She was the main character in a movie called *Little Shop of Horrors.* She was a gigantic Venus flytrap. Audrey had a big appetite. The monster plant would cry to her owner, "Feed me, Seymour!" And Audrey was picky about what she ate. Her favorite meal? *People.*

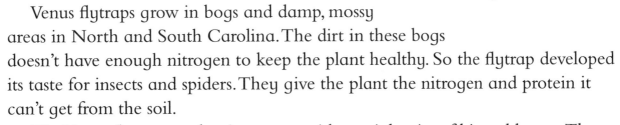

The Venus flytrap is a real plant. But don't worry. It's small, not huge. And it doesn't really eat people. It dines on insects and spiders. Still, don't try sticking your finger in a flytrap. *It* won't hurt *you.* But you could hurt or kill the plant.

Venus flytraps grow in bogs and damp, mossy areas in North and South Carolina. The dirt in these bogs doesn't have enough nitrogen to keep the plant healthy. So the flytrap developed its taste for insects and spiders. They give the plant the nitrogen and protein it can't get from the soil.

The Venus flytrap catches its supper with special pairs of hinged leaves. They look like sets of jaws, or very small bear traps. The edges of the leaves have long spikes. There are tiny hairs on the leaves of each trap. When a curious insect wanders along a leaf, it brushes against these hairs. The contact triggers the trap and the leaves clamp together. They snap shut faster than you can snap your fingers. Chomp!

It takes the plant about ten days to digest its unlucky prey. The flytrap makes chemicals that dissolve the trapped bug or spider. The plant absorbs nutrients from the prey's body.

The Venus flytrap gets its name from Venus, the Roman goddess of love. This might sound strange. After all, this toothy plant doesn't seem very loving. On the other hand, you *could* say that it really loves bugs.

VENUS FLYTRAP FACTS

- The leaves of the Venus flytrap produce a sweet nectar that attracts insects to the plant.

- In addition to capturing spiders and insects, Venus flytraps sometimes catch and digest small frogs.

- If a trap catches a falling leaf or something else that is not food for the plant, the trap will reopen in twelve to twenty-four hours.

TALK IT OVER

Use these questions to guide your students in considering analogies between Venus flytraps and self-regulation, positive decision-making, and other self-management and social behaviors in people.

The Venus flytrap adapted to living in boggy areas by eating insects. Can you make an analogy to the ways people show adaptability to changes in their lives?

👁 It can be hard to adapt to a new place or a new situation. Sometimes we need to come up with creative ways to deal with change. Creativity and imagination are part of emotional adaptability.

👁 People who have challenges in some areas of their lives can adapt to their situations and overcome these challenges. They can learn other skills to help them succeed.

👁 Sometimes we can help others adapt to new situations. For example, children can show leadership in helping new students adjust. They can take them around school, sit with them at lunch, and be friendly and kind to them.

Curious bugs that crawl along the Venus flytrap's hinged, spiny leaves may become lunch for the plant. Can you make a comparison to the way people act when they are curious? How can self-regulation help protect us from situations

that could become dangerous, such as giving in to negative social pressure?

👁 You might be curious about a new or unfamiliar place or activity. Curiosity is a natural emotion and can lead to exciting discoveries. But if you're not careful and don't make safe decisions, or if you don't exercise self-control, you might put yourself or someone else at risk. It's important to think carefully about your choices and consider the consequences.

👁 If you get too close to dangerous activities, you might be trapped and find it hard to escape. For example, if you try using smoking products, or if you spend time with people who get into fights, you could get caught up in a scary situation. Practice reading the facial cues and gestures of others to recognize emotions and behaviors like anger or deception. If you feel uneasy, leave. Remember to go to a trusted adult for help when you need it.

The Venus flytrap gets its name from the ancient Roman goddess of love. But in many ways, this plant doesn't seem exactly "loving." Do people ever make assumptions about others based on their names or appearances?

👁 Sometimes when we hear a person's name or learn about just one part of their life, we make assumptions about what the person is like. But everyone has different sides. One aspect of someone's personality is not the whole story.

👁 A person who seems very different from you at first might turn out to be a great friend. You can never be sure what people are like until you get to know them.

👁 Names and appearances can trick you. It's best not to make assumptions about people or places. What sounds good might be harmful, and what looks attractive might be danger in disguise.

The Venus flytrap can snag insects before the bugs know what has hit them. Can you compare this quick turn of events to the way people make decisions?

- Sometimes you might make a snap decision and then regret it. It's important to take responsibility for your choices, and use what you learn from your experiences to make better decisions next time.

- It's best not to flirt with fear and danger. If you get too close to danger, you might get hurt. Make positive decisions to keep yourself and others safe. And if you're not sure what to do, talk to a trusted adult.

- It's a good idea to think about possible consequences of an action before making a decision. Still, we can't always know or control what will happen, and we all make poor choices sometimes. It's part of being human.

ACTIVITIES

Activity 1: Social Dilemmas

Materials
None

Directions
Explain to kids that a dilemma is a situation in which you have more than one choice. These choices might be positive, negative, or a mixture of both. Difficult decisions occur when two positive choices seem to come into conflict with each other. Can you always be both honest and loyal, for example?

Discuss a few social dilemmas with your class. Ask how kids would react in each situation, and why. Explain that all choices have consequences, and that people need to take responsibility for their own choices. How can we know what the right decision is? *Is* there always a "right" decision? A few sample dilemmas follow. Feel free to add any others that you'd like.

- Your best friend cheats on a test. Should you stay loyal to your friend and not tell anyone, or should you be honest and tell the teacher? What are the possible consequences of each decision?

- You are home with your brother, and no grown-ups are home. You're writing a report about magnets. It's due tomorrow, and you've waited until the last minute to work on it. You don't have any books about magnets in the house, and it's too late to go to the library. You think you could find information online, though. You've always been taught to be responsible and get your homework done. But your mom has also told you never to use the internet unless an adult is home. You trust yourself to stay away from unsafe websites, but you'd still be breaking your mom's rule about not using the internet without a grown-up. What should you do? How can you be responsible about your homework and also obey your mom? If you can't do both, which do you think is more important?

- You're at a birthday party, and some of your friends are going to sneak away and watch a scary movie that they took from someone's older sister. They want you to come along. A little voice in your head tells you not to go. You have a bad feeling about it, but you don't know why. You really want to go with your friends, because you like them and you want them to like you. Plus, you're curious about what the movie will be like. Do you listen to that little voice, or do you go with your friends? What character traits are involved in making this decision? Are some of these traits in conflict with each other?

Variation: Hold a panel discussion about dilemmas. Ask three or four students to sit at the front of the room. Pose sample dilemmas to them and ask what each of them would do. Then invite kids in the audience to ask questions and share their own thoughts.

Activity 2: Flytrap Words

Materials
Slips of paper
Hat, bowl, or other container

Preparation
Play a game in which students have to give each other clues to guess certain words, without saying these target "Flytrap Words" themselves. For example, if Michaela is trying to get Cameron to guess

the word *flower*, Michaela could give hints such as *blossom* or *rose*. Or Michaela could go a different route and say *ingredient in bread*, to get Cameron to say the homonym, *flour*. This is a great game for encouraging teamwork and cooperation. It also can encourage self-management and self-regulation.

Before playing, write Flytrap Words on slips of paper. Choose enough words so that you have four for every two students. These don't have to be especially complicated or clever. Sometimes the simplest words and concepts can be the hardest to guess. If you like, some of your Flytrap Words could be related to the lesson. You could also mix in vocabulary or spelling words that your class is working on. For example, Flytrap Words might include *fly, happy, train, spider, stop sign, plant, writer, leaves, yellow, frog, ancient, magnet, teeth, neighborhood,* and *orange juice*. Fold the slips in half and place them all in a hat or other container.

Directions

Pair kids up and explain the idea behind the game. Tell them that each round will last two minutes, and kids will take turns being prompters and guessers. If the timer runs out for a round before the Flytrap Word is guessed, or if the prompting student says the Flytrap Word then, snap! The flytrap closes, and the team gets no points for that round. At the end of four rounds, whichever team has the most points is the winner.

Then walk around the room and ask one student from each pair to draw a slip and wait to look at it until you say it's time. When every team has a slip, start the timer for two minutes and tell the students with the slips that they can now look at their words and start giving clues.

You'll soon notice that the kids doing the prompting will have to control the urge to blurt out the answers, which can be especially difficult if it's taking other players a long time to guess correctly. In addition, with each round, kids will need to stay adaptable and flexible as they switch back and forth between being prompters and guessers.

After the game, ask kids if they found the game challenging. As prompter, how hard was it not to say the Flytrap Words? How hard was it to be the guesser? Which role did kids prefer, and

why? Discuss the fact that it's not always easy to show self-control, especially if we feel stressed or pressured in a situation. Talk about ways kids can practice and improve self-control in their lives, such as writing lists of tasks and priorities to help them decide whether they have time to watch a movie; setting a schedule for exercise, homework, or chores; or testing themselves by trying to go without something that tempts them (whether it's ice cream or video games) for a certain amount of time.

Activity 3: Flytrap Snaps

Materials

Venus flytrap

Pot

Peat moss

Sand

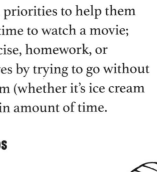

Preparation

Buy a Venus flytrap from a local nursery or online at sites such as petflytrap.com, flytrapstore.com, or californiacarnivores.com. *Note:* If you repot a Venus flytrap, do not use regular gardening soil, which can kill the plant. Venus flytraps grow best in a mixture of peat moss and sand, with no fertilizer. Also, water your flytrap with distilled water, rainwater, or reverse osmosis water, and be sure the pot allows the water to drain. Place the potted flytrap in your classroom.

Directions

Show students the toothy new addition to your classroom. Talk about how the Venus flytrap catches and digests its prey. Have kids take turns watering the plant. If desired, kids can also take turns catching insects and feeding them to the plant, or you can do this yourself. (*Note:* Warn kids never to put their fingers, or anything other than a small insect, into any of the plant's traps. They can hurt or even kill the plant or its traps this way.)

Once kids have had a few chances to observe the flytrap catching and digesting prey, you could also talk about the way it can be easy to get too close to danger when we're curious about something, someplace, or someone. You could then extend this analogy to explore the need to make good decisions and to be accountable for the consequences of our

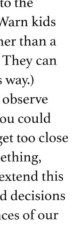

actions. You can also use the example of kids taking turns caring for the plant to discuss responsibility.

Watching the Venus flytrap in action will also help bring other social and emotional ideas and lessons to life. You might compare the flytrap's quick snap shut to how quickly someone can get angry. Snap! The wrong words come out in anger. Ask children to write down two or three times when they have "snapped" at someone out of anger, whether verbally or physically. What kinds of things tend to lead to these snaps? How do angry words or actions usually affect a situation? How do children feel after they snap?

On the other side of the paper, ask children to write down what they can do to prevent snapping or fighting. What words, thoughts, or actions could help them take charge of their emotions or redirect them in more productive ways? Children can share their intervention ideas about how to handle angry situations. As a group, you might develop these ideas into classroom guidelines and perhaps even set rewards for controlling angry outbursts.

Variation: If desired, you could introduce your group to the idea of peer mediation, a conflict resolution process that students mediate themselves. Students can learn the following steps of peer mediation and practice them through role-playing:

- **Introductions.** The mediator and disputants introduce themselves, and the mediator explains the guidelines for the process. (*Note:* Peer mediation must be voluntary and only works if both disputants want to discuss solutions.)

- **What happened?** Each disputant gets a chance to tell the story of what happened and how they felt about it. The mediator takes notes and may ask questions. The mediator can also help disputants stay focused on the issue and not engage in name-calling or finger-pointing.

- **See the other side.** Each disputant repeats the other's story to show that they understand that perspective. They don't have to *agree* with the other person's point of view, but this process of echoing shows that they've heard and understood it. The mediator may then summarize the situation, showing understanding of both disputants' feelings.

- **Brainstorm solutions.** The mediator asks both disputants to brainstorm ideas for resolving the conflict and writes down these potential solutions. The mediator might also guide discussion about the consequences of possible solutions. Both disputants must agree to a solution for it to remain under consideration. If they cannot agree to any solutions, the process will need to be repeated.

- **Agreement.** The mediator writes down the agreed-upon solution or solutions, and both parties sign this agreement. The mediator may offer the disputants praise for their efforts. Seeing another person's perspective and understanding others' feelings shows social and emotional growth.

- **Follow-up.** After an agreed-upon amount of time, the mediator and disputants will meet again and talk about how the solutions are working, whether both people are honoring the agreement, and what progress is being made.

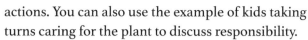

LESSON 24
WOLVES

Key Words

The behaviors, traits, and emotions below are just starting points for aligning SEL, character education, and this lesson's story. Most of these ideas can easily be connected with more than one competency or domain.

Self-Awareness: Fear • Gratitude

Self-Management: Honesty • Planning and Preparation • Trust and Trustworthiness

Social Awareness: Caring and Kindness • Communication • Service to Others

Relationship Skills: Citizenship • Cooperation, Collaboration, and Teamwork • Forgiveness • Friendship • Loyalty

Responsible Decision-Making: Analyzing and Evaluating • Identifying Challenges

Students will

 learn about wolves and some of their characteristics, such as the way pack members care for each other, forgive each other, or reconcile with each other, and make analogies to traits such as caring, cooperation, communication, trustworthiness, and loyalty among people

 draw comparisons between wolf behavior and people who serve others in need

 consider what can happen when people are kind and helpful to others and also discuss when it's better to ask for help from an adult

 understand the way wolves cooperate within the pack to support and care for all members, and make comparisons to people who cooperate in families, schools, and communities

Overview

Wolves are often viewed as dangerous animals, and many frightening stories describe attacks on people. The wolf's eerie howl has probably helped inspire such stories. But in reality—while wolves do hunt and eat many animals, from elk and deer to foxes and fish—they are very rarely aggressive toward humans.

Kids will be fascinated by the highly social and structured nature of wolf packs and the way pack members cooperate and care for each other. They'll also be intrigued by wolves' loyalty to their packs and to their mates. Discussing the behaviors and traits of wolves can encourage children's awareness and development of social skills, such as teamwork, cooperation, service, trust, and citizenship.

Story

Wild Wolves

WILD WOLVES

Eve and Norman Fertig are animal lovers. They rescue and care for animals that are hurt or sick. One day they found a two-week-old wolf dog. She was very sick. The Fertigs named her Shana and kept her as a pet. They saved Shana's life. They didn't know she would return the favor one day.

A few years later a huge winter storm hit their area. When the storm came, the Fertigs were outside on their large plot of land. Trees fell everywhere. Snow blanketed the ground. The Fertigs couldn't get back to their house and were freezing in the cold. They were afraid they would die.

Shana seemed to sense the danger. She appeared out of nowhere. The couple's faithful friend dug a tunnel under the snow and fallen trees, all the way to the house. Then the 160-pound wolf dog carried Eve on her back through the tunnel and pulled Norman behind her. The Fertigs say Shana saved their lives.

Lots of people live with dogs. Some, like the Fertigs, even have wolf dogs in their homes. But have you ever known someone who went out and lived with wolves? Shaun Ellis did this. First, he studied wolves. Then he wanted to get closer. Shaun took a big risk. He moved into the wild and began living near a wolf pack. In time, the wolves learned that Shaun wouldn't hurt them. They grew to trust him. They even brought him food to eat. In return, Shaun babysat the pack's wolf pups. A great bond of friendship connected the wild wolves to Shaun even though they were different. The wolves appeared to accept Shaun.

One day, Shaun wanted to get a drink from a nearby stream. But one of the wolves stopped him in his tracks. The wolf snarled. He nipped at Shaun. Shaun was scared. Had the wolves turned against him? The wolf didn't hurt him, but would not let Shaun pass. Later, Shaun did go to the stream. Guess what he saw? Bear tracks. Shaun realized the wolf had probably saved his life. The wolf had also protected the lives of the pack's pups. The bear might have followed Shaun's tracks or his scent back to the den where the pups played.

Shaun and the wolves trusted and protected each other, like members of the same pack. They were a team—a human–wolf team.

WOLF FACTS

- Wolves are close relatives of dogs. Thousands of years ago, humans began taming some wild gray wolves. Slowly, these tame wolves evolved into the dogs we know today. Sometimes wolves will mate with dogs. Their babies are half wolf and half dog.

- Have you ever heard of a *lone wolf*? It usually describes someone who likes to work and play alone. The idea of a lone wolf comes from the way wolves live in the wild. Most of the time, wolves are not alone. They live in family groups called packs. The main male and female in the pack are mates and they lead the pack. Wolf mates are very loyal to each other and usually stay together for life. Sometimes a pack *will* drive out a young male wolf who then becomes a lone wolf. Other times, male wolves leave to start their own packs. However, wolves have been seen to forgive members of their pack who come back after leaving, and to show reconciliation. Wolves need packs, because they hunt animals that are much bigger than they are, such as moose and elk. Wolves work together to hunt and bring down these large prey.

- Adult wolves help take care of the pack's babies, called pups. Wolf pups are very playful. Playing helps them learn how to be adult wolves. They learn how to hunt and how to communicate through sounds, posture, and facial expressions. They learn to be good members of the pack.

- Some experts think that wolves mourn when a pack member dies. The pack may howl as though they're calling for the dead wolf. The wolf's mate, especially, may seem to grieve for a long time.

TALK IT OVER

Use these questions to guide your students in considering comparisons between wolf behaviors and human emotions, such as caring, loyalty, friendship, and trust.

Sometimes a wolf leaves his pack or is driven away. Then he becomes a lone wolf. Lone wolves may be more aggressive than wolves in packs, because they have to fight harder for their food. Can you compare and contrast these ideas to situations people might be in?

- Everyone needs to be alone sometimes. Just because a person wants some privacy or some quiet time doesn't mean that they are unfriendly.

- Being alone and being lonely are different. When we're lonely, we may also feel very sad. If you feel sad and lonely a lot, talk to a grown-up you trust.

- If people are unkind and don't let someone play with them or join their group, that person might feel hurt and angry. If you're ever tempted to exclude someone else, think about how you would feel in their place. It's important to be kind to others. Just as the wolves in the story accepted Shaun, you include people who are different from you.

Wolves are very loyal to the members of their packs and especially to their mates. Can you compare this to human examples of loyalty?

- Family members are usually loyal to each other.

- True friends are usually loyal to each other. They stick up for each other and they are honest with each other.

- People often feel loyalty to groups they belong to, such as schools, clubs, faith communities,

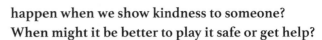

and nations. Loyalty can help these groups be stronger and more successful. But lasting loyalty must be earned. If people feel betrayed by someone or something they've been loyal to, they may be very angry or sad.

Wolves in the same pack help care for young pups. And wolves work together to hunt moose and other large animals. If pack members don't work together for the good of the group, they all suffer. Can you compare this to behaviors or situations among people?

- Every member of a family has responsibilities and chores, from parents to young kids. Without cooperation, the family wouldn't function well.

- Schools, communities, and governments need to all work together to make sure all citizens are cared for.

- Some jobs are a lot easier to do with help. Having other people around can make a job more fun too.

Every member of a wolf pack has to count on the other members for support. Living together and relying on each other this way takes trust. How can people build trust in each other?

- When you are honest, people are more likely to trust you.

- People will trust you more if you are dependable and do what you say you will do. If you promise to clean your room or help a friend with a project and then go back on your word, you might lose other people's trust.

- Being kind and caring can earn the trust of others over time.

- In a family, class, or community, everyone's success is connected. Cooperation and good citizenship are positive traits that can help everyone succeed.

Shaun lived safely with wolves. And Shana, a wolf dog, saved Eve and Norman's lives. But many people think of wolves as dangerous and wouldn't have rescued a wolf dog like Shana. What can

happen when we show kindness to someone? **When might it be better to play it safe or get help?**

- If you are kind and caring toward a person you don't know well, they might become your friend.

- If you help someone out, they might feel very loyal to you. That person might also be there for you someday when *you* need help.

- If you see someone being bullied, you can stand up for that person and be their friend. But if you feel afraid, don't confront the person doing the bullying. Get help from a grown-up.

- It is important to help people who need it. But sometimes the best way to help is by going to a grown-up. For example, if you see a person who seems to be drowning, you should never get into the water. It's not safe. Instead, you should call for help.

- Wild animals are not pets. Shaun's story is unusual. So is the story of Shana. You should never be cruel to an animal. But it's also important to be very careful around wild animals, or around any animals that you aren't familiar with.

ACTIVITIES

Activity 1: Wolf Book Club

Materials

Wolf book (1 copy per student, or 1 to read aloud as a group)

Directions

Choose a book about wolves that is suited to your students' ages and abilities. Options include *Look to the North: A Wolf Pup Diary* by Jean Craighead George (kindergarten through grade 3), *Wolf Island* (grades 1 through 4) by Celia Godkin, *Julie of the Wolves* by Jean Craighead George (grades 4 and up), *Summer of the Wolves* by Polly Carlson-Voiles (grades 5 and up), or *White Fang* by Jack London (grades 5 and up).

Kids can read the chosen book individually, or you can read it aloud as a group. In either case, hold regular "wolf book club" meetings during the course of reading the book. Gather kids in a circle

and talk about the story as a group. Consider the way wolves are portrayed. Focus on examples of wolf loyalty, trust, cooperation, and service to others or to the pack. Discuss the comparable social and emotional skills that people have. What were kids' favorite—and least favorite—parts of the story, and why? Why do they think the writer made the decisions that they did? What are some other ways the story might have gone?

If desired, end this activity by having kids write their own stories about wolves.

Activity 2: Good Question!

Materials
Good Question! handout (in digital content)

Directions
Pass out copies of the Good Question! handout and tell kids that they'll each be interviewing a family member or other adult. Ask them to focus their interviews on topics such as family, loyalty, and trust. As a group, brainstorm interview questions. For example, *Growing up, what family member did you feel closest to, and why?* or *When was a time you really had to trust someone?*

Once you have a list of ten questions or so, have each student write down on the handout three to five questions that they find most interesting. Tell kids that they can use these questions as starting points in their interviews, but also encourage them to tailor their questions according to the people they interview and where their conversations go. Explain that interviewers need to listen closely to answers and think about what their next questions should be. Remind kids that wolves communicate through sounds, and also through facial expressions and body language. People do this too. So as they conduct their interviews, kids can watch for what their interviewees are saying *without* words.

After kids have done their interviews, talk about the activity. Was it harder than kids expected to conduct an interesting and productive interview? Did they learn things that surprised them? Did they enjoy the experience of being interviewers?

Variation: Ask kids to write essays, articles, or stories based on what they learned in their interviews. If kids feel comfortable doing so, they can share these with the class.

Activity 3: Adopt a Wolf

Materials
Various

Directions
Wolves in the wild often need help. Explain to kids that wolves are endangered or threatened in many parts of the world. And we—humans—are their most dangerous predators. Humans have hunted and trapped wolves for many years. In addition, construction and other human activities have disrupted wolves' habitat.

Fortunately, kids can make a difference! As a group, brainstorm ways to raise money to "adopt" a wolf (through the World Wildlife Fund, for example) or to donate to a sanctuary or other organization that helps protect and care for wolves, such as the International Wolf Center (wolf.org). This can become a great problem-solving and planning experience. Fundraising ideas might include raking yards, holding a bake sale, selling raffle tickets to win wolf prizes (a book about wolves, a toy wolf, etc.), or putting on a play about wolves and charging admission.

Once you have a list of ideas, choose a few that look possible for your group, and ask kids to vote on their favorite. Then develop an action plan for carrying out this service project. Talk about what supplies you'll need, how much time it will take to organize and hold the event, and who could help.

After you hold your event, talk with kids about the experience. Did they succeed in reaching their goal? Are there things they would do differently next time? How did it feel to help wolves? Did this service project give them ideas for additional ways to help wolves or other animals?

GLOSSARY

You can use these kid-friendly definitions with students if some of the vocabulary in the stories and lessons is too advanced.

acceptance: caring about and including all people; liking people for who they are without trying to change them

adaptability: the ability to adjust your thoughts or actions as situations change

anger management: learning to recognize signs that you are getting angry and taking action to cool down

assertiveness: speaking up in a strong but polite way

balance: when the different parts of a person's life are in harmony; for example, if you have balance in your life, you have time for school and homework, having fun with friends, after-school activities, and family

bullying: behavior that is unkind and usually repeated, which hurts, threatens, or intimidates others, especially people who are vulnerable

caring: showing that you care about someone; showing concern, being friendly and kind, listening, sharing, helping, and giving are all ways that you show you care

citizenship: being a member of a community, state, province, or country; the way you act and the responsibilities you have as a member of a community

communication: sharing information, thoughts, or feelings with someone else by saying it out loud, writing it, or showing an example

conflict management and resolution: the process of handling arguments or disputes in a calm, effective, and productive way

consequences: the effects or results of an action, choice, or situation

conservation: protecting or saving something, especially related to our planet and environment; for example, recycling paper to keep more trees from being cut down to make new paper

cooperation: working and playing together peacefully; working together on a job or on a problem that needs to be solved

courage: braveness; boldness; doing something that is positive, even if it feels scary

curiosity: having questions about something new or something you don't understand; being interested in learning more

decision-making: the process of using good judgment to make positive choices about your own behavior and how you get along with others, which includes identifying and analyzing a problem, recognizing the consequences of your actions, considering the well-being of yourself and others, and knowing when something doesn't feel right

discernment: the ability to judge well, including sensing the feelings and emotions of others, identifying positive and negative choices, and knowing what needs to be done to address a situation

empathy: the ability to understand, sense, and share the feelings of another person

fairness and equality: treating other people the way you would like to be treated; giving everyone the kinds of rights and chances you have; when you're fair, you do your best to share, take turns, and treat each person with respect

forgiveness: the act of forgiving someone; giving up hurt and anger toward someone

friendship: the connection or tie you have with someone you care about and like to do things with

goal-setting: identifying something you want to accomplish and creating realistic steps toward achieving it

gratitude: the quality of feeling thankful and the desire to show kindness in return

hard work: dedication and commitment to a task; being willing to do a difficult job

helpfulness: willingness to help; offering help even when it's not asked for

honesty: truthfulness in word and action; sticking to the facts

inner strength: grit, resilience, or fortitude; being true to yourself; standing boldly for positive beliefs

integrity: being honest in words, thoughts, and actions; having strong principles and sticking to them

loyalty: being devoted and faithful; standing by someone; staying true to a belief or a cause

mindfulness: being aware of the present moment; calmly accepting one's feelings, thoughts, and bodily sensations

patience: being calm; the ability to wait for someone or for something to happen; the ability to see something through to the end

peacefulness: inner calmness; knowing how to work through disagreements; working together to solve problems

peer mediation: a process in which young people involved in a conflict meet with a trained student mediator to address the problem

perseverance: practicing until it's right; trying over and over again; never giving up

perspective: a point of view; the way a person feels, how they see the world, or how they evaluate reality

planning and preparation: figuring out ahead of time how to do something so it goes well; getting ready for a task ahead of time

playfulness: having fun; a positive, happy attitude; a good sense of humor

problem-solving: trying different solutions and thinking in new ways until you find something that works; part of problem-solving can also be accepting the consequences of your choices even when those choices don't turn out the way you want them to

relationship skills: learning how to keep healthy and rewarding relationships with other people, including those who have different backgrounds or needs; growing in the ability to communicate clearly; listening and cooperating with others; resisting social pressure; learning to handle conflicts in a positive way; knowing when to ask for help

respect: care and concern for others and yourself; when you respect someone, you care about the person's ideas, thoughts, and feelings

responsibility: the act of making good choices, being dependable, and taking charge of your own actions, words, and thoughts

safety: being free from harm or risk

self-awareness: understanding your own feelings and emotions; creating inner peace, developing self-confidence; understanding personal strength and weaknesses

self-confidence: trust in your own abilities, qualities, and judgment

self-management: being able to accept and manage your own thoughts, emotions, and actions; make decisions without direction from others; doing the right thing on your own, without a teacher or parent telling you to; resisting temptation; having the motivation to set and pursue your own your goals; learning to adapt and grow. Sometimes this is also called self-regulation or self-control.

service: a kind act that you do for people, animals, or the environment

social awareness: understanding the perspectives and feelings of others and empathizing with them, including those who are from different backgrounds; understanding how to behave positively in social situations; recognizing where you can get support from others

teamwork: the social ability to work together with others to pursue a common goal

trust: believing that someone is there for you; depending on someone; counting on someone to do what they say they will do

trustworthy: capable of being counted on to do what you say you'll do; dependable

wisdom: appreciation for the value of learning, all throughout life; using your knowledge and experience to grow and be a better person

RESOURCES

BOOKS FOR KIDS

These resources, both fiction and nonfiction, explore the animals and plants in *Social Emotional Stories*. While not all of these books directly discuss social and emotional learning, you can use the ideas within them to explore concepts with your students and spark meaningful discussion about positive traits, SEL skills, and behavior, as well as to further investigate these fascinating animals and plants.

Apes

Ape Escapes! And More True Stories of Animals Behaving Badly by Aline Alexander Newman (Washington, D.C.: National Geographic Children's Books, 2012). Fu Manchu is an orangutan that outwits zookeepers and picks locks so he can break out of his habitat and wander the Omaha Zoo. Fu Manchu even makes his own lock-picking tool, which he hides in his mouth so he won't be caught. This book also contains two other stories about resourceful animals. *Grades 2 and up; nonfiction.*

Koko's Kitten by Dr. Francine Patterson (New York: Scholastic, 1985). When Koko, a great ape fluent in sign language, asks her trainer for a kitten, the trainer buys a toy kitten. But Koko wants a real, live kitten, and when her wish is finally granted, she grooms and cuddles the kitten she names All Ball. When All Ball is run over by a car, Koko grieves in a way that humans can relate to. *Grades K–3; nonfiction.*

The One and Only Ivan by Katherine Applegate (New York: HarperCollins, 2012). This award-winning book tells an unforgettable story of a transformative friendship between a gorilla and an elephant. The book has a sequel, *The One and Only Bob. Grades 3–7; fiction.*

Bamboo

Baby Panda Chews Bamboo by Ben Richmond (New York: Sterling Children's Books, 2018). This informative picture book follows a baby panda from birth through adulthood. *Grades K–4; nonfiction.*

Life Cycles: Bamboo by Julie K. Lundgren (Vero Beach, FL: Rourke Publishing, 2011). Students will be guided through the complete life cycle of bamboo. *Grades 2 and up; nonfiction.*

Box Jellyfish

The Box Jellyfish by Colleen Sexton (Minneapolis: Bellwether Media, 2011). The box jellyfish, also called the sea wasp, is full of toxin. Each of its tentacles has five thousand sting cells with enough poison to kill sixty people! In this book, young readers will discover what makes the box jellyfish one of the ocean's most beautiful but terrifying creatures. *Grades 3 and up; nonfiction.*

Bristlecone Pine Trees

Bristlecone Pines by Kelli M. Brucken (Farmington Hills, MI: KidHaven Press, 2005). Bristlecone pines manage not only to survive through the hottest heat and coldest cold, they thrive and are the world's oldest living trees. Kids will learn how these trees grow and why they must be protected. *Grades 4 and up; nonfiction.*

Cats

The Cats of Roxville Station by Jean Craighead George (New York: Dutton Juvenile, 2009). Rachet the cat is thrown into a river, but she doesn't drown—she is able to climb her way up the riverbank and find a new home with a group of feral cats by the Roxville train station. Soon Rachet meets a foster child named Mike, who wants to be her friend—but first he must gain her trust. *Grades 4–6; fiction.*

Dewey the Library Cat by Vicki Myron and Bret Witter (New York: Little, Brown, 2010). Dewey the cat was left in a library book drop slot on the coldest night of the year and managed to survive. Named Dewey Readmore Books by his new caregivers, he gained many new friends and fans and inspired library-goers with his winning spirit. *Grades 4–8; nonfiction.*

Fifty Nifty Facts about Cats by J. M. Chapman and S. M. Davis (Quincy, IL: Vulpine Press, 2016). Readers will discover a wide variety of great facts about this fascinating animal. *All ages; nonfiction.*

Coconut Crabs

Crabs by Mary Jo Rhodes and David Hall (New York: Scholastic, 2007). Chock-full of dramatic photos and fascinating facts about crabs, this book will teach kids about coconut crabs and many other crabs. *Grades 2 and up; nonfiction.*

Crows

Crows! Strange and Wonderful by Laurence Pringle (Honesdale, PA: Boyds Mill Press, 2010). Crows have a remarkable way of communicating with one another, using at least twenty-five distinct sounds to get their messages across. Children will learn how crows "talk," behave, and survive. *Grades 2 and up; nonfiction.*

The Summer of the Crows: Not Your Typical Boy Meets Crow Story by Tony Ducklow (Amazon Digital Services, 2011). When Tucker McNeal happens upon baby crows orphaned by a summer storm, the experience turns into an adventure that teaches him about the amazing intelligence of crows. *Grades 4 and up; fiction.*

Dandelions

A Dandelion's Life by John Himmelman (New York: Children's Press, 1998). This picture book takes readers through the dandelion's life cycle, from seed to blossom and back to seed. *Grades K and up; nonfiction.*

The Dandelion Seed by Joseph Anthony (Nevada City, CA: Dawn Publications, 1997). This picture book takes kids on a journey with a dandelion seed that is afraid to leave its flower when autumn comes. *Grades K and up; fiction.*

Dogs

Along Came a Dog by Meindert DeJong (New York: HarperCollins, 1980). In this book illustrated by Maurice Sendak, a homeless dog takes it upon himself to protect a little red hen, and the two become friends. *Grades 3 and up; fiction.*

Because of Winn-Dixie by Kate DiCamillo (Cambridge, MA: Candlewick Press, 2000). Winn-Dixie is a big, ugly dog that teaches ten-year-old Opal about her absent mother, helps her make new friends in her new hometown, and makes her feel happier and less alone. *Grades 4 and up; fiction.*

The Call of the Wild by Jack London (New York: Macmillan Company, 1903). In this classic novel set during the Alaska Gold Rush, a heroic dog must decide whether to answer the call of the wild or to live with humans. *Grades 4 and up; fiction.*

Everything Dogs: All the Canine Facts, Photos, and Fun You Can Get Your Paws On! by Becky Bains with Dr. Gary Weitzman (Washington, D.C.: National Geographic Society, 2012). This book introduces readers to a range of fun and fascinating facts about dogs, and includes engaging photographs. *Grades 3–7; nonfiction.*

Hachiko Waits by Lesléa Newman (New York: Henry Holt, 2004). Based on the true story of loyal Hachiko, the Akita dog that waited for his owner at a train station in Japan, long after his owner had died. *Grades 3–5; fiction.*

Nubs: The True Story of a Mutt, a Marine & a Miracle by Brian Dennis, Mary Nethery, and Kirby Larson (New York: Little, Brown, 2009). Nubs was the leader of a pack of wild dogs in Iraq when he was befriended by Marine Major Brian Dennis. When Major Dennis and the Marines were relocated 70 miles away, Nubs showed up. Because the Marines aren't allowed to have pets, Major Dennis arranged for Nubs to stay with a family in the United States until Dennis could return home and take Nubs in as his own. *Grades 3–5; nonfiction.*

Shelter Dogs: Amazing Stories of Adopted Strays by Peg Kehret (Morton Grove, IL: Albert Whitman & Company, 1999). This book shares the individual stories of eight stray dogs that were left at animal shelters, were adopted by loving families, and went on to thrive and prove how amazing dogs can be. *Grades 3–6; nonfiction.*

Shiloh by Phyllis Reynolds Naylor (New York: Atheneum, 1991). Marty Preston finds a beagle in the hills behind his home and promptly names him Shiloh. But he soon learns that Shiloh belongs to someone else, a man who drinks too much, has a gun, and abuses his dogs. Marty finds himself in a dangerous ethical dilemma when Shiloh's angry owner wants him back. *Grades 3 and up; fiction.*

Where the Red Fern Grows by Wilson Rawls (Garden City, NY: Doubleday, 1961). In this classic novel for children Billy Colman and his hound dogs roam the Ozarks, hunting for a raccoon Billy hopes to enter in an annual raccoon hunt contest, fighting a mountain lion in the process, a clash that ends tragically. Billy finds peace in the Native American legend of the sacred red fern that grows over the graves of his dogs. *Grades 4 and up; fiction.*

Dolphins

Dolphin Adventure: A True Story by Wayne Grover (New York: Greenwillow Books, 2000). The author shares his encounter with a dolphin family of three, a mother, father, and baby, off the Atlantic coast of Florida. Upon discovering that the baby dolphin is trapped because its tail has been wound in fishing line and its flesh pierced with a hook, Grover dives underwater to free it with his diving knife. The blood from the dolphin's injury attracts two sharks that the father dolphin attacks, saving Grover's life. *Grades 3 and up; nonfiction.*

Nine True Dolphin Stories by Margaret Davidson (New York: Scholastic Educational, 2004). Included in this collection of true stories about dolphins—one that gives children rides on her back, and another that is trained to save lives—are facts about how dolphins survive and how scientists study them. *Grades 3–5; nonfiction.*

One White Dolphin by Gill Lewis (New York: Atheneum, 2012). Kara and her family are dedicated to protecting marine life and saving the reef, which causes problems with Jake and his family, because fishermen need to dredge the reef in order to make a living. Kara soon meets a boy named Felix, who hopes to sail in the Paralympics. Felix and Kara work together to save a baby albino dolphin caught in a fishing net, an act that has interesting results for the reef. *Grades 3 and up; fiction.*

Winter's Tail: How One Little Dolphin Learned to Swim Again by Craig Hatkoff, Isabella Hatkoff, and Juliana Hatkoff (New York: Scholastic, 2009). Winter the dolphin was caught in a crab trap when she was a baby, seriously injuring her tail. She was rescued, but her tail eventually fell off. With the help of a prosthetic tail, Winter was able to swim again, and has been an inspiration to young amputees. *Dolphin Tale*, starring Harry Connick Jr., Ashley Judd, and Morgan Freeman, came out in 2011. *Grades 3–5; nonfiction.*

Elephants

Elephants by Seymour Simon (New York: HarperCollins, 2018). Award-winning science writer Seymour Simon investigates the many characteristics and behaviors of one of the world's most beloved animals. *Grades 1–5; nonfiction.*

An Elephant in the Garden by Michael Morpurgo (New York: Feiwell and Friends, 2011). In this wartime novel, a zoo-keeping family decides to save an elephant named Marlene rather than allow her to be euthanized with the other animals so they don't run wild if the zoo is bombed. Marlene will stay in the family's garden instead, until the city is bombed and they must flee—with an elephant. *Grades 5 and up; fiction.*

Elephant Talk: The Surprising Science of Elephant Communication by Ann Downer (Minneapolis: Twenty First Century Books, 2011). Elephants may not talk the way humans do, but scientists have found that they have a unique way of communicating with one another, even when separated. The author examines this communication and its possible impact on the dwindling population of elephants due to poaching. *Grades 3 and up; nonfiction.*

Tarra & Bella: The Elephant and Dog Who Became Best Friends by Carol Buckley (New York: G. P. Putnam's Sons, 2009). Tarra the elephant has retired from the circus and moved to the Elephant Sanctuary of Tennessee, where she is a loner until she meets a stray dog named Bella. The other elephants have paired up with each other, but Tarra and Bella bond as an unlikely but inseparable duo. *Grades 3–6; nonfiction.*

Fireflies

Fireflies by Mary R. Dunn (Mankato, MN: Capstone Press, 2012). This simple book introduces readers to facts about fireflies. *Grades K and up; nonfiction.*

Fly, Firefly! by Shana Keller (Ann Arbor, MI: Sleeping Bear Press, 2020). This lyrical story—based on an event witnessed by nature writer and ecologist Rachel Carson—illustrates the wonder and delight the natural world can offer. Includes a section of science facts about fireflies. *Grades 1 and up; fiction.*

Horses

Black Beauty by Anna Sewell (New York: Hurst and Company, 1903). A classic with the unique twist of a horse for a narrator, this book follows the life of Black Beauty, from colt to carriage horse to cab horse. Readers will see how some people treat animals very well and others abuse them, and how the animal might be affected. *Grades 4 and up; fiction.*

Goliath: Hero of the Great Baltimore Fire by Claudia Friddell (Ann Arbor, MI: Sleeping Bear Press, 2010). The Great Baltimore Fire of 1904 is often overshadowed by the Great Chicago Fire, but it caused considerable destruction. Goliath, the huge horse from Engine Company 15, endured an explosion and then pulled a fire rig to safety—by himself. *Grades K–5; nonfiction.*

Horses: The Definitive Catalog of Horse and Pony Breeds by Scholastic (New York: Scholastic, 2019). This is a visually rich guide explores the characteristics of horse and pony breeds from around the world. *Grades 3–7; nonfiction.*

Moths

Eyewitness: Butterfly & Moth by DK Publishing (New York: DK Children, 2000). Using photographs to document the life cycle of moths and butterflies, this book will teach young readers about where these insects live, what they eat, and how they survive. *Grades 3 and up; nonfiction.*

Parrots

Alex the Parrot: No Ordinary Bird by Stephanie Spinner (New York: Alfred A. Knopf, 2012). In 1977, most scientists figured parrots' small brains equaled limited intelligence. But Irene Pepperberg, a graduate student interested in studying the African gray parrot, bought one of her own and named him Alex, short for Avian Learning EXperiment. Pepperberg soon realized that Alex had a great capacity to learn. *Grades 3 and up; nonfiction.*

Parrots Over Puerto Rico by Susan L. Roth and Cindy Trumbore (New York: Lee & Low Books, 2013). Puerto Rican parrots were in danger of extinction in the 1960s. This compelling book recounts the efforts of the scientists of the Puerto Rican Parrot Recovery Program to save the parrots and ensure their future. *Grades 2–5; nonfiction.*

Penguins

March of the Penguins by Luc Jacquet (Washington, D.C.: National Geographic Children's Books, 2006). The book version of the impressive documentary follows emperor penguins as they journey across the Antarctic to hatch and raise their chicks. *Grades 3 and up; nonfiction.*

My Season with Penguins: An Antarctic Journal by Sophie Webb (New York: Sandpiper, 2004). The author shares her experience of living in the Antarctic with Adélie penguins for two months, including being slapped by one of the hardy birds. *Grades 4–8; nonfiction.*

The World of Penguins by Evelyne Daigle (Plattsburgh, NY: Tundra Books, 2008). Readers will learn about all kinds of penguins living in and through all kinds of situations, aided by realistic acrylic paintings and photos. They will read about where penguins nest and what they eat, as well as who wants to eat them. *Grades 4 and up; nonfiction.*

Pigs

Ace: The Very Important Pig by Dick King-Smith (New York: Crown Publishers, 1992). Ace isn't like the other piglets in his litter: not only does he have a black mark like a club from a deck of cards, he can understand Farmer Tubbs when he talks. When Ace wants something, he grunts, making different sounds depending on what he is trying to communicate. Soon Ace has made himself comfortable in the farmer's house, where he watches TV and spends time with his friends, a house cat and a dog. *Grades 3–5; fiction.*

Charlotte's Web by E. B. White (New York: Harper, 1952). Kids will love getting to know Wilbur and Charlotte, and if they've already read this classic tale at home they'll be happy to get reacquainted. In an attempt to save Wilbur the pig from becoming bacon, Charlotte the spider begins spinning webs with persuasive messages woven in. The side characters—the other farm animals—add to the charming story. *Grades 3–5; fiction.*

Quaking Aspens

Quaking Aspen by Bonnie Holmes (Minneapolis: Carolrhoda Books, 1999). Kids will learn about the quaking aspen's life cycle, its role in the ecosystem, and the threats it faces. *Grades 3 and up; nonfiction.*

The Tree Book for Kids and Their Grown-Ups by Gina Ingoglia (Brooklyn, NY: Brooklyn Botanic Garden, 2008). This book features thirty-three different trees that grow in North America. Each profile includes a beautiful botanical watercolor illustration by the author. *Grades 3–7; nonfiction.*

Squirrels

Gooseberry Park by Cynthia Rylant (Boston: Sandpiper, 2007). Kona, a Labrador retriever, and Stumpy, a squirrel, meet one day in Gooseberry Park, and they become fast friends. When Stumpy needs help, Kona comes to the rescue, and shows what a true and loyal friend he is. *Grades 3–5; fiction.*

Squirrels in the School by Ben M. Baglio (New York: Scholastic, 2000). When Mandy and James find a family of squirrels nesting inside the school, they have to work together to keep the squirrels safe from school officials who are eager to get rid of them. *Grades 3–5; fiction.*

Turkeys

Wild Turkeys by Dorothy Hinshaw Patent (Minneapolis: Lerner, 1999). This book introduces kids to the life cycle and behavior of turkeys, and also explores some of the similarities and differences between wild turkeys and farm turkeys. *Grades 2–4; nonfiction.*

Venus Flytraps

Hungry Plants by Mary Batten (New York: Random House, 2000). This book gives kids an up-close look at Venus flytraps and other carnivorous plants. *Grades 2–3; nonfiction.*

Wolves

Journey: Based on the True Story of OR7, the Most Famous Wolf in the West by Emma Bland Smith (Seattle: Little Bigfoot, 2016). This beautiful picture book is inspired by the journey of a young gray wolf who garnered nationwide attention when he became the first wild wolf in California in almost a century. *Grades 1 and up; fiction.*

Julie of the Wolves by Jean Craighead George (Carmel, CA: Hampton-Brown, 1972). Miyax lives in a small Eskimo village—until her life there becomes dangerous and she runs away. Instead of fleeing to safety, however, Miyax finds herself wandering in the Alaskan wilderness. In her struggle for survival she joins a pack of wolves, becoming one of their wild family. When she finally reaches civilization, Miyax longs for her role as Julie of the wolves. *Grades 4 and up; fiction.*

White Fang by Jack London (New York: Macmillan Company, 1906). Set during the Klondike Gold Rush at the end of the nineteenth century, *White Fang* is narrated by a wolf dog as he transforms from wild animal to domesticated pet. Readers will gain insight into the world of wolves and how they might view humans. *Grades 5 and up; fiction.*

Miscellaneous

125 True Stories of Amazing Animals: Inspiring Tales of Animal Friendship and Four-Legged Heroes, Plus Crazy Animal Antics by National Geographic Kids (Washington, D.C.: National Geographic Children's Books, 2012). This book is packed with inspiring, hilarious, and touching stories about incredible animals, including a sea otter that kayaks, a bear that stole a family's car, and a cat that called 911 to save its owner. Kids will also get to read true stories of unlikely animal friendships and learn facts about each different animal. *Grades 3 and up; nonfiction.*

Animal Heroes: True Rescue Stories by Sandra Markle (Minneapolis: Millbrook Press, 2008). Included in this collection of true animal stories are accounts of a guide dog that saves her blind owner on 9/11, a group of dolphins that saves swimmers from a shark attack, and a cat that saves its family from carbon monoxide poisoning. *Grades 4–7; nonfiction.*

Dog Finds Lost Dolphins, and More True Stories of Amazing Animal Heroes by Elizabeth Carney (Washington, D.C.: National Geographic Children's Books, 2012). Cloud is a special black Lab—the only dog certified to sniff out stranded dolphins, some that are more than a mile away from her super sniffer. Cloud often waits on the dock for the dolphins to emerge from the water and give her a kiss. This book also includes two other stories about amazing animals. *Grades 2 and up; nonfiction.*

Owen & Mzee: The True Story of a Remarkable Friendship by Isabella Hatkoff, Craig Hatkoff, and Dr. Paula Kahumbu (New York: Scholastic Press, 2006). Owen, a baby hippo, was stranded after the 2004 tsunami and rescued by villagers in Kenya. He soon forged an unbreakable bond with a 130-year-old giant tortoise, Mzee, and the two can be seen swimming, eating, and playing together all over the preserve they call home. *Grades K–5; nonfiction.*

ORGANIZATIONS AND WEBSITES

Character Counts!
charactercounts.org
This initiative based at Drake University develops and delivers services and materials to increase ethical commitment, competence, and practice in all segments of society. Based on Six Pillars of Character (trustworthiness, respect, responsibility, fairness, caring, and citizenship), the organization provides practical strategies, curricular resources, and training.

Character Lab
characterlab.org
Author and professor Angela Duckworth founded the Character Lab with the goal of advancing the science and practice of character development. The website provides weekly tips for exploring character, as well as ready-to-use classroom resources targeting specific character strengths.

Character.org—Character Education Partnership
character.org
This national nonprofit organization is dedicated to promoting character education at all grade levels. The website offers downloadable publications, lesson plans, a character education blog, and a substantive list of resources—including the *11 Principles of Effective Character*, which you can use as a road map to help direct your group's character building (including SEL lessons).

Collaborative for Academic, Social, and Emotional Learning (CASEL)
casel.org
CASEL is the leading organization for development of academic, social, and emotional competence for all students. The organization aims to improve and transform American education through SEL.

Engaging Schools
engagingschools.org
Formerly Educators for Social Responsibility, Engaging Schools is a national nonprofit organization that works with educators to integrate academic, social, and emotional learning.

The Foundation for a Better Life
passiton.com
The organization seeks to inspire people to live good values, seek out positive role models, and live a better life. On their website you'll find their motivational PSAs, images of their inspiring billboards, and stories of real-life heroes.

GoodCharacter.com
goodcharacter.com
Recommended by the Parents' Choice Foundation, this website contains resources for character development and service learning. Includes articles, tips, teaching guides, lesson plans, and resource lists. The website offers free lesson plans for character education and social emotional learning, activities, programs, and resource lists.

Idealist

idealist.org

This site offers a good starting place to explore volunteer opportunities for your class or for interested students. Find resources, project ideas, and organizations that can help you get started.

Mindset Scholars Network

mindsetscholarsnetwork.org

This interdisciplinary research network is dedicated to improving student outcomes and expanding educational opportunity by advancing scientific understanding of students' mindsets about learning and school.

Mindset Works

mindsetworks.com

Mindset Works provides resources and training to cultivate a growth mindset school culture, including the Brainology curriculum and other resources for students, teachers, and administrators.

National Commission Social, Emotional, and Academic Development

aspeninstitute.org/programs/national-commission -on-social-emotional-and-academic-development

In partnership with CASEL, the Aspen Institute National Commission on Social, Emotional, and Academic Development is uniting leaders to re-envision what constitutes success in our schools. With the help of teachers, parents, and students in communities across the country, the commission will explore how schools can fully integrate social, emotional, and academic development to support the whole student.

PERTS (Project for Education Research that Scales)

perts.net

This organization empowers educators to improve student outcomes—especially for underserved populations—by applying research-based practices, including the power of mindset. The website offers resources including a "Mindset Kit" and "Mindset Meter."

Search Institute

search-institute.org

Through dynamic research and analysis, this independent nonprofit organization works to promote healthy, active, and content young people and communities through asset building.

The SEL School

gtlcenter.org/sel-school

This initiative (formerly part of the Center on Great Teachers and Leaders at American Institutes for Research) is dedicated to translating research into practice. The website offers a useful primer on SEL and teaching the whole child, including detailed information on instructional practices that support social and emotional learning.

Six Seconds: The Emotional Intelligence Network

6seconds.org/education

Six Seconds helps promote positive change by researching and sharing current science about emotions and the brain. Their work focuses on scientific research around skills of emotional intelligence (EQ)—and how these skills are teachable.

Social-Emotional and Character Development Lab (Rutgers SECD Lab)

secdlab.org

The SECD Lab at Rutgers University focuses on understanding the relationship of academic achievement, social and emotional competencies, and the development of character. Its website offers a wide range of resources including podcasts, videos, and articles.

Start Empathy (Ashoka Changemakers)

startempathy.org

As part of the Ashoka Changemaker Schools Network—a global community of elementary, middle, and high schools that prioritize empathy, teamwork, leadership, problem-solving, and changemaking as student outcomes—the Start Empathy initiative is dedicated to helping every child master the skill of empathy. The website provides resources for teachers, school districts, young people, and families.

Teaching Tolerance

tolerance.org

A project of the Southern Poverty Law Center, this national education initiative is dedicated to helping teachers foster respect and understanding in the classroom. The website contains resources for educators, parents, teens, and kids.

Youth Service America

ysa.org

This organization supports a global culture of engaged young people committed to a lifetime of meaningful service, learning, and leadership. The website includes resources such as toolkits and guides to help young people enact change; project ideas; and facilitator materials.

Youth Frontiers

youthfrontiers.org

Youth Frontiers is a nonprofit, nonpartisan organization that partners with schools to build cultures of respect where students thrive socially, emotionally, and academically. Its vision is to change the way kids treat each other in every hallway, lunch line, and classroom of every school in America.

REFERENCES

Agosto, Denise E. 2013. "If I Had Three Wishes: The Educational and Social/Emotional Benefits of Oral Storytelling." *Storytelling, Self, Society* 9 (1): 53–76. jstor.org/stable/10.13110/storselfsoci.9.1.0053.

Angier, Natalie. 2009. "Pigs Prove to Be Smart, if Not Vain." *New York Times*, November 10, 2009. nytimes.com/2009/11/10/science/10angier.html.

Anthony, Lawrence. 2009 *The Elephant Whisperer: My Life with the Herd in the African Wild*. New York: Thomas Dunne Books.

Anwar, Yasmin. 2017. "How Many Different Human Emotions Are There?" *Greater Good Magazine*, September 8, 2017. greatergood.berkeley.edu/article/item/how_many_different_human_emotions_are_there.

Athan, Mattie Sue. 2010. *Guide to Companion Parrot Behavior.* New York: Barron's Educational Series.

Barker, Shane. 2017. "The Little-Known Relationship Between Emotional Intelligence and Success." *Forbes*, November 7, 2017. forbes.com/sites/forbescoachescouncil/2017/11/07/the-little-known-relationship-between-emotional-intelligence-and-success/#2a3351cf696d.

Bradshaw, John. 2011. *Dog Sense: How the New Science of Dog Behavior Can Make You a Better Friend to Your Pet.* New York: Basic Books.

Brusca, Richard C., and Gary J. Brusca. 2003. *Invertebrates.* Sunderland, MA: Sinauer Associates.

CASEL. 2019. "Core SEL Competencies." Accessed March 31, 2020. casel.org/core-competencies.

CASEL. 2019. "Overview of SEL." Accessed March 31, 2020. casel.org/overview-sel.

CASEL. 2019. "What Is SEL?" Accessed March 6, 2020, casel.org/what-is-sel.

The Cornell Lab of Ornithology. birds.cornell.edu.

D'Amato, Peter. 1998. *The Savage Garden: Cultivating Carnivorous Plants.* Berkeley, CA: Ten Speed Press.

Davies, Hazel, and Carol A. Butler. 2008. *Do Butterflies Bite? Fascinating Answers to Questions about Butterflies and Moths.* New Brunswick, NJ: Rutgers University Press.

Davis, Karen. 2001. *More Than a Meal: The Turkey in History, Myth, Ritual, and Reality.* New York: Lantern Books.

Dunlop, Colin, and Nancy King. 2009. *Cephalopods: Octopuses and Cuttlefish for the Home Aquarium.* Neptune City, NJ: TFH Publications.

Farrelly, David. 1984. *The Book of Bamboo: A Comprehensive Guide to This Remarkable Plant, Its Uses, and Its History.* San Francisco: Sierra Club Books.

Firth, Perry. 2015. "Wired for Empathy: How and Why Stories Cultivate Emotions." *Firesteel*, July 23, 2015. firesteelwa.org/2015/07/wired-for-empathy-how-and-why-stories-cultivate-emotions.

Future of StoryTelling. 2012. "Empathy, Neurochemistry, and the Dramatic Arc: Paul Zak at The Future of StoryTelling." October 3, 2012. youtu.be/q1a7tiA1Qzo.

Goodall, Jane. 1996. *My Life with the Chimpanzees.* New York: Pocket Books.

Grant, M., and J. Mitton. 2010. "Case Study: The Glorious, Golden, and Gigantic Quaking Aspen." *Nature Education Knowledge.* 1(8): 40.

Holland, Jennifer S. 2011. *Unlikely Friendships: 47 Remarkable Stories from the Animal Kingdom.* New York: Workman Publishing.

Hollenhorst, John. 2010. "Central Utah's Pando, World's Largest Living Thing, Is Threatened, Scientists Say." *Deseret News*, October 7, 2010. deseretnews.com/article/700071982/Central-Utahs-Pando-worlds-largest-living-thing-is-threatened-scientists-say.html.

Horowitz, Alexandra. 2009. *Inside of a Dog: What Dogs See, Smell, and Know.* New York: Scribner.

The Humane Society of the United States. humanesociety.org.

Hutto, Joe. 2006. *Illumination in the Flatwoods: A Season Living Among the Wild Turkey.* New York: Lyons Press.

International Oleander Society. oleander.org.

Jacobs, Tom. 2014. "Reading Literary Fiction Can Make You Less Racist." *Pacific Standard.* Last updated June 14, 2017. psmag.com/social-justice/reading-literary-fiction-can-make-less-racist-76155.

Johnson, Dan R., Brandie L. Huffman, and Danny M. Jasper. 2014. "Changing Race Boundary Perception by Reading Narrative Fiction." *Basic and Applied Social Psychology* 36 (1): 83–90. tandfonline.com/doi/abs/10.1080/01973533.2013.856791.

Jonsson, Patrik. 2005. "Close Encounters of the Fluttering Kind: A Rise in Bird Attacks." *The Christian Science Monitor*, June 10, 2005. csmonitor.com/2005/0610/p01s03-usgn.html.

Krakovsky, Marina. 2008. "Chimps Show Altruistic Streak." *Discover Magazine*, January 15, 2008. discovermagazine.com/planet-earth/84-chimps-show-altruistic-streak.

Lanner, Ronald M. 2007. *The Bristlecone Book: A Natural History of the World's Oldest Trees.* Missoula, MT: Mountain Press.

Lemonick, Michael D.. 1997. "Young, Single, and Out of Control." *Time*, October 13, 1997. content.time.com/time/magazine/article/0,9171,987172,00.html.

Lin, Pei-Ying, Naomi Sparks Grewal, Christophe Morin, Walter D. Johnson, Paul J. Zak. 2013. "Oxytocin Increases the Influence of Public Service Advertisements." *PLoS ONE* 8 (2). doi.org/10.1371/journal.pone.0056934.

Lynch, Wayne. 2007. *Penguins of the World.* Buffalo, NY: Firefly Books.

Maller, Cecily Jane. 2009. "Promoting Children's Mental, Emotional and Social Health Through Contact with Nature: A Model." *Health Education.* researchgate.net/publication/228722999_Promoting_children's_mental_emotional_and_social_health_through_contact_with_nature_A_model.

Marzluff, John, and Tony Angell. 2012. *Gifts of the Crow: How Perception, Emotion, and Thought Allow Smart Birds to Behave Like Humans.* New York: Free Press.

Masson, Jeffrey Moussaieff, and Susan McCarthy. 1995. *When Elephants Weep: The Emotional Lives of Animals.* New York: Bantam Doubleday Dell.

Mydans, Seth. 2008. "Talking to Fireflies Before Their Flash Disappears." *New York Times*, September 10, 2008. nytimes.com/2008/12/11/world/asia/11fireflies.html.

Narrative IQ. 2014. "What Stories Do to Our Brain." Accessed March 31, 2020. narrativeiq.com/what-stories-do-to-our-brain.

National Geographic. nationalgeographic.com.

National Oceanic and Atmospheric Administration: National Ocean Service. oceanservice.noaa.gov.

National Park Service. nps.gov.

NOVA. 2011. "Kings of Camouflage." *NOVA*, aired July 13, 2011. Accessed March 4, 2020. pbs.org/wgbh/nova/nature/kings-of-camouflage.html.

Ovans, Andrea. 2015. "How Emotional Intelligence Became a Key Leadership Skill." *Harvard Business Review*, April 28, 2015. hbr.org/2015/04/how-emotional-intelligence-became-a-key-leadership-skill.

Paul, Annie Murphy. 2012. "Your Brain on Fiction." *New York Times*, March 18, 2012. nytimes.com/2012/03/18/opinion/sunday/the-neuroscience-of-your-brain-on-fiction.html.

Pepperberg, Irene. 2008. *Alex and Me: How a Scientist and a Parrot Discovered a Hidden World of Animal Intelligence—and Formed a Deep Bond in the Process*. New York: HarperCollins.

Powell, Joanna. "Hero Pet of the Year." *Reader's Digest*. Accessed March 6, 2020, rd.com/advice/pets/hero-pet-of-the-year.

Pryor, Karen. 1995. *On Behavior: Essays and Research*. North Bend, WA: Sunshine Books.

Raffaele, Paul. 2010. *Among the Great Apes: Adventures on the Trail of Our Closest Relatives*. New York: Smithsonian Books.

Rodriguez, Giovanni. 2017. "This Is Your Brain on Storytelling: The Chemistry of Modern Communication." *Forbes*, July 21, 2017. forbes.com/sites/giovannirodriguez/2017/07/21/this-is-your-brain-on-storytelling-the-chemistry-of-modern-communication.

Rota, Jadranka, and David L. Wagner. 2006. "Predator Mimicry: Metalmark Moths Mimic Their Jumping Spider Predators." *PLoS ONE*, December 20, 2006. journals.plos.org/plosone/article?id=10.1371/journal.pone.0000045.

Sanchez, Anita. 2006. *The Teeth of the Lion: The Story of the Beloved and Despised Dandelion*. Blacksburg, VA: McDonald and Woodward.

Savage, Candace. 1995. *Bird Brains: The Intelligence of Crows, Ravens, Magpies, and Jays*. San Francisco: Sierra Club Books.

Schlegel, Alexander, Peter J. Kohler, Sergey V. Fogelson, et al. 2013. "Network Structure and the Dynamics of the Mental Workspace." *Proceedings of the National Academy of Sciences* 110 (40): 16277–16282. doi.org/10.1073/pnas.1311149110.

Schorger, A.W. 1966. *The Wild Turkey: Its History and Domestication*. Norman, OK: University of Oklahoma Press, 1966.

Siebert, Charles. 2006. "An Elephant Crackup?" *New York Times Magazine* October 8, 2006. nytimes.com/2006/10/08/magazine/08elephant.html.

Smithsonian. "Famous Horses." *Smithsonian*. Last updated January 2011. Accessed March 4, 2020. si.edu/encyclopedia_si/nmnh/famehors.htm.

Stephens, Greg J., Lauren J. Silbert, and Uri Hasson. 2010. "Speaker-Listener Neural Coupling Underlies Successful Communication." *Proceedings of the National Academy of Sciences* 107 (32): 14425–14430. doi.org/10.1073/pnas.1008662107.

Stewart, Amy. 2009. *Wicked Plants: The Weed That Killed Lincoln's Mother and Other Botanical Atrocities*. Chapel Hill, NC: Algonquin Books.

Thorington, Richard W., and Katie E. Ferrell. 2006. *Squirrels: The Animal Answer Guide*. Baltimore, MD: The Johns Hopkins University Press.

Time. "Top 10 Heroic Animals." Accessed March 6, 2020.content.time.com/time/specials/packages/completelist/0,29569,2059858,00.html.

Treher, Elizabeth, David Piltz, and Steven Jacobs. 2011. *A Guide to Success for Technical Managers: Supervising in Research, Development, and Engineering*. Hoboken, NJ: Wiley.

Waldbauer, Gilbert. 2009. *Fireflies, Honey, and Silk*. Berkeley, CA: University of California Press.

Watson, Lyall. 2004. *The Whole Hog: Exploring the Extraordinary Potential of Pigs*. Washington, D.C.: Smithsonian Books.

Weaver, Janelle. 2010. "Monkeys Go Out on a Limb to Show Gratitude." *Nature: International Weekly Journal of Science*, January 12, 2010. nature.com/news/2010/100112/full/news.2010.9.html.

Western Watersheds Project. 2019. "What's Eating the Pando Clone? Monitoring Project Shows Two Weeks of Cattle is Decimating the Understory." June 27, 2019. westernwatersheds.org/2019/06/whats-eating-the-pando-clone-monitoring-project-shows-two-weeks-of-cattle-is-decimating-the-understory.

Yuan, Ye, Judy Major-Girardin, and Steven Brown. 2018. "Storytelling Is Intrinsically Mentalistic: A Functional Magnetic Resonance Imaging Study of Narrative Production Across Modalities." *Journal of Cognitive Neuroscience* 30 (9): 1298–1314. mitpressjournals.org/doi/full/10.1162/jocn_a_01294.

Zak, Paul. 2013. "How Stories Change the Brain." *Greater Good Magazine*, December 17, 2013. greatergood.berkeley.edu/article/item/how_stories_change_brain.

Zins, Joseph E., and Maurice J. Elias. 2006. "Social and Emotional Learning: Promoting the Development of All Students." *Journal of Educational and Psychological Consultation* 17 (2–3): 233–255. doi.org/10.1080/10474410701413152.

INDEX

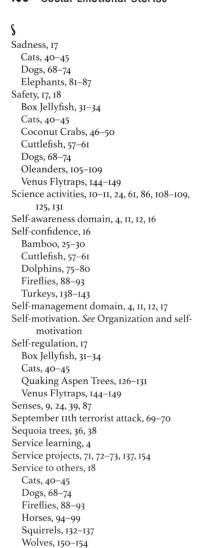

To download the reproducible forms and other digital content for this book, visit freespirit.com/stories. Use the password 4SEL.

ABOUT THE AUTHOR

Barbara A. Lewis is a national award–winning author and educator who teaches kids how to think for themselves and solve real problems. Her students at Jackson Elementary School in Salt Lake City, Utah, initiated the cleanup of hazardous waste, improved sidewalks, planted thousands of trees, and fought crime. They instigated and pushed through several state laws and an amendment to a national law, garnering ten national awards. They have also been recognized in the Congressional Record three times.

Barbara has been featured by many national newspapers, magazines, and news programs, including *Newsweek*, the *Wall Street Journal*, *Family Circle*, *CBS This Morning*, *CBS World News*, and CNN. She has received many awards for teaching and writing, including Professional Best Leadership Award (*Learning Magazine*), Distinguished Alumnus Award (University of Utah), the Annemarie Roeper Global Awareness Award (NAGC). She is the author of *What Do You Stand For? For Kids*, *What Do You Stand For? For Teens*, *The Kid's Guide to Service Projects*, *The Teen Guide to Global Action*, and *Social Emotional Stories*. Her books for Free Spirit Publishing have garnered many honors, including being on the VOYA Nonfiction Honor List and being selected for the YALSA's Popular Paperbacks for Young Adults.

Barbara has lived in Indiana, New Jersey, Switzerland, Belgium, Utah, and Poland. She and her husband, Lawrence, currently reside in Park City, Utah. They have four wonderful children and ten perfect grandchildren. They live in a forest among shy deer, bold moose, scolding squirrels, and feathered friends.

Other Great Resources from Free Spirit

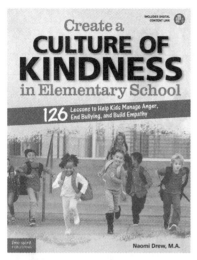

Create a Culture of Kindness in Elementary School
126 Lessons to Help Kids Manage Anger, End Bullying, and Build Empathy
by Naomi Drew, M.A.
For educators, grades 3–6.
304 pp.; PB; 8½" x 11"; includes digital content.

The SEL Solution
Integrate Social-Emotional Learning into Your Curriculum and Build a Caring Climate for All
by Jonathan C. Erwin, M.A.
For K–12 administrators and teachers.
200 pp.; PB; 8½" x 11"; includes digital content.

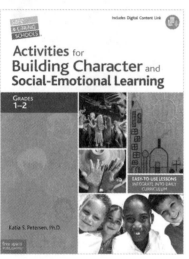

Activities for Building Character and Social-Emotional Learning Grades 1–2
Safe and Caring Schools Series
by Katia S. Petersen, Ph.D.
For educators, group leaders, caregivers.
208 pp.; PB; 8½" x 11"; includes digital content.

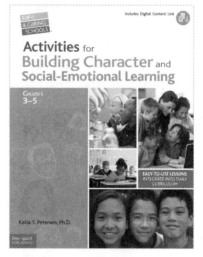

Activities for Building Character and Social-Emotional Learning Grades 3–5
Safe and Caring Schools Series
by Katia S. Petersen, Ph.D.
For educators, group leaders, caregivers.
208 pp.; PB; 8½" x 11"; includes digital content.

The Kid's Guide to Service Projects
Over 500 Service Ideas for Young People Who Want to Make a Difference
(Updated 2nd Edition)
by Barbara A. Lewis
For ages 10 & up.
160 pp.; PB; 2-color; 6" x 9".

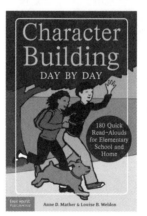

Character Building Day by Day
180 Quick Read-Alouds for Elementary School and Home
by Anne D. Mather and Louise B. Weldon
For teachers, grades 3–6.
240 pp.; PB; illust.; 6" x 9".

Interested in purchasing multiple quantities and receiving volume discounts?
Contact edsales@freespirit.com or call 1.800.735.7323 and ask for Education Sales.

Many Free Spirit authors are available for speaking engagements, workshops, and keynotes. Contact speakers@freespirit.com or call 1.800.735.7323.

For pricing information, to place an order, or to request a free catalog, contact:

Free Spirit Publishing Inc. • 6325 Sandburg Road, Suite 100 • Minneapolis, MN 55427-3674
toll-free 800.735.7323 • local 612.338.2068 • fax 612.337.5050
help4kids@freespirit.com • freespirit.com